SAMUEL JOHNSON
& his World

SAMUEL JOHNSON

& his World

Margaret Lane

Hamish Hamilton
London

This book was designed and produced by
George Rainbird Ltd
Marble Arch House
44 Edgware Road
London W2 2EH

Published in Great Britain in 1975 by
Hamish Hamilton Ltd
90 Great Russell Street
London WC1B 3PT

House editor: Yorke Crompton
Picture research: Andrea Stern
Indexing: Ellen Crampton
Design: Pauline Harrison

Filmset, printed, and bound in Great Britain
by Jarrold & Sons Ltd, Norwich

ISBN 0 241 89270 8

Endpapers Details from Rocque's *Plan of the Cities
of London and Westminster and Borough of Southwark*, 1746,
showing (front) Fleet Street and (back) Holborn

Frontispiece The last portrait of Johnson
painted by Reynolds, in 1783

Contents

Colour Plates

Author's Note

The field of Johnsonian studies is now so intimidatingly vast that one approaches it, however simply, with a sense of apology. The published works on which I have chiefly relied in my own modest excursion are listed in the Bibliography, for the benefit of the reader who cares to explore further. Of the many people who have generously helped me in one way or another I would like especially to thank Mr Kai Kin Yung, who first as Curator of the Johnson Birthplace Museum and then as Registrar of the National Portrait Gallery, has been unfailingly helpful, and also kind enough to read my proofs and to make valuable suggestions; Dr Graham Nicholls, the present Curator at Lichfield, who with unfailing patience answered a great many diverse questions; Professor Philip Rhodes and Dr Ronald MacKeith for elucidating for me some of the mysteries of eighteenth-century medicine; Mr Stanley Bray, of Messrs Sangorski & Sutcliffe, for demonstrating and explaining the methods of eighteenth-century bookbinding; Mr Eric Bellamy, Librarian of the National Motor Museum at Beaulieu, for tracing the somewhat obscure history of the rule of the road; Mrs Mary Hyde, for generously allowing items from the famous Hyde Collection to be used in illustration; Captain H. E. Widnell, the Beaulieu historian, for permitting me to reproduce the 'Dame School' drawing from his family album; Mr Stanley Gillam, for kindly letting me photograph pages from the London Library's first folio edition of Johnson's Dictionary; and Mr Douglas Matthews, the Deputy Librarian, whose patience as the recipient of endless troublesome visits and interrogatory postcards is an example to us all.

M.L.

1

The House in Breadmarket Street

ICHFIELD in 1709 was by no means an unpleasant place to be born in. In size no greater than a prosperous village, lying in a level country of fields and woods, it was in fact, as it still is, a calm and elegant little city. A beautiful and somewhat eccentric cathedral, constructed of faded rose-red stone and displaying not one spire but three – 'the like of which', said Defoe, 'are not to be seen in one Church, no, not in Europe' – rose up in Gothic majesty above the low roofs and outlying marshes of this otherwise unremarkable midland town.

In the seventh century an Anglo-Saxon bishop, St Chad, had arbitrarily chosen this primitive settlement (at that time a huddle of daub-and-wattle huts) as his episcopal see, and the first holy edifice had eventually been built there, covering the saint's bones. Since then a succession of cathedrals had risen and fallen, maintaining the ecclesiastical notability of the place, and Lichfield in consequence thought very well of itself. However small and humdrum the town might be, there was always the Cathedral and the Close to give it consequence; and although the clerical incumbents, like most of their contemporaries, were far from brilliant, the place attracted at least a sprinkling of men of intellectual standing. Daniel Defoe, near the end of his life making a lively tour 'through the whole Island of Great Britain', had been impressed by it. 'There are in the Close, besides the Houses of the Clergy Residentiaries, a great many very well-built Houses, and well inhabited too; which makes Litchfield a Place of good Conversation and good Company, above all the Towns in this County or the next.'

By the time that Samuel Johnson was born there, in an imposing house on the corner of the market square, the Cathedral, the city's only claim to dignity, had gone through some bad times and was in a state of decay. The Civil War, which all but the very young remembered only too painfully, had done more wanton and deliberate damage to Lichfield Cathedral than to any other in the country. The reason for this was that Lichfield itself was in the main Royalist and Tory, so that when the Parliamentarians overran it they felt it a Protestant duty to degrade and deface the Cathedral as much as

OPPOSITE The Cathedral, Lichfield, in 1782 still only partly restored after the wanton damage inflicted by the Civil War possible. 'They profaned the church vilely,' we are told, 'chasing cats with hounds through it, and committing worse excesses too coarse to be mentioned'; and when Prince Rupert temporarily expelled the vandals he found that their commander, with a sharp eye on profits, had already carried off the Communion plate and linen. The central spire was destroyed in this siege, and when Cromwell's men returned they broke up the building with determined thoroughness, stripping the lead from the roofs, breaking up the bells for metal, dislodging and throwing down the statues with which, both inside and out, the Cathedral had been piously encrusted.

From then until the Restoration the building was a ruin, every part of it roofless except the Chapter House; to restore it seemed an almost impossible task. Only two clerics remained who had known and loved the Cathedral in its former glory, and these two, William Higgins the precentor and Zechariah Turnpenny the subchanter, stout Lichfield men, saw to it that the rebuilding was in fact a faithful restoration of the ancient structure. To underline Lichfield's Tory and monarchist principles, which had been sufficiently humiliated during the Commonwealth, a gigantic statue of Charles II was carved out of the local sandstone and erected in a central position on the west front. Here, with the faintest of smiles on his highly intelligent and self-indulgent face, and lacking only the iron haloes of the surrounding saints, King Charles remained throughout the whole of Johnson's lifetime and for three-quarters of a century after. It was not until 1860 that the Victorian dean and chapter, uneasily aware of a certain incongruity, had Charles II taken down and replaced by the more suitable figure of Christ in Majesty. Since that day King Charles has stood in a dark corner within the west door, and more recently in an outside cranny among central-heating pipes, where nobody seems to pay him much attention. A pity; for now that the statue can be closely seen, it is remarkable how much the stone expresses; the rough-hewn features are alive with sensuality and character.

Shortly after the Restoration young Michael Johnson, later to become a respected bookseller and father of a famous son, left the small village of Cubley in Derbyshire and moved twenty miles south to settle with his parents and brothers in the town of Lichfield. Very little is known about this family; Johnson himself told Boswell that he could hardly say who was his grandfather; yet they seem, though poor, to have been a cut above the anonymous illiterate farm labourer that this remark suggests, since all three boys as soon as they were old enough were apprenticed to booksellers, in a trade demanding education as well as intelligence. William Johnson, the father, is described in the Stationers' Company records of the boys' apprenticeships as a 'yeoman' and 'gentleman', which is perhaps overstating it. ('The truth is,' said Boswell, 'that the appellation of Gentleman . . . was commonly taken by those who could not boast of gentility.')[1] Most probably he was a small freeholder with no pretensions to gentle birth but anxious to rise above the level of the cottage farmer. It was a difficult time for such people, when the whole style and method of agriculture was changing from open common-land

OPPOSITE The statue of Charles II deposed from the West Front of Lichfield Cathedral to its interior in 1860, and recently removed to an obscure corner outside

II

Lichfield in 1771, with the tower of St Mary's Church in the centre and the
three spires of the Cathedral on the left

farming, in which whole villages shared, to a system of enclosed fields, vastly increased wheat-growing, and large privately owned farms.

How he supported himself in Lichfield we do not know. He died soon after the move, and the first Johnson of note in the little town is his son Michael, returned from his long apprenticeship in London and at the age of twenty-four already established in Sadler Street as a bookseller. Even at that early age his seriousness was remarkable. He had scraped up a fair education during his apprenticeship, could read and write Latin, was a staunch High Churchman and Royalist and showed a creditable interest in civic responsibility. He was only twenty-seven when he became a warden of the Conduit Lands Trust (an old-established Lichfield charity which had helped his widowed mother and her children in the worst years of their distress), and not much older when he was appointed churchwarden of St Mary's, the church dominating the market place. This was the period, first under James II and then under Protestant William and Mary, when efforts were made to restore the ruined Cathedral, and in 1687 we find Michael Johnson and other Lichfield worthies contributing towards the recasting of the great bells. Their efforts were not enough. The bells could toll again and frequently did, sounding to a great distance over the flat fields, but the fabric itself remained in more or less a state of ruin until late in the eighteenth century, when even the medieval library was demolished.

The Cathedral clergy, of course, continued to inhabit the Close and to live in a world of their own. The Bishop himself had moved out of the way into great comfort at Eccleshall Castle, his palace being in part rented to a wealthy layman; but the rest of the Close was soberly populated by clerics of every grade, carrying out their undemanding duties and creating something of the atmosphere of a university precinct. Their

12

presence was of great importance to Michael Johnson, for these men at least, in an age when literacy in country districts was not to be relied on, would be customers for books; theological works in the main, Fathers of the Church, Latin and Greek texts, doctrinal arguments and accounts of exotic voyages, with perhaps an occasional up-to-date medical treatise if the author of the theory – *The Preternatural State of the Animal Humours*, for instance, or *An Enquiry into the Right Use of Baths* – happened to be a Lichfield man.[2]

The stock-in-trade of Michael Johnson's bookshop would strike a modern customer as forbidding. He catered exclusively for the educated reader, since there were practically no others, and the regular patron of that day would be either a cleric, a lawyer, or a man of means who had read Latin and Greek at one of the great universities and was now improving his leisure by forming a private library. There would be very little frivolous reading in Johnson's shop. Theological literature abounded, outweighing even the classics, and all of it, naturally, unimpeachably Protestant, since Popery was now considered as dangerous as witchcraft. Sermons were frequently published as topical reading, while for the rest there was an endless supply of texts and learned commentaries on the classics. Michael Johnson may not have been the first bookseller ever to trade in Lichfield, but he was the first to achieve respect and reputation. His professional life was certainly an arduous one, for booksellers were few (even Birmingham had next to none) and publishers as we know them scarcely existed. People could hardly be expected to travel vast distances over the rough roads of England to buy a book, and his trade, therefore, made it necessary for him to keep his own horses and to travel perpetually into the surrounding counties and beyond, saddle-bags bulging with stock, visiting and offering his wares to likely customers. Another good way to promote bookselling was to set up a market-day stall in as many country towns as possible. We know that Michael Johnson, a man of formidable energy, had established stalls in Trentham, Uttoxeter, Birmingham and Ashby-de-la-Zouch, and there may have been others. He was constantly on the move, leaving his shop in the care of an apprentice while he rode off in all weathers to expand the business by acting as his own traveller.

By the time Michael Johnson was forty he felt sufficiently well established to start a small parchment factory on a stretch of reclaimed marshy ground on the outskirts of the town. Today the word 'factory' suggests something more imposing: Michael Johnson's was probably no more than a huddle of wooden sheds where the sheep- and calf-skins that he purchased were scraped, split, tanned and treated by a journeyman currier. The skins were needed for bookbinding, which he had taken up as a necessary sideline and which had now become an important part of the business. Most serious booksellers of the day ran their own bindery, since books were generally issued from the printer's in primitive paperback, the sheets folded and 'stab-stitched' together, or at best protected by blue or brown paper covers. In this form they could be cheaply bought by those who wanted nothing better, but a gentleman forming his own library (a new and fashionable hobby even in country districts) needed something more durable and handsome; he might even have ideas about the binding – coats of arms to be stamped and gilded, special ornamental tooling applied, and so on. It is unlikely that Michael Johnson went in for anything elaborate, but he was at least able to produce the plain calf bindings that were in general use in the early eighteenth century, together with the limp vellum-covered account books in which everyone recorded his business or household expenses, and an endless supply of parchment for legal purposes. Paper, even the beautiful strong hand-made paper of the period, was not considered durable enough for wills, birth certificates, indentures, deed-polls, or any form of document. (The legal obsession with parchment lasted, in fact, until well into the twentieth century.)

Exactly what the bookshop and bindery were like in the early years we do not know, but from the start of his married life (he married in 1706, at the age of forty-nine) we have a remarkably clear picture, since the house he built soon after this auspicious occasion is still much as it was, and the modern visitor can reconstruct, room by room and floor by floor, the house in which Samuel Johnson first saw the light.

Michael Johnson had married late, after a broken engagement at the age of twenty-nine and no other amorous adventures that we know of. His bride, Sarah Ford, was a spinster of thirty-seven, small and slight, the last daughter left at home to look after her widowed father in a substantial house in Warwickshire. The Fords were a fairly prosperous Birmingham family who had made money as millers and farmers, and could boast of sons and cousins who had profited by education and gone into the legal, medical and clerical professions. They were, and certainly felt themselves to be, a cut above the Johnsons, but Michael was already doing well as an enterprising tradesman, and at thirty-seven Sarah cannot have felt hopeful of better offers. It was not uncommon for the unmarried daughters of large middle-class families to go into service as housekeepers in the homes of the gentry, and this might well have been her lot if she had not fallen in with the tall and powerfully built Lichfield bookseller, who in his silent and sombre way was not unimpressive. Her father, Cornelius Ford, bestowed on her a marriage settlement of several hundred pounds, and with this windfall Michael Johnson felt justified both in expanding his business and building the handsome house which still stands on the corner of Lichfield's market square.

From this point the financial fortunes of the family are something of a mystery. In later years Samuel Johnson spoke always of his childhood and youth as a period of great poverty, and his lifelong sympathy for the poor clearly had its roots in early experience. Yet in the three years before his birth everything seems to have been moderately prosperous. No one knows how Michael Johnson himself had risen from humble poverty, in which the family was several times relieved by Lichfield charities, his mother even on one occasion being awarded one of the 'women's waistcoats' handed out in St Mary's parish to 'the poor inhabitants of the city'. Some benevolent Lichfield citizen may have paid for his apprenticeship in London, may even have invested in the small stock with which he opened his first shop, and have helped him by introducing likely customers. But by the time of his marriage and the establishment of the bookshop on the ground floor of the new house, he was certainly one of Lichfield's most respected tradesmen, and it is puzzling that from this point he should have been endlessly bedevilled by debt.

In spite of the cheapness, by present standards, of labour and building materials, it is probable that the house cost a good deal more than he intended. He was never a good man of business in the financial sense, never kept proper accounts or showed much caution in the laying out of money, and the house had no fewer than eleven bedrooms, two kitchens, a spacious shop with ground-floor parlour, and generous storage space in the cellars. Clearly he was reckoning on rapid expansion, on servants and apprentices lodged in the attics, a possible nursery of children on the second floor, a bedroom and parlour to let to his friend Dr Swinfen for his Lichfield visits, space for the bookbinding presses in the basement, as well as comfortable living quarters for the family. In theory it sounded highly practical and sensible: in fact he had undertaken more than he could manage.

Michael Johnson, the Lichfield bookseller who
was the father of Samuel Johnson

Then, as well as the house there was the parchment factory, another potential source of difficulty, since the work had to be farmed out and Michael, apart from buying the skins, lacked the knowledge and manual dexterity to deal with it. And as if these financial risks were not enough, he had invested, only three months after his marriage, in the most ambitious purchase of his career – nearly three thousand volumes from the late Earl of Derby's library at Knowsley, a professional venture of unknown price which it is surprising to find within the scope of a country bookseller. Altogether it seems that Michael Johnson at the beginning of his married life got himself into diffi- culties which he was never afterwards able to disentangle. By the time his son was born the trouble had become a nagging worry, and it was to grow steadily worse as time went by. Samuel Johnson was born into a home which, on the face of it, should have given him all the stimulus and encouragement he needed. As things turned out, his youthful experience was largely of the frustration and bitterness of poverty.

Sarah Johnson was forty when this longed-for child was born. In the first two years of her marriage there had been no pregnancy, and the couple may well have thought they would be childless. Even now, as her time approached, there was anxiety, for a first birth in middle age could be dangerous, and of all the babies born in England at this period, one in four died. When the day came Michael Johnson did what he could. Instead of running for the local midwife he called in the celebrated George Hector, a Lichfield surgeon who had made himself into that strange novelty, a 'man-midwife', and was now regarded as being of 'great reputation'. It was as well he did so, for the labour was prolonged, difficult and dangerous, and might have been beyond the skill of the local wise-woman. Obstetrics was still a comparatively new science, still largely beneath the notice of the medical profession. In the view of most physicians and surgeons delivery was women's work, childbirth a domestic risk which only exceptionally merited their attention. If a surgeon did conduct a difficult delivery he had nothing but his hands and his experience to help him, since even that most simple device, the obstetric forceps, was still unknown. (It had been invented by a Dr Chamberlen early in the seventeenth century, but he and his sons had thought it profitable to keep their life-saving discovery a family secret, and so it remained for a hundred and twenty years.)

When at last the child was born it was almost dead, and the surgeon's hopeful 'Here is a brave boy!'[3] was uttered as he worked to get the breathing started. It was some time before the child was able to cry. Even then his life seemed so precarious that the Vicar of St Mary's across the way was brought in within a few hours to perform baptism, with Dr Swinfen, the Johnsons' lodger, standing as godfather. Next day the child was still alive, and Michael Johnson exuberant. Two months before, he had been elected Sheriff, and this was the day of the traditional civic ceremony, 'the Riding', when the city dignitaries made a perambulation of the Lichfield boundaries in a ride of sixteen miles, after which the Sheriff gave a public feast of bread, cakes, cheese and ale. He would, he told his wife, 'Invite all the town, *now*', and the son in whose honour he decided to be extravagant recorded long after that 'he feasted the citizens with uncommon magnificence, and was the last but one that maintained the splendour of the Riding.'[4]

It was Michael Johnson who decided that Sarah must not attempt to suckle the baby, who should be put out to nurse. Mrs Johnson needed time to recover, but it is also possible that Michael's decision was in part a feeling for gentility. Ladies of any social standing preferred not to be bothered with nursing, and there were plenty of robust young women available who were glad to take on the task for a modest fee. 'They generally seek for nurses among the farmers' and plowmen's wives', wrote Defoe, who disapproved of the practice, 'on pretence of strong, healthy and wholesome women. Nay, they often choose the poorest of them too, whose food is coarse and their drink hog-wash and belch, not generous wines as the lady herself drinks.'[5] The Johnsons decided on a certain Joan Marklew who lived nearby, married to a brickmaker who worked for Michael Johnson. She had been nursing her own son for eighteen months and was willing to wean him and take on the Johnsons' baby. She seemed a healthy young woman and possibly was so; in those days nobody dreamed of a medical examination. 'If the woman looks but wholesome,' said Defoe, 'and has a good full breast, a pair of duggs like a cow and a tollerable skin, 'tis all well; she's deem'd wholesome.' For two and a half months Mrs Marklew nursed the baby in the brickmaker's cottage, his mother visiting him every day and never discovering 'any token of neglect'.[6] When he was finally brought home, however, it was soon noticed that his eyesight was defective; the left eye, indeed, appeared completely blind. There were swellings on his neck, too, which perhaps had been previously hidden by shawls or clothing. This, at least, is what Johnson later believed he remembered his mother telling him, but it now seems, on medical evidence,[7] more probable that he contracted scrofula (tuberculosis of the lymphatic glands, particularly of the neck) when he was one or two years old. Johnson's own recollection, which after fifty years he admitted might be confused, seems to bear this out, for he knew he had had an 'issue' cut in his arm to drain the noxious humours in which doctors still believed, and recalled that he 'took no great notice' of the operation, 'having my little hand in a custard'.[8] A child of a few weeks would hardly have been given a custard to divert him, but it might well have comforted a child of two years old.

Scrofula, at all events, was a common enough disease and was known as the 'King's Evil', the royal touch being still regarded as a possible miraculous cure when everything else failed. It is now known that the usual source of infection is cow's milk, and the milk sold even in country towns in the early eighteenth century must often have been a rich source of disease, the animals being often kept in filthy conditions and tuberculin-testing or any compulsory standard of cleanliness undreamed of. Johnson would have been given cow's milk after weaning, and this may have been more to blame than Mrs Marklew, though the fact that her own son was near-sighted and scrofulous convinced Dr Swinfen that she must be responsible. We now know that scrofulous infections are not passed on to children through mother's milk, but in Mrs Marklew's day the 'humours' of the body were still believed to be sucked in by this method, and a good deal more besides. 'If the nurse has been of a leud and loose disposition,' wrote Defoe, still pursuing his vendetta against the wet-nurse, 'the heir is ruined in his virtue . . . if she is drunken, he inherits her unquenchable apetite; if she is a termagant, he is a bully; if a scold, he becomes talkative and a rattle; if a lyar, he seldom proves a man of sincerity.' Poor Mrs Marklew got the blame, though Mrs Johnson had an uneasy suspicion that the blunted sight and wretched health of her little son might derive from her own family. It seemed at times that the child would never thrive, and indeed he was born in a difficult season, when the winter came early and was cruelly long and hard. 'A very severe frost set in,' a chronicler of the time tells us, 'after which there fell an immense quantity of snow, the frost continuing with scarcely any intermission for three months. The Thames was, in consequence, frozen over, and booths erected, while every species of pastime was carried on upon the ice. . . .'[9] The Johnsons' lofty house would be difficult to keep warm, and the care of an ailing child through such a winter must have meant endless trouble. Dr Swinfen in after years was fond of saying that 'he never knew any child reared with so much difficulty'.[10]

Was it he, perhaps, who made the incision or 'issue' in the child's arm, which was kept open for several years? The operation sounds alarming, but in fact it was very slight. A small cut would be made on the same side of the body as the diseased area (in Johnson's case the left arm, since it was the left eye which was chiefly damaged) and kept open by some foreign body, sometimes a bead, more usually a twist of horsehair or silk threaded through the skin. The perpetual slight weeping of the tiny wound was sup-

17

posed to stimulate the discharge of 'noxious humours' from the body, and so drive out the disease. In this instance, not surprisingly, it did nothing of the kind, and the child was taken by his mother the twenty miles or more to Worcester, for a consultation with a physician who also practised as an oculist. What that practice consisted in at that date, beyond recommending some form of magnifying glass to the short-sighted, or an infusion of fennel or vervain, it is difficult to say. No good came of the visit, and as the scrofula had developed unsightly sores and the child was perpetually ailing, the Johnsons decided as a last resort to take him to London to be touched for the King's Evil.

This was a serious undertaking, involving a three-day coach journey and two official inspections of the patient. It was Sir John Floyer, Lichfield's most eminent doctor and a former physician to Charles II, who recommended the royal treatment, and there is no doubt that he, like many thousands of loyal subjects, still believed in it. 'Touching' or 'stroking' as a method of healing was not confined to royalty; faith-healers and quacks practised it, often with success, but the royal touch was naturally held to be the most magical and efficacious, and James II in August 1687 had actually touched in Lichfield Cathedral itself. Charles II had touched almost a hundred thousand persons during his reign, and his healing ceremonies had cost ten thousand pounds annually. Not all the sufferers were cured, needless to say, but a good many were, either through the healing powers of faith or, as the more sceptical doctors of the day believed, because the monarch sensibly advised them to 'wash their sores'. Scrofula is, besides, a disease which often clears up by itself, or appears to do so. And instant cures were not expected: if the sores abated six months after the ceremony this was a miracle.[11]

Queen Anne had resumed the touching after a lapse of years, probably to emphasize her hereditary right to the throne, since the Pretender over the water was busily continuing the practice in France and Italy to stress the divine nature of his claim. After her death, less than two years after Johnson's attendance at the ceremony, the touching fell into disuse and its special service was removed from the Prayer Book; but in 1712, when Mrs Johnson took her child to London, the performance drew crowds to St James's Palace and the air was full of rumours of cures and miracles. Small wonder, as Macaulay observed, 'that when men of science gravely repeated such nonsense, the vulgar should have believed it. . . . Nothing is so credulous as misery.'[12]

Before leaving Lichfield Mrs Johnson had to have a parish certificate and a signed statement from a physician, confirming that the child had the King's Evil and had not been touched before. (One of the attractions of the ceremony was that each person received a specially minted gold coin or 'touch-piece', and this naturally encouraged the enterprising to try to attend the service more than once.) Arrived in London and settled in their lodgings with a bookseller in Little Britain, a favourite street with the book trade (an area, also, noted for its whores), they had to attend at the house of one of the royal physicians, who verified the disease. The next step, the day before the touching, was to call at an office in Whitehall, present the certificate, and be issued with an entry ticket to St James's Palace. They would then be admitted in the crowd of two hundred persons who were to be touched on the morning of March 30th 1712.

OPPOSITE The order of service for the 'Royal Touch', printed as a broadsheet in 1679

18

The Manner of His Majesties Curing the Disease
CALLED THE
KINGS-EVIL.

THE Ministers of the Kings Majesties Chappel reading the Common-Prayers and Liturgy allowed in the Church of *England*, when the Ordinary Prayers with the Epistle and Gospel is ended, the diseased persons are brought by the Kings Chyrurgeons into His Majesties presence, where by Faith and fervent Prayer they desire help. Then is read this Gospel next following; and when these words are read, *viz. They shall lay their hands, &c.* The King layeth both his hands on the diseased persons, and with his bare hands doth stroke them: which being done, the diseased persons stand a little aside. Then the rest of this Gospel is read, *viz. So then when, &c.*

The Gospel written in the xvj of *Mark*.

*J*Esus appeared unto the eleven as they sate at meat, and cast in their teeth their unbelief and hardness of heart, because they believed not them which had seen that he was risen again from the dead. And he said unto them, Go ye into all the world, and preach the Gospel to all creatures: He that believeth and is baptized, shall be saved: but he that believeth not, shall be damned. And these tokens shall follow them that believe: In my Name they shall cast out devils, they shall speak with new tongues, they shall drive away serpents; and if they drink any deadly thing, it shall not hurt them: THEY SHALL LAY THEIR HANDS ON THE SICK, AND THEY SHALL RECOVER. So then when the Lord had spoken unto them, he was received into heaven, and is on the right hand of God. And they went forth, and preached every where, the Lord working with them, and confirming the word with miracles following.

Repeat the same as often as the King toucheth the sick person.

Which Gospel being read, then this Gospel next following is also read: And when these words are read, *That light was the true light, &c.* The King ariseth, and the diseased are again brought before him; then he taketh a piece of Gold called an Angel, of the value of 10 shillings, with a hole made therein, and making the sign of the Cross on the diseased place, with Prayer and Blessing, he hangeth the Gold in a Silk-string about the Neck of every diseased person. When the King hath so put an Angel of Gold about the Neck of every one of the diseased persons, then the rest of this Gospel is read, *viz. He was in the world, &c.* The diseased persons standing in the mean time a little aside.

The Gospel written in the first of St. *John*.

*I*N the beginning was the Word, and the Word was with God, and God was the Word. The same was in the beginning with God. All things were made by it, and without it was nothing made that was made. In it was life, and the life was the light of men and the light shineth in the darkness, and the darkness comprehended it not. There was sent from God a man, whose name was John: the same came as a witness to bear witness of the light, that all men through him might believe. He was not that Light, but was sent to bear witness of the light. THAT LIGHT WAS THE TRUE LIGHT, WHICH LIGHTETH EVERY MAN THAT COMETH INTO THE WORLD. He was in the world, and the world was made by him, and the world knew him not. He came among his own, and his own received him not. But as many as received him, to them gave he power to be made sons of God, even them that believed on his Name, which were born, not of blood, nor of the will of the flesh, nor yet of the will of man, but of God. And the same word became flesh, and dwelt among us, and we saw the glory of it, as the glory of the only begotten Son of the Father, full of grace and truth.

Repeat same as the Angel their n...

This Gospel being ended, then the King with the whole company of the Church upon their knees do pray thus:

*L*Ord have mercy upon us.   Christ have mercy upon us.   Lord have mercy upon us.
Our Father which art in Heaven, hallowed be thy Name, Thy Kingdom come, Thy will be done in Earth, as it is in Heaven, Give us this day our dayly bread, And forgive us our trespasses, as we forgive them that trespass against us, And lead us not into temptation: Answer. But deliver us from evil. Amen.
Minister, O Lord save thy servants.   Answer. Which put their trust in thee.
Min. Send unto them help from above.   Ans. And evermore mightily defend them.
Min. Help us O God our Saviour.   Ans. And for the glory of thy Names sake deliver us, be merciful unto us sinners for thy Names sake.
Min. O Lord hear our prayers.   Ans. And let our cry come unto thee.

*A*Lmighty God, the eternal health of all such as put their trust in thee, hear us we beseech thee on the behalf of these thy servants for whom we call for thy merciful help, that they receiving health, may give thanks to thee in thy holy Church, through Jesus Christ our Lord, Amen.

Then the Prayers are concluded with this Blessing, *viz.*

*T*HE peace of God which passeth all understanding, keep your hearts and minds in the knowledg and love of God, and of his Son Jesus Christ our Lord: And the blessing of God Almighty, the Father, the Son, and the Holy Ghost, be amongst you, and remain with you always. Amen.

Which being ended, the healed persons depart, first giving thanks to God, and to the Kings Majesty, and congratulating one another for their recovery.

LONDON: Printed for *Dorman Newman*, at the *Kings-Arms* in the *Poultrey*, MDCLXXIX.

The ceremony, of which Johnson in after life retained only 'some confused Remembrance of a Lady in a black Hood',[13] was solemn and impressive. The Queen, middle aged, stout and ailing, sat under a state canopy attended by her chaplains, while prayers and liturgical verses and responses were intoned and the sick were brought up singly to kneel before her. As one of the chaplains solemnly pronounced. 'He put his hands upon them and He healed them',[14] the Queen stroked the cheeks and neck of the sick person. When all had been touched, they were brought up again in the same order, and the second chaplain, kneeling, handed the gold touch-pieces, threaded on white ribbons, to the Queen, who placed them round their necks. (Johnson wore his under his shirt for the rest of his life.) The first chaplain then chanted, 'God give a blessing to this work: and grant that these sick persons, on whom the Queen lays her hands, may recover, through Jesus Christ Our Lord.' Finally, after an epistle, more prayers and a last blessing, the Lord Chamberlain and the Comptroller of the Household brought a basin, a ewer and a towel to the Queen, who washed her hands – a fitting end to a ceremony which must often have been distasteful to perform.

The visit had involved Mrs Johnson in some expense, which determined her to make the return journey as economically as possible. Instead of travelling by stage-coach, as they had come, they returned by wagon ('a heavy carriage for burthens'),[15] which was comfortless and slow. His mother made Sam's troublesome cough the excuse for the change, since it might annoy the stage-coach passengers, but 'the hope of saving a few shillings', as he afterwards recorded, 'was no slight motive; for she, not having been accustomed to money, was afraid of such expenses as now seem very small. She sewed two guineas in her petticoat, lest she should be robbed.'[16] Nevertheless she was resolved that the visit should be commemorated by a few lasting purchases, and bought Sam a little silver mug and spoon engraved with his Christian name and initial, 'Sam. I', 'lest if they had been marked S. I. which was her name, they should, upon her death, have been taken from me.'[17] This cup seems to have been the only treasure of his early life, and to part with it in the days of his married poverty must have been painful. 'The cup was one of the last pieces of plate which dear Tetty sold in our distress. I have now the spoon.' His mother also bought for herself, he remembered, 'two teaspoons, and till my manhood she had no more'.[18]

Whatever hope the Johnsons entertained of the good results of the visit, it would not be long before they had to admit to failure. The swellings and sores in the child's neck continued, so they resorted at last to an operation, which was none too skilfully performed, since it left disfiguring scars which remained for life. (The portraits painted in Johnson's years of fame do not stress these, but in the eloquent and moving death-mask[19] they are plainly visible.) Gradually the effects of the scrofula faded away, and although Sam's eyesight remained defective and he caught and survived the usual childish ailments, he began to grow into a large and sturdy boy. Not many months after the visit to London, when he had just passed his third birthday, his brother Nathaniel was born, and Michael Johnson's family was complete.

Domestic life at the bookseller's was humdrum, respectable, and not particularly happy. Michael and Sarah Johnson liked each other no better and no worse than the partners of

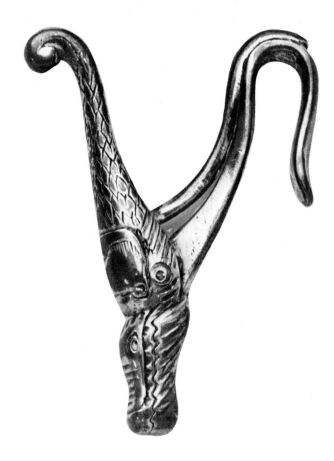

Johnson's silver bib-clip
(about 1½ inches long),
used to fasten a table napkin to
the lapel of his coat

innumerable ordinary marriages, but they were basically ill-suited, both temperamentally and practically. 'My father and mother had not much happiness from each other.
They seldom conversed; for my father could not bear to talk of his affairs; and my
mother, being unacquainted with books, cared not to talk of anything else. Had my
mother been more literate, they had been better companions.'[20]

Michael Johnson hated to talk of his affairs because they were usually chaotic. 'The
truth was, that my father, having in the early part of his life contracted debts, never had
trade sufficient to enable him to pay them, and maintain his family; he got something,
but not enough.' His solid reputation as a bookseller and his civic appointments (first as
sheriff, then as magistrate) did him no good financially: the first involved him in constant travelling to markets and the houses of customers, leaving bookshop and bindery
in his wife's care; the other increased his expenses without bringing in either salary or
profits. How the business lasted as long as it did is a wonder, with both the Johnsons
admittedly hopeless at book-keeping and accounts. 'Neither of them ever tried to
calculate the profits of trade, or the expenses of living. . . . It was not till about 1768
that I thought to calculate the returns of my father's trade, and by that estimate his
probable profits. This, I believe, my parents never did.'[21] How could they imagine a
business could be run in such a style? Sarah Johnson's habit was to worry and complain,

21

Michael's to be gloomily silent or, better still, absent from home for as long and as often as possible. He was 'a very pious and worthy man', Johnson told Mrs Thrale, 'but wrong-headed, positive, and afflicted with melancholy.'[22] Such a man was impatient of argument, not very cheerful company, a withdrawn and silent presence about the house. 'My father had much vanity,' Johnson considered, 'which his adversity hindered from being fully exerted',[23] and his mother, quick to press home her small and only advantage, was apt to make wounding references to his family. 'My mother had no value for his relations; those indeed whom we knew of were much lower than hers.'[24] (Not that the Fords were at all grand: then as now, there was quite as much snobbery at humble levels as elsewhere.)

It is not surprising that the child loved his mother better than his father. Though her talk, when her husband was present, was largely of 'complaint, fear and suspicion', she seems to have had a warm and simple relationship with her children, and Johnson's lifelong affection (though he confessed he did not always respect her – 'Poor people's children, dear lady, never respect them')[25] is the best possible evidence that, within the limits of her nature and understanding, she was a good mother. Of course there has been no lack of theorists anxious to prove that the later disturbances of Johnson's psyche, his abnormal sense of guilt, the tics and involuntary movements that made him seem such an oddity, were entirely his mother's fault; that he hated her and suffered from obsessive guilt on that account. 'Johnson's fears' – to quote a recent example – 'were the most puissant of the offspring of his repressed mother-hate, and he needed them to assuage the guilt he felt for hating his mother.'[26] All the evidence of Johnson's own recollections, his letters and his lifelong devotion to her memory make this appear as the great nonsense that it probably is. Her telling him stories in bed, of Heaven, 'a fine place, filled with happiness', and 'a *sad* place, called Hell'; her teaching him his letters, with the servant-girl,[27] who sat him on her lap and explained about St George and the Dragon; her buying him coffee she could ill afford when he hankered for it as a boy – all these accounts breathe warmth and affection, never hatred. As to Johnson's physical and psychological peculiarities, it must be said at once that it is fairly useless to speculate about them, since we have to admit in the end that *we cannot know*. 'There is no agreement as to the cause,' says J. L. Clifford, one of the best of Johnson's latter-day interpreters. 'There is even less agreement as to the source of the tensions. Freudians, when they sift the evidence, find an Oedipus complex. . . . Others have suggested an inferiority complex which had its origin in his physical and social handicaps. Still others find in him an unresolved conflict between an uncompromising rationalism and his strong emotional drives. Each describes the disorder according to the terminology of his own school of thought.'[28] Speculation is irresistible, but no one who reads carefully can doubt that Johnson was fond of his mother as a child, and ever afterwards felt for her a tender and grateful affection.

His father was another matter. Often either absent or preoccupied, he could be exasperating to the child when he was present, praising his cleverness to strangers, making him recite or show off when he had no wish to, generally causing resentment and embarrassment. 'That', he said to Mrs Thrale one day, 'is the great misery of late marriages; the unhappy produce of them becomes the plaything of dotage. An old man's child leads much such a life, I think, as a little boy's dog, teased with awkward fondness, and forced, perhaps, to sit up and beg, as we call it, to divert a company, who at last go away complaining of their disagreeable entertainment.'[29]

There was not, however, much company to be entertained in this or any other fashion, for even giving tea to neighbours was expensive and Michael Johnson discouraged it, as also his wife's paying visits about the town, since hospitality accepted must be returned. This was not as mean as it sounds, for tea was still an expensive luxury costing anything from ten to twenty shillings a pound. (To judge this price by present-day standards one must multiply the twenty shillings by six or seven.) Most of the tea still came from China and was heavily taxed; it was gradually falling in price with the introduction of new varieties from India, but was still a luxury, and both sorts were sparingly drunk in the Chinese manner, as a weak infusion without milk.

Any imported delicacy, even sugar, was likely to run a hazardous course before it reached the Johnsons' table, for England, as usual, was at war; the apparently peaceful life of Lichfield was set against a background of battles, treaties, declarations, naval skirmishes and piracy. Only a week before Samuel Johnson was born Marlborough had defeated the French at Malplaquet, and from then until Johnson's death the succession of wars was practically unbroken, involving France, Spain, Austria, Scotland and America. Yet, since communications were mercifully slow, these international rivalries and massacres had little effect on ordinary life: unless a press gang came through a village and carried off a labourer from the tavern, the inhabitants would hear more rumours than hard news, and in the absence of local newspapers might know nothing precise even of defeat or victory until the belated news arrived by the mail-coach, followed soon by fancy accounts in broadsheet or ballad.

So the Johnsons' life would be reasonably peaceful and, apart from increasing money worries, modestly comfortable. There would be at least one female servant living at the top of the house (we never hear of more than one, despite the eleven bedrooms), and a manservant or bookbinding apprentice. Dr Swinfen came and went, and the Johnsons cooked and ate and spent most of their private hours in the basement kitchen. It is likely that the bindery was in the basement too, for there was plenty of space and in winter the kitchen fire and the charcoal stove for 'finishing' would keep it warm. There would not be much light, of course, but bookbinders and their apprentices were accustomed to work long hours in poor conditions, usually by candlelight. 'As to the Work itself,' says a trade description of the time, 'though a great many parts of it are seemingly but piddling, yet there are others that are laborious, and together they require a Lad of Strength, as well as to be ready and neat in his working.'[30] The minimum equipment of such a bindery would be the lying-press and 'plough', a heavy standing-press worked by a massive screw with descending plates, a sewing-frame for stitching the sheets together and a charcoal stove for heating the finishing tools. There would also, for the decorating of expensive bindings, be a rack of little brass or iron stamps with wooden handles, each bearing a different ornament or armorial device for pressing into the leather.[31] A supply of water was a necessity, and this would have to be brought in buckets from a street pump, since indoor running water was a luxury Lichfield would not see for many years. There was no town drain or sewer either; a house as well designed as the Johnsons' would have a privy, but this would be no more than a wooden seat over a cesspit, probably in a closet in the basement. Many of these indoor cesspits could never be dug out, and the cloacal smells which were a domestic commonplace of the eighteenth century were only one of many disagreeable details which today we have mercifully forgotten. Water, too, was a difficulty, when every bucketful had to be brought from a pump perhaps a distance of two streets away; town houses like the Johnsons', with no garden or yard, could not aspire to the luxury of a private well. In such conditions it is not extraordinary that respectable citizens washed no more than they were obliged to, especially in winter, and that nobody dreamed of taking a weekly bath at any season of the year, unless they followed the precepts of an advanced physician like Sir John Floyer, who held that for certain disorders a bath was actually beneficial.

The disposal of refuse was another problem for the householder, for without sewers or drains and with no organized collection of garbage the city's sanitary regulations had little effect. Michael Johnson was more than once fined for leaving a 'muck-heap' in the alley behind his house, which was what everyone did when no one else was looking. The law required people to convey their 'muck' to the open ditch on the outskirts of the town, a laborious and disagreeable operation. It was much easier to empty slops into the gutters of the roadway and hope that the next good fall of rain would carry everything away. Fortunately Lichfield was well supplied with ponds and streams, and it rained as often in the midlands then as now, so that the city was sometimes reasonably clean and never intolerable. Pigs and poultry, wandering haphazard in the streets, were the best scavengers.

An 18th-century bookbinder at work, with a
heavy standing-press behind him on the right and a row
of finishing-tools in the rack above

2

Dame School and Grammar School

HEN the time came for Sam to go to school there was one conveniently near, across the road and round the corner in Dam Street. It was very humble and very small, the living-room of a shoemaker's cottage, where 'Dame' Oliver the cobbler's widow gave lessons to a handful of infants whose shrill repetitious chant could be heard by the passers-by. Johnson was not yet five years old, so was generally taken to and from school by the maidservant while his mother looked after the baby and minded the shop. His eyesight was still so poor that it was thought dangerous for him to make even this journey of less than two hundred yards alone.

Dame Oliver was poor, but had evidently had some education, for she could read the heavy Gothic type in which early books were printed, and borrowed a 'black-letter' Bible from Michael Johnson to prove her skill. Her tiny earnings as schoolmistress she supplemented by baking and selling cakes, especially gingerbread, so that the school-room must often have smelt delicious enough to worry the class. Though strict she was also kind, and might well have sat as the model for Shenstone's *Schoolmistress*, her birch-rod and sugary rewards both near at hand. William Shenstone, who just missed being Johnson's contemporary at Pembroke College, Oxford, had himself been to a dame-school of the same sort, and poignantly remembered both the sweetmeats and the punishments. There would be little in Mrs Oliver's schoolroom but a chair for herself and a bench for the children; they would repeat their lessons standing round her in a semicircle, their hornbooks in their hands, as Shenstone in his Spenserian stanzas remembered –

> Eftsoons the Urchins to their Tasks repair:
> Their Books of Stature small take they in Hand,
> Which with pellucid Horn securèd are;
> To save from Finger wet the Letters fair.

He also described the beatings which were such an accepted commonplace of school life, even in the infant class, when a boy of four or five could be whipped for wandering attention – 'And thro' the Thatch his Cries each falling stroke proclaim.'

After two years of this, at about six years old, Sam Johnson was promoted to the class

25

LEFT *A Dame School*: a drawing from a family album belonging to Captain H. E. Widnell, and RIGHT Lichfield Grammar School, where Johnson was a pupil between the ages of seven and sixteen: an early 19th-century print

of a retired shoemaker, whose curriculum, if one can judge by his having published a spelling-book dedicated 'To the Universe', was more ambitious. And a year later again, being already marked out as a boy of exceptional intelligence, he entered the lowest class of Lichfield's celebrated grammar school, which had educated such famous men as Ashmole the antiquary and Joseph Addison, to say nothing of a number of learned judges and other legal luminaries.

Here for two years in the lower school he seems to have been happy, for Humphrey Hawkins, the usher in charge of the younger boys, was a gentle creature whose miserable poverty (the school paid him only five pounds a year) had failed to sour his temper. He taught elementary Latin to the boys by day and in the evenings managed the local churchwarden's accounts and helped his wife to wash the choir surplices. Under his indulgent guidance Sam found it fairly easy to learn, and outdistanced the other boys without much effort. Progress in Latin, however, was no simple matter, for the dreary method of learning by rote was still universal in schools as it had been in the Middle Ages, and attention failed very often from sheer boredom. Once, he remembered in old age, he had been afraid of the next day's test on the conjugation of verbs, and his mother had successfully encouraged him. '"We often," said she, dear mother! "come off best, when we are most afraid."' Though his speech was still childish she was proud, she told him, that she actually 'had a boy who was forming verbs'. Looking back over more than half a century Johnson recorded the incident with tenderness, adding, as though to justify the setting down of such small matters, 'These little memorials soothe my mind.'[1]

Promotion to the upper school came unexpectedly, when he was nine years old. This change was not due to good progress on his part, but to a complaint from the town clerk, who disapproved of the headmaster's practice of keeping the free local boys in the lower

26

school as long as possible, so as to make room in the upper school for fee-paying pupils from further afield, whom he profitably boarded in his own and neighbouring houses. Johnson wept at parting from the kindly Hawkins and soon found that his tears were justified, for he was now under the discipline of a sadistic headmaster. Much has been said in extenuation of the Reverend John Hunter's brutality: that he was a good scholar, had a taste for music and field sports, and was in general considered a credit to the Church and his profession. But even Johnson, who like most of his contemporaries accepted the beating of children at home and at school as a necessary part of education, never got over his dread and dislike of Hunter, or excused the gleeful enthusiasm of his thrashings. He was 'very severe, and wrong-headedly severe. He used to beat us unmercifully; and he did not distinguish between ignorance and negligence; for he would beat a boy equally for not knowing a thing, as for neglecting to know it. He would ask a boy a question; and if he did not answer it, he would beat him, without considering whether he had an opportunity of knowing how to answer it.'[2] Such wanton severity would not, at the time, have been generally condemned, even by parents; most of them would have accepted Hunter's dictum, as he warmed to his work, 'This I do to save you from the gallows.' (And it is worth remembering that in Johnson's boyhood there were no fewer than a hundred and sixty capital offences.) John Wesley's mother, bringing up a family of children in these same years in godly strictness, wrote of the good effects of her severity: 'When turned a year old (and some before), they were taught to fear the rod, and to cry softly; by which means they escaped abundance of correction they might otherwise have had.' It was not for another thirty years or so that a more humane system began to gain ground, so that Lord Chesterfield in middle age could write without fear of ridicule, 'Pray let my godson never know what a blow or a whipping is.'

Johnson's punishments under Hunter were not generally for ignorance. Though he was constitutionally lazy (and to a degree that was to torment him all his life), his powers of memory and concentration were so exceptional that he could perform in a short time tasks which cost the other boys hours of anguish. Too blind to be good at games, he soon found out that his only hope of dominating the others lay in intellectual superiority, in appearing to learn without effort, in being willing, as a special favour, to help his friends. So that although he told the scholarly Bennet Langton, 'My master whipped me very well. Without that, Sir, I should have done nothing', his beatings, according to his schoolfriend, Edmund Hector, were generally 'for talking and diverting other boys from their business, by which, perhaps, he might hope to keep his ascendancy'.[3] This Edmund Hector, nephew of the man-midwife who had brought Johnson into the world, was his chief companion during the grammar-school years, and has left us a vivid account of Johnson's extraordinary domination over his schoolfellows. 'As his uncommon abilities for learning far exceeded us, we endeavoured by every boyish piece of flattery to gain his assistance, and three of us, by turns, used to call on him in a morning, on one of whose backs, supported by the other two, he rode triumphantly to school. He never associated with us in any of our diversions, except in the winter when the ice was firm, to be drawn along by a boy bare-footed.'[4] (Boswell added a detail to the barefoot boy, 'who pulled him along by a garter fixed round him; no very easy operation, as his size was remarkably large'. The garter need not puzzle us, since this was a pre-elastic age, and a garter was a stout knitted tape a yard or more in length and very strong. Goldsmith, after all, wrote of the suicide who would 'deliberately nooze himself up in his garters'.)[5]

Johnson's intellectual ascendancy was a source of some vanity; he liked it to appear that he spent little or no time accomplishing the set tasks, and when he was not conspicuously idle he worked fast. 'His ambition to excel was great,' Hector remembered, 'though his application to books, *as far as it appeared*, was very trifling. I could not oblige him more than by sauntering away every vacation that occurred in the fields, during which time he was more engaged in talking to himself than his companion.' Already there were signs of that 'dismal inertness of disposition' which was to plague him all his life, and which Boswell, who also suffered from melancholy, understood only too well. But the idleness of the school holidays brought a special pleasure; he and Hector would lounge away the time in the fields with an Eastern romance or borrowed tale of adventure, or swim in Stowe Pool near his father's parchment factory, or gorge themselves on the summer fruit which Shenstone remembered as one of the inalienable pleasures of a schoolboy's life – apples, pears, cherries, plums, nuts –

These must be bought, tho' Penury betide.

This idleness in the fields extended even to Sundays, for from the time of his first attending the Grammar School Johnson had won the concession from his father that he need not always attend church with his parents. The services were long and tedious, the sermons often read droningly from a book and incomprehensible, so that the boy became first bored and then impatient. 'Sunday', he remembered, 'was a heavy day to me when I was a boy. My mother confined me on that day, and made me read *The Whole Duty of Man*, from a great part of which I could derive no instruction.'[6] Small wonder that he 'fell into an inattention to religion, or indifference about it' in his ninth year, and was glad of the alarming accident which let him off church attendance altogether. This was a sudden crumbling of the stonework in the steeple of St Mary's Church, of which his father was churchwarden and where the family occupied a rented pew. Some stones and mortar fell into the aisle one Easter Sunday, and although no one seems to have been hurt there was a panic. 'The people (being a numerous congregation) crowded so fast', a London newspaper reported, 'that they tumbled upon one another, and lay crawling in heaps. . . . Hats, books, hoods, scarfs, cover-sluts or long riding-hoods, headdresses, spectacles, gloves, clogs, snuff-boxes, fans etc., were left in abundance. . . .'[7] The writer perhaps was comically making the most of it, but the steeple in fact was found to be in so dangerous a condition that the only remedy was to pull it down and use the stone for repairing the rest of the structure. The church was closed and the wooden pews removed to the chapel of St John's Hospital on the outskirts of the town, where loyal members of the congregation attended in cramped conditions for the next five years. But Johnson, 'having bad eyes and being awkward about this', was not compelled to go. Instead he was allowed to help himself to books and to lie reading in the fields on Sunday mornings. 'This habit continued till my fourteenth year; and still I find a great reluctance to go to church.'[8] The dispensation was a valuable one, for what more could an obsessive reader want than hours of solitude and leisure, with his father's bookshop

28

serving as private library? Thus was established a habit of rapid, random, miscellaneous reading from which his extraordinary memory absorbed and retained varieties of learning which would never have come his way in any grammar school.

When Johnson was just sixteen there was a break in the routine of home and school which was to have a significant influence on his life. He was invited to stay with one of his Ford cousins at Pedmore in Worcestershire, and by making this short journey of about twenty miles stepped into another world. Cornelius Ford, son of Mrs Johnson's physician brother, was a young man of a type the boy had not yet encountered – agreeable, intellectual, pleasure-loving, highly educated and a stimulating talker. The occasion of their first meeting was another of Michael Johnson's financial ineptitudes. Cornelius's father had been trustee of Mrs Johnson's small marriage settlement; Michael had not yet performed his part of the bargain, and now that the physician was dead, Cornelius, who had succeeded to the trusteeship, travelled to Lichfield with the purpose of settling the matter. In this he succeeded, and himself made a lively impression on the Johnson family. Small, plump, sophisticated, funny, he struck an immediate spark of response from his young cousin, and the sense of congeniality was mutual. He invited Sam to return with him to Pedmore for a brief stay. In the tall, heavy-boned, moody boy who suddenly came to life when for once there was lively talk round the bookseller's table he seems to have recognized a kindred spirit.

Though the intellectual attraction was strong, they were temperamentally as different as possible. Ford had had everything that Johnson could reasonably wish for, and had wasted it. Brought up in a prosperous professional family he had gone from grammar school to Cambridge, where he distinguished himself as a classical scholar and made some attractive friends, among them Philip Stanhope, who would soon succeed his disagreeable father as Earl of Chesterfield. A fellowship at Peterhouse was the next step, and for several years Ford had led the snugly convivial life of a Cambridge don, pursuing the pleasures of good conversation and the more dangerous satisfactions of heavy drinking. His head was as good for the one as for the other; he was never seen to be at all the worse for his wine and soon had a reputation for wit into the bargain. These talents at last made him impatient of university life and drew him to London, where social gaiety and the excellence of the taverns round Covent Garden soon ran through his modest patrimony. Nothing if not practical, he prudently retreated to his small estate at Pedmore, married the following year (he was now thirty) a Quaker lady of forty-three who had a nice settlement, paid off his debts with her money, and finally, with a view to a comfortable existence without much labour, took deacon's orders. The plan bore fruit in 1727, when Lord Chesterfield,[9] who had made him his chaplain for a brief period, appointed him rector of South Luffenham in Rutland.

At the time of young Johnson's visit, however, he had only just been ordained deacon and was living quietly at home, awaiting preferment. His marriage had served its purpose and was now not particularly interesting: to have his strange young cousin for a few days' visit would be a diversion. And so it proved, for the boy responded to all the brilliance and wordly wisdom that his cousin had to offer, and their companionship became so absorbing that the visit of a few days extended into weeks and then months, and still young Johnson remained happily at Pedmore. There was good company, too, in the neighbourhood, quite apart from Cornelius Ford; all those solid relations that Mrs Johnson was so proud of, and whose houses he visited now with his clerical friend, forgetting shyness. He even made a good impression on these respectable families, so that, 'although little better than a schoolboy, he was admitted into the best company of the place, and had no common attention paid to his conversation.'[10] But it was 'Neely' Ford himself whose influence was important, the charm of a man of learning who had no use for pedantry and thought good conversation the art most worth learning in life. He had mixed in London with poets and writers, had even known Pope in his heyday and was full of entertaining memories and stories. He was well versed, too, in the classical learning that Johnson found so attractive, and it seems likely that, as the weeks slipped pleasantly away, he may have resumed his old role of classical tutor, so that the time that was lost from the Grammar School should not be wasted. He believed in a broad approach to knowledge, as an enhancement of life rather than a programme of drudgery. 'Nealy Ford', wrote Mrs Thrale in her journal more than fifty years later, '. . . was, he told me, the man who advised him to study the principles of everything, that general acquaintance with life might be the consequence of his enquiries. "Learn", said he, "the leading precognita of all things. No need perhaps to turn over leaf by leaf; but grasp the trunk hard only, and you will shake all the branches."'[11] First impressed on him at Pedmore, this became one of Johnson's guiding principles.

The side of Ford's character which he got no hint of during these six months of studious pleasures was the passion – a very eighteenth-century one – for drink, late hours and disreputable company, which only six years later would destroy him. Mrs Thrale had noted him down, from Johnson's talk, as 'the profligate parson immortalized by Hogarth', and that is the character in which, thanks to Hogarth's satiric genius, he became famous. Only four years after his appointment as rector of South Luffenham he was found dead in the Hummums in Covent Garden – the Hummums being a bagnio (steam-bath and sweating establishment) to which gentlemen resorted to recover from their hangovers, and to be bled or 'cupped'. Nobody knows what killed him, but as he was only thirty-seven and already so corpulent as to appear at least fifty, it was possibly a stroke. A waiter claimed that the ghost of Ford appeared twice to him in the cellars, charging him with a farewell message to certain women of the town.) *The Daily Post* for August 24th 1731 carried the announcement: 'On Sunday morning last died, at the Hummums in Covent Garden, the Rev. Mr Ford, well known to the World for his great Wit and Abilities.' His principal haunts had been the Bedford Coffee House and the Bedford Arms Tavern (Hogarth's favourite) in the arcaded Piazza, Covent Garden, and the Hummums were only a few doors away. The neighbourhood had latterly, despite (or perhaps because of) the fashionable Opera House, become gaily disreputable, and the appearance there night after night of a prosperous-looking parson in gown and bands earned 'Parson' Ford a reputation which did him harm. 'One would imagine', wrote Sir John Fielding, who as magistrate did his best to impose a little law and order on London street life, 'that all the prostitutes in the kingdom had picked upon that blessed neighbourhood for a general rendezvous, for here are lewd women enough to fill a mighty colony. . . . These and the taverns afford ample supply of provision for the flesh, while others abound for the consummation of desires which are thus decided.

Covent Garden Piazza and Market, at the time of 'Parson' Ford's death in the Hummums

For this design the bagnios and lodging houses are near at hand.'[12] It is unlikely that Ford did anything more improper than drink, smoke and talk all night, for lively conversation was his passion, and this was where it was to be found. The Bedford Coffee House, the *Connoisseur's* gossip-writer of the time tells us, 'is every night crowded with men of parts. Almost every one you meet is a polite scholar or wit. Jokes and *bons mots* are exchanged from box to box, every branch of literature is critically examined and the merit of every production of the press, or performance at the theatre, weighed and examined.'[13] But the drinking of those days, and in such company, was horrific, and when Hogarth a year after Ford's death engraved his outrageous *Midnight Modern Conversation*, he pilloried Ford and his companions in such a manner as to make it difficult to conceive of any company looking more disgusting.

The scene is a saturnalia of drunkenness which has lasted into the small hours of the morning. As with all Hogarth's satires there are clues to be read in every area of the picture, eloquent details telling all we need to know and underlining the moralist's disgust. Thus, the clock tells us it is four o'clock in the morning (such places stayed open all night so long as there was custom) and half the company have long been incapable. Only Hogarth's bookbinder, phlegmatically smoking in a white nightcap, a crafty looking barrister called Kettleby, and Parson Ford himself, are still tolerably sober. At least twenty empty bottles can be counted, and the punch-bowl, like the huge piss-pot in the foreground, is brimming full. A staggering doctor pours wine on a sprawling prizefighter, a sodden politician sets fire to his ruffles as the candle he fumbles misses the bowl of his pipe. Other characters (Hogarth meant them all to be recognized, as indeed they were) are either vomiting or passing out, or, in the case of John Harrison

31

Hogarth's *Midnight Modern Conversation*: the Reverend Cornelius Ford and his friends in the St John's Coffee House, Temple Bar, at four o'clock in the morning

the tobacconist, yelling a raffish song as he claps his snatched-off wig on the parson's head. In the midst of all this obscene disorder the parson himself sits serene, decorous and contented, one plump little hand stirring the punch with a ladle, the other supporting the pipe he has been smoking all night. He is rational, alert, collected, undismayed at the horrid goings-on, still bright at this awful hour and benevolently presiding. Hogarth has drawn his face with affection, as though in spite of his failings he were fond of him, as Johnson continued to be long after he knew the truth of his disreputable end. At least Ford had never countenanced profane talk, and when anything of the kind started would check it with a tactful reminder – 'So you are resolved, I see, to send the poor parson to bed.' Johnson remembered him always with tenderness, and the six months at Pedmore which had shown him what good conversation was really like. In his seventieth year, composing his *Lives of the Poets*, he recalled how the poet Elijah Fenton went to see *The Merry Wives of Windsor* in the company of one 'Ford, a clergyman, at that time too well known, whose abilities, instead of furnishing convivial merriment to the voluptous and dissolute, might have enabled him to excel among the virtuous and the wise'.[14] Undoubtedly Ford could have excelled in the Church if he had taken his duties seriously, but would he have found it amusing? As one of his cronies, faithful to convivial memory, wrote a month after his death –

32

FORD is not dead, but sleepeth: spare his fame, I charge ye,
One ounce of Mother-Wit is worth a pound of Clergy.[15]

After six months of Ford's agreeable company Johnson returned to Lichfield to find
that his headmaster, angered by the impertinence of this long absence, refused to have
him back. What was to be done? Ford was urgently communicated with and obligingly
set about writing letters and pulling strings, with the result that the boy was admitted to
Stourbridge Grammar School, not far from Pedmore, which normally took boys only
from its own district. It was not a particularly happy solution, for the headmaster, with
whom Johnson lodged, was an irritable clergyman bored with education and more
interested in discipline than in learning. (Nevertheless he preserved a number of
Johnson's Latin exercises, which suggests that he thought this peculiar sixteen-year-old
somehow remarkable.) The one bright spot in the arrangement was that the boy was
within easy reach of Ford and his friends, and of those comfortable relations of his
mother's who had given him his first experience of a civilized provincial life in which
young people were not always obliged to hold their tongues before their elders. This was
a social experience to which Johnson responded. The only other time in his life when he
had been away from home was in 1719, when he was nine years old, and with his younger
brother Nathaniel had been sent to Birmingham to stay with other relatives of his
mother's who had been less congenial. These Ford and Harrison relations were all shopkeepers and tradespeople, amiable in their way but rather boring. One, his uncle
Nathaniel Ford, kept a clothier's shop; his wife was so amazed at the amount Sam ate one
day of a boiled leg of mutton that his mother told him 'it would hardly ever be forgotten'.
Another uncle by marriage, John Harrison, was a saddler in the High Street – 'a very

Birmingham High Street in the late 18th century, looking towards St Martin's

33

mean and vulgar man,' his nephew remembered, 'drunk every night, but drunk with little drink; very peevish, very proud, very ostentatious'. And there was his father's younger brother, Andrew, a bookseller like Michael Johnson and, like him, always in the coils of debt and worry. All their shops were in or near the main street of what was already a busy and expanding manufacturing town. There too, also in the High Street, was the mercer's shop belonging to Harry Porter, in whose back parlour Johnson would eventually meet the woman he was to marry. But all this was very small beer compared with the families around Pedmore and Stourbridge, on whom, in spite of his uncouth appearance, he seems to have made a memorable impression.

At the end of six months of school he returned to Lichfield and a period of semi-idleness that was to last for two years. Nothing much seemed to have changed since he went away. His mother now had a young servant, Catherine Chambers, only a few months older than himself, who was to serve the family devotedly for life. His brother Nathaniel was presumably still at school; so little is known about this shadowy figure that it is difficult to remember him as part of the family. The brothers had little if anything in common; there is no record of any mutual interest or affection. Earlier rivalry for their mother's love there may have been, and therefore jealousy; all that is apparent is that there was no love lost between them. For company Sam turned again to Edmund Hector, his old schoolfriend, now a medical student, and to John Taylor, another grammar-school crony, son of an Ashbourne attorney. These two, so different from one another and from himself, were to remain his devoted friends for life, and are important in his story. Hector's young sister Ann was even his first love, the object of a romantic fervour which came and went and was never quite forgotten. Some fifty years later he took Boswell to call on her, now a clergyman's widow in Birmingham, and told him, 'She was the first woman with whom I was in love. It dropped out of my head imperceptibly, but she and I shall always have a kindness for each other.'[16]

Hector was busy with his studies; Taylor, two years younger than Johnson, was in an upper form in the grammar school and would soon be at Oxford. What, then, was to be done with Samuel Johnson? It began to look as though the answer would be – nothing. The trouble, as usual in the bookseller's family, was financial. Michael Johnson had finished his year of office as senior bailiff, when he had basked in a certain import-ance as Lichfield's first citizen, and since he worked as hard and travelled as tirelessly as ever, all should have been well. Nothing, however, could save him from his own incompetence in matters of profit and loss. The parchment factory had been a financial folly from the start, and had got him into trouble with both the excise and the city authorities; yet he obstinately refused to give it up, and so continued to lose money. He was now deep in debt, borrowing money from friends and more than ever intent on domestic economies. There was simply no money to spare for Sam's further education: he must give up all thought of a profession and, as tradesmen's sons had always done, make himself useful in the shop.

Without enthusiasm, gloomily recognizing the necessity of earning his keep, he worked with the apprentice in the basement and learned to stitch and bind books and to handle the parchment and skins that his father dealt in. It is impossible to imagine that with his poor sight and general clumsiness he was much good at the craft, even though the standards of his father's trade were not exacting. (One of their best local customers, Sir William Boothby, had complained crossly, 'Your books do open very ill so that it is troublesome reading, pray mend this great fault.') Yet we do know that he actually learned to stitch and bind, and that his work, however imperfect, found its way on to the shelves of the shop, since that is where, many years later, when his father had long been dead and the business been taken over by another, Johnson with amazement identified a book that he had bound with his own hands. Its long shelf-life may have been due to poor workmanship, but more probably it had come back to the shop at second hand. Eighteenth-century bindings were made to last, and prove their point today in the world's libraries.

The shop itself was more congenial than the basement bindery, for here at least was an endless supply of reading matter, and Sam seems to have spent the best part of his two years as a shop assistant standing about in corners turning pages. He was often 'chid', it was remembered in Lichfield, for being inattentive to some of his father's best customers, being so deep in a folio as to be quite unaware that they might want something.[17] And books were not the only things they wanted: a provincial bookseller's shop carried all kinds of articles besides to which Sam was indifferent – stationery of sorts, rolls of wallpaper, patent medicines, even a few simple children's toys such as wooden dolls and peg-tops. It was not only the boredom that distressed him; there was also the pain of frustration that was hard to bear, for he had long been conscious of his own exceptional powers, and to see his friends launched towards distinction and learning while he himself dragged out this dead-end existence was bitterly depressing. There was only one aspect of life in Lichfield during these two years which from time to time cheered and stimulated him, and that was a new friendship (if 'patronage' is not the better word) offered from an unexpected quarter.

Gilbert Walmesley was the rich and respected layman who lived in the Bishop's Palace (the Bishop preferring, as we have seen, to live in remote state at Eccleshall Castle) and was considered Lichfield's most important citizen. Officially he was Registrar (or Judge) of the Ecclesiastical Court, which dealt with the proving of wills and suchlike matters; he also held one or two profitable sinecures besides possessing a comfortable fortune of his own, so that, still a bachelor at the age of forty-seven, he was able to live well and indulge his intellectual bent by collecting an admirable library and keeping whatever company he found congenial. As a young man he had been fashionably wild among like-minded wits, all known for their bawdy talk and heavy drinking, but Walmesley had also been sufficiently serious to spend some time at Trinity College, Oxford, to become a barrister of the Inner Temple, and to return to his native Lichfield (his father had been a Member of Parliament and Chancellor of the Diocese) and professional respectability. He was a staunch Whig, which as a great modern lexicographer[18] defines it, 'expresses the antithesis of everything expressed by *Tory*'. That is to say, Protestant, progressive, for Parliament and against royal prerogative, in favour of the new Hanoverian dynasty and passionately opposed to the Stuart Pretenders and all Papists; politically articulate in a style that we might now call left-wing Liberal. Whigs were no great respecters of either persons or traditions; they wanted a new world, new freedoms, new advances, and discussed Whig politics and read Whig newspapers in

35

LEFT As it is today: the Bishop's Palace, Lichfield, in Johnson's youth the home of Gilbert Walmesley, and later of Canon Seward and his daughter Anna, the 'Swan of Lichfield'. RIGHT Gilbert Walmesley of Lichfield, the friend and patron of young Samuel Johnson and David Garrick

Whig coffee-houses with all the vehemence of a still young and rather boisterous political party. They carried their politics even into their drinking, preferring port above other lighter and better wines as a token of friendship for Portugal and hostility to France, whose Tory partisans continued to drink claret. (For Whig political reasons much heavier duties had been imposed on French wines than on those now shipped in great cargoes from Oporto.) Gilbert Walmesley's loyalty to the Whigs in this respect had crippled him with gout by the age of thirty-one, when he confessed himself unable to move without crutches. By the time Johnson first saw him in middle age he had sobered up and reformed to the point of being able to walk normally, with only the occasional aid of a stout stick, but the gout continued to bedevil him from time to time, and gout-stool and gout-cage would be among the normal furniture of the Bishop's Palace.

Literature and good conversation were now Walmesley's chief pleasures; he was a frequent visitor to Michael Johnson's bookshop and parcels of books and periodicals were constantly on their way to the Cathedral Close. It was not long before he discovered that the bookseller's son was no ordinary slouching shop-boy but a youth of unusual and unexpected gifts who, once drawn into conversation, proved to be both a serious and a striking talker. Walmesley took a benevolent interest in the young, provided they were intelligent; he would have liked children of his own, but at this period was still unmarried and contenting himself with benevolence towards the more promising sons of a number of Lichfield neighbours. There was Robert James, for instance, at twenty-two studying

The Earl of Squanderfield's gout-stool, from Hogarth's *Marriage à la Mode*

medicine at Cambridge and in the vacations frequenting Mr Walmesley's house, where his manners were remembered as being none of the best. (He was later to invent a 'fever powder' and publish a vast *Medicinal Dictionary*, and is perhaps unlucky in being remembered chiefly by Johnson's reference to 'a physician who for twenty years was not sober'.) The favourite of the household was ten-year-old David Garrick, son of an army captain of modest means who lived nearby; the boy was still at the Grammar School and was so lively and amusing that Walmesley allowed him to run in and out of the house almost as though it were his own. He was even encouraged to get up an amateur production of Farquhar's *The Recruiting Officer*, in which he played the comic Sergeant Kite, and which was performed in the great drawing-room of the Bishop's Palace.

Sometimes alone, sometimes with others, young Johnson found comfort and stimulus in Walmesley's company. Walmesley was trained in law, and made the subject attractive; his devotion to literature had sharpened his critical sense; in political talk his fanatical Whiggery made him a formidable opponent.

With all this, Johnson became deeply attached to his kind patron, and never ceased to feel gratitude for Walmesley's encouragement and kindness. 'Of Gilbert Walmesley', he wrote at seventy, when his old friend had long been dead, '. . . let me indulge myself in the remembrance. I knew him very early; he was one of the first friends that literature procured me. . . . He was of advanced age' – forty-seven can seem old to seventeen – 'and I was only not a boy; yet he never received my notions with contempt. He was a Whig, with all the virulence and malevolence of his party; yet difference of opinion did not keep us apart. I honoured him, and he endured me.'

It is curious, perhaps, that Walmesley's radicalism failed to influence, let alone convert him, since he respected his judgment in other things and himself had a streak of rebel in him, especially in this youthful period of frustration. Perhaps it was his innate scepticism which preserved him? The panaceas of reformers, he considered, had not been proved; a brave new world might well have its own undreamed-of evils and problems. Besides, where government was to do all, the individual was bound to diminish in stature, to lose the essential human responsibility of man for man. The Whigs, like many of their political descendants, believed in human perfectibility. If the Establishment were overthrown and the system changed, men, they believed, would reveal their noble nature and the civilized world would become a happier place. Whereas Johnson, even at seventeen, was deeply sceptical of all such romantic notions, and remained so all his life – eventually startling Lady McLeod at Dunvegan some fifty years later by replying, when she doubtfully asked him if no man were naturally good, 'No, madam, no more than a wolf.'

Johnson's inherited Toryism, then, was in no great danger: it was even strengthened by his own ingenuity in countering Walmesley's arguments, so that those Bishop's Palace evenings saw the absolute high-water of his conservatism. Looking back in his fifties he told Boswell that 'after the death of a violent Whig, with whom he used to contend with great eagerness, he felt his Toryism much abated'. And Boswell added, 'I suppose he meant Mr Walmesley.'

The time spent with Walmesley was not wasted. Nor were the two years idled away in the bookshop, where Johnson had paid less attention to his duties than to a random exploration of history, poetry, classical literature – whatever came to hand in Latin, Greek, French, English: those sombre bookshelves were in a sense his university. And at last, unexpectedly, the chance of Oxford suddenly presented itself, and the whole scene changed.

One of Mrs Johnson's well-to-do cousins had died earlier in the year, and now that the will was proved she received a pair of Mrs Harriotts' best flaxen sheets and pillow-cases, a pewter dish and plates and the sum of forty pounds 'for her own use'. This lady had disapproved of Michael Johnson as a man who made more loss than profit, and he was obliged to sign an undertaking that he would not touch the money; he surely shared, however, in his wife's decision to spend it by giving Sam a start at the university.

If this sounds reckless – to enter a young man at Pembroke College on the strength of so modest a windfall – we must remember that forty pounds was worth at least ten times as much in 1728 as it is today. It was about enough, in fact, to pay his college expenses for the first year, and after that, they probably argued, Michael would be over his troubles and they would manage. Besides, there had been a handsome offer from one of Sam's schoolfellows, one Andrew Corbet, who had been at Oxford now for the past eighteen months and expressed himself willing to help with expenses for the sake of Sam's company. (As it turned out, he left Oxford a week after Johnson's arrival and forgot all about his promise, but nobody, oddly enough, foresaw that.) So approaches were made to the Master of Pembroke College, of which Dr Swinfen and one or two connections of Mrs Johnson's had been members, and clothes and books were packed and the great enterprise much discussed among the neighbours. On the day of departure, when Sam and his father were preparing for the long ride to Oxford (his chosen collection of books following by wagon) his old schoolmistress, Dame Oliver, came to bid him good-bye with a present of gingerbread, and told him he was the best scholar she had ever had. He never forgot either her kindness or her compliment, for when he told Boswell about it he added, with a smile, that 'this was as high a proof of his merit as he could conceive'.

Why Michael Johnson should have accompanied his nineteen-year-old son to Oxford is not clear. Possibly to confer a little dignity on the young man's introduction, which might otherwise be awkward; more probably, because his pride in the event made it impossible for him to stay away. He was now seventy-two, and in a life continually threatened by failure the triumph of getting his brilliant son into Oxford and therefore well on the way to a gentleman's profession must have seemed a miracle. So he accompanied him to the university and made himself known to the Fellows of Pembroke, whom he regaled with accounts of Sam's precocity, of his having been quite a poet at school, both in English and Latin, while his son sat silent, awkwardly embarrassed. One of the Fellows, Dr William Adams, thought the young man's appearance and manner strange, but when the conversation took a particular turn and he suddenly broke in with a felicitous quotation from the fifth-century grammarian Macrobius, the hitherto critical dons exchanged glances. The youth was more widely read, it seemed, than most of the young men whose tongue-tied presence each autumn had to be suffered. Perhaps they had not made the mistake they feared by admitting him as a commoner of the College?

Oxford

HE University of which young Johnson now found himself a member was perfectly recognizable, in some respects, as the Oxford we know today; in others it was very different. It had not yet wholly discarded its medieval shell, and now, in the increasingly rational daylight of the eighteenth century, found itself with a political and warlike past of some importance (having been the principal Cavalier stronghold in the Civil War) and a comfortable reluctance to give up its ancient habits for the sake of keeping abreast of the modern world.

Most of the colleges then extant looked much as they do now, the stone of their façades and quadrangles still beautiful in its original pale colour, to which, happily, expert cleaning has recently restored some of them. Pembroke had been in existence for only a century, and was still small; the original foundation had been for ten Fellows and ten scholars, and in Johnson's time the college housed no more than forty. Christ Church, huge and imposing on the opposite side of St Aldate's, had recently spent a fraction of its riches in building Peckwater Quadrangle, a great square of honey-coloured Cotswold stone, and Queen's College, also loaded with royal benefactions, had restyled itself with a massive classical screen confronting the High Street. Within all these walls, ancient or grandly new, the inheritors of a learned monastic tradition preserved the forms and discipline of university life without caring as much as they had done in the past (or as they were to do later in the century) for the drudgery of teaching. Some outstanding and scholarly teachers, of course, there were, who did well with the more earnest and studious of their pupils; but there were also many who found it pleasanter to live on their fellowships with a minimum of exertion. This was easy, since there were few obligatory lectures and degrees were given for statutory periods of residence, not for passing examinations – the theory being that since a university is a place of study, serious study is what invariably occurs in it. Most of the dons were in holy orders, living in their colleges in enforced celibacy, many of them merely passing the time while waiting for preferment, since the University was rich in benefices and Oxford never lacked for young men of good family who might have the gift of livings. And a Fellow's life, apart from the privations of clerical bachelorhood, was not neces-sarily dull. They attended chapel and dined together in hall, and once these two functions were disposed of the day was pretty much their own. Drinking, smoking and argument occupied endless agreeable hours in company, and if solitude were preferred a man could pace gravely across the quadrangle in cap and billowing gown, ascend his particular staircase and shut himself in with his books, his unfinished odes and future sermons, his Greek, Latin, Hebrew and Early Fathers. There were personal feuds and legal wrangles enough to heat up even the dullest common-room. 'There are such differences now in the University of Oxford,' wrote Hearne the Oxford antiquary in his diary, 'hardly one college but where all the members are busied in law business and quarrels, not at all relating to the promoting of learning.'

The University was Tory almost to a man (unlike the town, which was largely pro-Hanoverian), and since the good old Tory days of Anne were not forgotten, Jacobite sentiment and contempt for the German monarch and his ministers would be carried on in a haze of pipe-smoke into the small hours of the morning. George I had died only the preceding year, and his ill success with the people was a favourite topic. Only a few months before his death, a record of the time relates, 'The equestrian statue of His Majesty in Grosvenor Square was much defaced, the left leg being torn off, the sword and truncheon carried away, the neck hacked, as if it had been designed to cut off the head, and a libel left attached to the same.'[1] This was a joke to be enjoyed to the full, with Latin quips and scurrilous references, before turning to more serious matters. George II had still to prove himself; it was too soon to tell, but at least he had shaken his fist at the criminal classes. All magistrates had been instructed to apprehend the thieves

Pembroke College, Oxford, showing Johnson's room, the upper one over the gateway

who infested London and Westminster, and to abolish the night-houses where they lay concealed by day. Lord Chesterfield had been appointed Ambassador to France, a choice disapproved of in Oxford, since he was a Cambridge man. The London newspapers were full of the nefarious tactics of the Spanish, whose men-of-war were seizing British ships in the Caribbean in spite of a peace treaty being on the way. And what scandals at home the papers revealed, in almost every issue! General Oglethorpe (soon to be famous for founding the colony of Georgia) had led an investigation into the state of the Fleet Prison which discovered such fascinating horrors, such corruption and brutality on the part of its notorious warden, Bambridge, that for a while the common-rooms could talk of little else; unless perhaps it were the smallpox and the awful weather, since this was a year in which storms, epidemics, floods and 'calamities affecting many countries' swept ominously over Europe. The coffee-houses of Oxford, where newspapers could be read for nothing, did a thriving trade with the senior members of the University, who for dignity's sake kept their port and claret for consumption in their own colleges, avoiding the town taverns.

The junior members of the colleges, whom we now call undergraduates, were divided into five sorts – gentlemen-commoners, commoners, scholars, battelers and servitors – according to the fees they paid and the status allowed them. Noblemen and rich men's sons were gentlemen-commoners: they paid double fees and were privileged to dine with the Fellows at high table. Peers and peers' sons could, as an additional distinction, wear silk gowns of whatever colour they chose: Lord Fitzwilliam, for example, sported pink, ornamented with gold lace and gilded tufts. The gentleman-commoner's gown was of plain black silk, worn with a velvet cap. [2]

Johnson had entered Pembroke as a commoner, one of the most numerous class in the University. Commoners paid their way entirely, had their own rooms in college, dined in hall, and were waited on by college servants and 'servitors'. With the forty pounds which was to see him through his first year he was no worse off than a great many others, since commoners' fees were modest, their battels (college accounts for food and service) cheap, and his 'caution money' – a sum deposited in advance against miscellaneous charges – was only seven pounds. Wesley at Christ Church, a much richer and grander college, had scraped along on the same sum, and Richard Congreve later in the century, when living was dearer, still managed comfortably on sixty pounds a year.

Scholars were those who had special grants of one sort or another, while battelers fetched their own meals and looked after themselves in return for a reduction in fees. Servitors were the humblest class, and were not encouraged to fraternize with the others. They paid next to nothing in college fees, in compensation performing certain menial services, carrying meals to the commoners' rooms, fetching their ale, cleaning their shoes and making themselves generally useful. This grading of students according to their means was a relic of the Middle Ages, the work of the servitors having been intended as a way to higher education for the poor and humble. They corresponded, according to the historian of Pembroke College, to the lay brethren of a monastery. 'They were not

OPPOSITE Academic dress in the 18th century: a Bachelor of Arts of the University of Oxford

42

43

poor gentlemen, but came from the plough and the shop.'[3] By the time of Johnson's arrival in Oxford, however, this was no longer strictly true, and there were some poor clergyman's sons and others among the servitors who had come to resent the social discrimination. George Whitefield, the famous Methodist preacher who was at Pembroke a year or two later, was a servitor during his four years, and having worked as a drawer in his father's inn at Gloucester found, he said, 'my having been used to a public-house was now of service to me.'[4] (Whitefield, of course, being something of a holy masochist, would have welcomed anything that degraded him in a worldly sense, since humiliation brought spiritual profits.) There was even a Bishop of Worcester who as a youth had arrived at Oxford on foot and during his terms of study turned the spit in Exeter College kitchen.

The academic gown which Johnson and other commoners wore in college, about the town, and even when sauntering in the fields or along the river, was of plain black woollen stuff and by modern standards imposingly voluminous. Their caps were square black 'trenchers', forerunners of the mortarboard, with a tuft on top instead of the later tassel. Johnson's gown and cap, probably second-hand, would cost him little; apart from this necessary expense, and the modest sums recorded against his name in the Pembroke buttery books, he must have spent next to nothing. He would breakfast in his room (up two flights of stairs in the tower, over the gateway) according to the habit of the time, on 'a glass of ale and a crust'; dine at eleven or twelve in hall, where the commoners had wooden platters and the smell of past meals was usually noticeable; and sup later in his own room, or with one of his companions, on a tray brought from the buttery by a servitor. There could be no expenditure on clothes, not even on shoes when his own began to wear out, and the extravagance of a wig or expense of a barber was not to be thought of. 'Every schoolboy,' wrote Richard Graves, a Pembroke man and near-contemporary of Johnson's, 'as soon as he was entered at the University, cut off his hair, whatever it was; and, without any regard to his complexion, put on a wig, black, white, brown or grizzle, as lawless fancy suggested.'[5] The tie-wigs of the undergraduates, long and natural-looking curls tied at the back with a black silk bow, were elegant and attractive; the 'grizzle' wigs of the older men, stiff rows of grey curls powdered, conferred an appropriate dignity; but Johnson at the time of his marriage six years later was still wearing his own hair, 'straight and stiff and separated behind'.[6]

At nineteen he was older than the average freshman, and must sometimes have thought himself back again at school. The age of matriculation varied, and until much later in the century was much younger than would be thought sensible today. Gibbon, a Magdalen man, matriculated at fourteen; Jeremy Bentham and at least one of his contemporaries entered Oxford at the age of twelve. The average first-year 'man' was sixteen or seventeen, an age particularly susceptible to the excitements of grown-up foppery and extravagance. 'Raw, unthinking young men,' Nicholas Amherst the poet wrote of these years at Oxford, 'having been kept short of money at school, care not how extravagant they are, while they can support their extravagance upon trust . . . *running upon tick*, as it is called, especially when they have numberless examples before their eyes, of persons in as mean circumstances as themselves, who cut a tearing figure in silk gowns, and bosh it about town in lace ruffles and flaxen tie-wigs.'[7]

44

There were no organized amusements in those days, no crews practising on the river, no football or other regular games to take part in or watch, and the ways in which the students amused themselves were often childish. Sliding on the ice in Christ Church meadow, for which Johnson cut his tutor's lecture in his first week, giving this amusement as his excuse, was fairly typical. (And if it seems strange that there should be shallow ice on a flooded meadow as early as mid-November, it is worth recording that 1728 had an exceptionally hard and early winter.) Wealthier undergraduates could go fox-hunting or steeplechasing, ride over to Bicester races or attend a ball, but a young man with no money to spend had to be content with simpler pleasures. Johnson's comment on his own careless reply, when his tutor mildly asked him why he had absented himself, has become famous. When Boswell remarked that it showed great fortitude of mind, Johnson replied, 'No, Sir: stark insensibility.'[8]

In one sense at least he was fortunate in his tutor, for William Jorden, though no great scholar, was an amiable man who went out of his way to show kindness to his students. ('A noted pupil-monger', an unkind contemporary called him.) In middle age, visiting Oxford again for the first time since those early days, Johnson remembered his own rudeness to him, and what had followed. 'I once had been a whole morning sliding in Christ Church meadow, and missed his lecture in logic. After dinner, he sent for me to his room. I expected a sharp rebuke for my idleness, and went with a beating heart. When we were seated, he told me he had sent for me to drink a glass of wine with him, and to tell me, he was *not* angry with me for missing his lecture. This was, in fact, a most severe reprimand. Some more of the boys were then sent for, and we spent a very pleasant afternoon.'[9] The phrase 'some more of the boys' gives a simple clue to the age of Johnson's group.

Six months after Johnson's initiation John Taylor, now seventeen, arrived in Oxford with the intention (following the casual proceeding of the time) of joining his friend as a commoner of Pembroke. Johnson, however, had by this time formed a poor opinion of the college tutors and thought none of them good enough for the well-to-do attorney's son who was intended for the law. He made inquiries, therefore, all about the University until he had settled it in his own mind that Edmund Bateman of Christ Church was the man for the job. Taylor accordingly was entered at that College. Since only the width of the street divided them the friends were able to pass much of their time together, and Johnson formed the habit of going to Taylor's rooms after each of Bateman's lectures so that his friend could relate the gist of it while it was fresh in his mind.

This was characteristic of Johnson's intellectual curiosity and also of his haphazard methods of satisfying it. He was still abnormally idle, as he had always been, performing such tasks as were given him in sudden bursts of brilliant application. He had brought with him quite a library of books, more than a hundred volumes from Lichfield, and with these in his solitary room over the gateway, reading late into the night, he would accomplish prodigies of memory and performance while seeming to do little or nothing during the day. What he 'read *solidly* at Oxford', he told Boswell, 'was Greek; not the Grecian historians, but Homer and Euripides, and now and then a little epigram.'[10] His favourite subjects were classical literature, ethics and theology, and the ease with which he brought classical analogies and poetical images into his translations and college

Dr William Adams, Johnson's nominal tutor at Pembroke College, Oxford,
and from 1775 Master of the College

exercises surprised his tutors, who too frequently saw him lounging in the college gateway 'with a circle of young students round him, whom he was entertaining with wit, and
keeping from their studies, if not spiriting them up to rebellion against the College
discipline.'[11]

It may seem strange, when we remember how much it meant to him to go to Oxford,
and how lovingly he praised the University in later life, that he should play the rebel;
but at nineteen he was not the experienced and rational man he was to become, and as
term and vacation went by he was increasingly tormented by financial anxiety and
depression. Dr Adams, a junior don who later became Master of Pembroke, remembered
him as a 'gay and frolicsome fellow'; others had stories of his leading the sort of student
jape that seems funny at the time, but in later years has a way of seeming heartless.
There was, for instance, a rule at Pembroke that a servitor should go round the students'

46

rooms at night, knocking at the doors to make sure they were in College; those who made no reply were reported absent. Johnson resented this detail of college discipline, refused to reply to the knock and thus made trouble for himself; he also took a revengeful pleasure in 'hunting the servitor' as the college bloods called it, chasing the poor wretch down the stairs to the banging of pots and candlesticks. Whitefield, performing this unnerving duty in his turn, found the ordeal so terrifying that he 'thought the devil would appear to me every stair I went up'. And there were other evidences of a desire of 'vexing the tutors and fellows', who seem to have been singularly tolerant of Johnson's hostile behaviour, evidently recognizing in him, as Dr Adams said, 'the best qualified for the University that he had ever known come there', and so entitled to some indulgence when he felt 'frolicsome'. But Johnson remembered his year at Oxford as on the whole unhappy. 'Ah, Sir, I was rude and violent,' he told Boswell. 'It was bitterness which they mistook for frolic. I was miserably poor, and I thought to fight my way by my literature and my wit; so I disregarded all power and all authority.'[12]

The nagging fear always present in his mind was that when he got to the end of the forty pounds there was no possible means of raising another penny. There had not even been enough to take him home in the vacations; when the other students drove off at the end of term he remained, with a few in a like situation, to pass the time largely in boredom and idleness in a college that was all but lifeless. Andrew Corbet, as we have seen, had disappeared long ago without fulfilling any of his promises. No further financial help could be expected from Lichfield: his father's affairs were becoming desperate and the prospects of the bookshop increasingly gloomy. The hopeful enterprise of sending young Johnson to Oxford at all began to look like a piece of ostentatious folly, without a future. His clothes were wearing out, his feet in their woollen stockings showed through the cracks in his shoes, and this evidence of poverty inspired an act of kindness which, solely because of Johnson's furious repudiation of it, has become famous. A gentleman-commoner of Pembroke, one William Vyse, seeing the sad state of Johnson's footwear, sent a new pair of shoes to be left outside his door, but Johnson 'threw them away with indignation'. He was not in a state of mind to accept charity – always a stumbling-block to the temperament which reacts with rage to the humiliations of poverty.

This prolonged anxiety about the future, made worse by loneliness in the vacations and by that recurring tendency to depression which the eighteenth century defined as 'inherited melancholy', reduced him at last to such a state that there was nothing for it but to go back to Lichfield and know the worst. That he intended, or at least hoped, to return seems certain from the fact of his leaving his precious books behind. But to know the truth was only a part of his motive in quitting Oxford. To move, to escape, even from himself, was the blind instinct behind this unhappy journey. 'He felt himself overwhelmed with an horrible hypochondria, with perpetual irritation, fretfulness and impatience; and with a dejection, gloom and despair, which made existence misery.'[13] For the first time in his life (though not the last) he faced the appalling conviction that he was going mad. 'It is a common effect of low spirits or melancholy,' wrote Boswell, who understood such neurotic disturbances better than most, 'to make those who are afflicted with it imagine that they are actually suffering those evils which happen to be most strongly presented to their minds. . . . Insanity, therefore, was his most dismal apprehension; and he fancied himself seized by it, or approaching to it, at the very time when he was giving proofs of a more than ordinary soundness and vigour of judgement.'[14] What form his delusions took, with one exception, we do not know; but the desire for home and the lost security of childhood must have played their part, since one day at Pembroke, 'as he was turning the key of his chamber', he heard his mother distinctly call 'Sam!' – though he knew she was far away in Lichfield. This was a mystery he would never try to explain.[15]

Only one comfort (and it proved at times a harsh one) came to his aid in those last months as the horizon darkened: that indifference to religion which had been so marked a characteristic of his youth suddenly dissolved, and he found himself able to believe and pray, to find moments of relief in imploring help from an 'Almighty and most merciful Father'. This, then, was at least one boon which Oxford had afforded him, for he confessed that for a long time he had been 'a sort of relaxed talker against religion . . . and this lasted until I went to Oxford, where it would not be suffered.' It would not be suffered, that is, if one talked about it; there was a good deal of freethinking in the University but free-speaking in that High Church stronghold was another matter. Form and observance were everything, attendance at services more important than genuine piety. It was only by chance that Johnson picked up a religious book which unexpectedly fixed his idle attention. 'When at Oxford I took up Law's *Serious Call to a Holy Life*, expecting to find it a dull book (as such books generally are) and perhaps to laugh at it.'[16] But this newly published work by a clergyman of singular piety and directness proved 'quite an overmatch' for Johnson's apathy, and set him for the first time 'thinking in earnest of religion', and at the beginning of that long and often terrifying spiritual struggle which was both a solace and a torment and from which he would never afterwards be free.

He was not alone in responding to the mystic and emotional power of Law's appeal: the book was new and being eagerly read at Oxford. John Wesley, at this time a Fellow of Lincoln, was moved by the eloquent force of Law's arguments. 'The light', he confided to his journal, 'flowed in so mightily upon my soul that everything appeared in a new view.' Whitefield, borrowing the book he could not afford to buy, found as he read it that 'God worked powerfully upon my soul'. The ferment was already working in Oxford which was to explode in the religious eruption of the Methodist movement.

Johnson was neither of Wesley's circle nor attracted by the Methodists' 'enthusiasm', which he was later to define as 'a vain belief of private revelation'. But he was no less than Wesley and Whitefield stirred by this quickening pulse of religious fervour, and through William Law had stumbled on the spiritual concept which was to colour his whole experience.

Early in December 1729, at the end of term, Johnson packed his books and left them in Taylor's care at Christ Church. He was already a full quarter in arrears with college fees and must have guessed that he might not return to the familiar room over the gateway where he had lived continuously for the past thirteen months. Taylor accompanied him as far as Banbury, the second coaching stage, then returned to Oxford.

What discussions took place in the family once Johnson reached home we do not know, but there was evidently no possibility of his returning. His father had borrowed money from a London bookseller and was struggling on as usual, gloomy and anxious but still taking an active part in civic affairs. He seems by now to have been on the verge of bankruptcy, yet managed to stay on the brink and to retain his respected place on the Lichfield bench. He was sufficiently hard pressed, however, to be grateful for a grant of ten pounds as a 'decayed tradesman' from the Conduit Lands Trust, the charity of which he himself had been a warden; and with such aid he just managed to keep the tanning sheds and bindery going as well as the shop, and was probably thankful to have his elder son at home again, to strengthen and perhaps eventually expand the business.

Sam, however, was in no condition to be useful. Cut off at twenty from his one hope of intellectual achievement, obsessed by secret fears and misery to a point which would now be described as anxiety hysteria, he was more of a burden than a help. He was haunted by a nightmare dread of mental breakdown, and spent days on long solitary walks – often to Birmingham and back, a distance of over thirty miles – in the vain hope that physical exhaustion would prove the remedy. On one of these Birmingham marches he appealed for help to his godfather, Dr Swinfen, even writing out for him a long statement in Latin of his hypochondriac symptoms and fears of insanity. This analysis so impressed the good doctor with its acuteness and clarity that he committed the unpardonable indiscretion of passing it round, with admiring comments, among his friends. This breach of confidence reached Johnson's ears soon enough and not unnaturally made him extremely angry: according to Dr Swinfen's daughter he was never entirely reconciled to his godfather.

Apart from the recurring depression, which may have had its origin in some undefined physical disorder (possibly, as he himself suspected, in part inherited from his father) there was the very real anxiety of wondering what he was to do with his life, since Oxford and all it offered was now relinquished. Without a degree the further study of law, to which his disputatious temperament attracted him, was out of the question; so, too, was the Church, if he had ever seriously considered it. It was not just a question of earning a living: he was intellectually ambitious, aware (as he had been even in his schooldays) of possessing unusual powers, and convinced that life would be meaningless if he failed to make use of them. He had thought to make his way by his literature and wit, but how was he to do that if he were condemned to his father's bookshop and basement bindery? He had written poems at school and at Oxford that had impressed his tutors; had made excellent translations of Horace and Virgil and could write and discourse fluently in Latin; he had even, as a college exercise, turned the whole of Pope's *Messiah* into Latin verse; so well, indeed, that it was eventually published in a miscellany of poems and Pope was said to have spoken kindly of it. But in order to write one must live, however meanly, and in order to live as a writer one must earn money. Teaching, for which he had no real aptitude or liking, was a possibility, but in any reputable school a degree was usually necessary. But there were rumours that the usher, or under-master, of Stourbridge Grammar School was leaving, and remembering the circle of acquaintance he had made there while staying with 'Parson' Ford he decided to make the journey and see what could be done.

Before he could leave, however, the London *Daily Post* for Tuesday August 24th 1731 arrived with the brief announcement of Cornelius Ford's death, and the shock of this sudden news was not lessened by the whispered gossip which soon reached Lichfield. Ford's reputation had not improved in the six years since his young cousin had stayed with him at Pedmore. Neglect of his clerical duties, long absences in London and reckless spending had finally, earlier in the year, landed him as a debtor in the Fleet Prison. He had been bailed out by some of his acquaintance and a few months later, in circumstances which nobody seemed to know, had died in his favourite bagnio. This was a horrid blow, but Johnson made the journey nevertheless, hoping that the recommendations of Ford's friendly half-brother might have weight with the school governors. The application was made, supported by recommendations from his connections, and he whiled away the time of waiting among Ford's little group of amiable acquaintance. There was no lack of gossip or news from London to be talked about, some of it tantalizing (since he longed to go there), some of it alarming. Five kings of the Cherokee Indians had been brought to England from Carolina and presented to George II, submitting themselves, with a quaint ritual, to the British Crown. The popular actor, Colley Cibber, had been made Poet Laureate with a salary of a hundred pounds a year and a butt of sack, 'or £50 in lieu of the latter beverage'. Sir Thomas Pengelly, chief baron of the exchequer and one of the finest barristers of the day, had died with several others at Blandford during the Lent Assizes, as a result, it was said, of 'the pestilential stench of some prisoners brought to their trials'. (This 'stench', against which nosegays were provided for judges on the Bench, was in fact gaol fever

From a coloured bust: Colley Cibber, Poet Laureate,
dramatist and actor, whom Johnson held in low esteem but
considered 'by no means a blockhead'

or typhus, a disease spread by body-lice in crowded prisons.) And in London an 'alarm' with a singularly modern ring about it had been created 'by incendiaries who sent letters to people possessing great wealth, ordering them to leave sums at certain places, or that their houses would be fired and themselves murdered, which gave rise to considerable terror and uneasiness among the rich'. Stourbridge, being nearer to Birmingham, was a more immediate source of news and newspapers than Lichfield.

The period of waiting ended in disappointment: Johnson was turned down for want of a degree, and a young Bachelor of Arts from Oxford duly appointed. He returned home in a mood of despondency, more than ever determined to think of some way out of the impasse in which he found himself. Burying himself in books as his only solace, absent-minded and inattentive in the shop, he cannot have been much help to his father, still less to his distracted mother during Michael's absences. To this aimless period, in fact, belongs an incident that has become legendary, so revealing is it of his contumacy at the time and his remorse for ever after. Michael's health had been deteriorating for some time past, though no one seems to have realized that he was ill. One day, feeling worse than usual, he stayed in bed, asking Sam to go to Uttoxeter in his place to attend the bookstall. Johnson refused, feeling it beneath his dignity to sell goods from a barrow in the open market. 'Pride was the source of that refusal, and the remembrance of it was painful.' So painful, even in his seventies, that on an impulse fifty years later he 'went to Uttoxeter in very bad weather, and stood for a considerable time bareheaded in the rain, on the spot where my father's stall used to stand. . . . And I hope,' he added, 'the penance was expiatory.'[17] His feeling of guilt over the years was made even more distressing by the fact that within a few weeks of the incident his father died suddenly of 'an inflammatory fever', a condition which, like many other diseases, the medical jargon of the time shrouds in mystery. Michael Johnson died early in December 1731 and was buried at St Michael's Church on the eastern edge of Lichfield, since nearby St Mary's, of which he had been churchwarden, had no burial-place.

After the funeral the house in Breadmarket Street must have seemed unnaturally large and quiet, but the bookselling business, what was left of it, had to be carried on, and Sarah Johnson took charge. Michael had left no will, and indeed, apart from the house and the shop with their contents there was little to leave. These, by the marriage settlement, were Sarah's for life, and as Nathaniel was now nineteen and quite happy to become a bookseller it became urgent that Sam should find some means of subsistence. He cannot have had much hope of anything from his father's estate; when six months later this was settled his share proved to be twenty pounds. One pound went to pay off a pressing debt, the rest he divided carefully between saving and spending. 'June 15 – I laid by eleven guineas,' he wrote secretively in Latin in his diary, 'on which day I received all of my father's effects which I can hope for till the death of my mother (which I pray may be late), that is to say, nineteen pounds; so that I have my fortune to make, and care must be taken that in the meantime the powers of my mind may not grow languid through poverty, nor want drive me into wickedness.'[18]

He took the remaining eight pounds back with him to Market Bosworth, where a few months before, through the recommendations of family friends, he had at last obtained a post as usher in the local grammar school. The statutes required a university degree, but this was brusquely waved aside by the squire of Bosworth, Sir Wolstan Dixie, whose word was law in the school as well as in most other matters pertaining to his property. The job carried a salary of twenty pounds a year with a house or cottage suitable for an under-master. This last requirement Sir Wolstan also chose to ignore, having a fancy for an unpaid lay chaplain in his own household, who would say grace before meals and be useful in one way or another. So Johnson found himself lodged amid the imposing furnishings of Bosworth Hall, treated as though he were something between a servant and a poor relation. Sir Wolstan was well known to be a selfish and bullying man, the very type of hard-drinking, fox-hunting boor so often satirized in the stage comedies of the period; his boon companions were men of the same sort, and being unmarried he felt under no obligation to observe good manners or indeed any sort of civilized behaviour. John Taylor, knowing him well enough and most of the disagreeable stories told about him, described him as 'an abandoned, brutal rascal', and there is no reason to suppose that he exaggerated. The yeomen and small farmers with whom he associated were probably even rougher than their landlord. 'The inhabitants set their dogs at me,' wrote Hutton the local historian after a visit to Bosworth, 'merely because I was a stranger. Surrounded with impassable roads, no intercourse with man to humanize the mind, no commerce to smooth their rugged manners, they continue the boors of nature.'[18] This may have been an exaggeration, since another contemporary refers to Bosworth as 'the genteelest part of the county', but the awfulness of the roads, especially in winter, was one of the accepted miseries of country places. At Market Bosworth a walk of twenty-five miles lay between Johnson and home, deepening his sense of isolation in what he afterwards described as the unhappiest period of his life. And if twenty-five miles of road seems not worth considering today we can hardly do better than glance at a description of the highways of England on which John Wesley, perpetually travelling on horseback through this same period, was beginning to spend the greater part of his days: 'Not upon such roads as we ride over today, but on ways muddy, rocky and wet; grassy or marshy tracks, full of pits, deep-rutted, narrow . . . covered with loose flintstones, or not covered at all, darkened by overhanging, unlopped trees, or washed away on the open moors. On these highways coaches were stranded, broken or over-turned frequently; trees for Chatham shipyards were sometimes two or three years on their way from Sussex; old ladies were hauled laboriously to the parish church in winter by teams of oxen. The account of a journey of a prince and his retinue, travelling in carriages from Windsor to Petworth, reads like the voyage of a convoy in rough weather, with many wrecks.'[19]

Teaching in the Bosworth school was tedious and unrewarding. The headmaster was an elderly parson set in his ways, the hours were long, the rules strict, and no language but Greek and Latin was allowed to be spoken. Of the pupils we know nothing except that Johnson found them insufferably dull, as they no doubt found the rules of grammar it was his duty to hammer into them. It was hard to say, he wrote to Hector, whose difficulty was the greater – his to explain nonsense, or theirs to understand it. And when school was over there was no alternative to the restrictive and distasteful life at the Hall, where his host was frequently drunk and invariably quarrelsome. Johnson made the best of a hateful situation by reading late into the night in his own room, but it was not always possible to absent himself without inviting abuse; and this led to some explosive clashes. Finally, after little more than six months at Bosworth, the moment came when he could bear it no longer, and putting his few belongings together he left without ceremony, retracing the twenty-five miles of rutted roads that lay between him and Lichfield with all the feelings, as he wrote to Taylor, of a man coming out of prison. These miserable few months, when he had been treated with what he felt to be 'intolerable harshness', left a traumatic impression; it had been an experience 'which all his life afterwards he recollected with the strongest aversion, and even a degree of horror. But it is probable', Boswell sensibly observed, 'that at this period, whatever weariness he may have endured, he laid the foundations of much future eminence by application to his studies.'[20]

Within a few days of reaching home he heard of another possibility of employment. The usher of the school at Ashbourne had died suddenly, and since his friend John Taylor was now carrying on his father's practice there as an attorney, and he had other acquaintances in the place, he sent off a batch of letters begging for recommendations. If it would help for him to come to Ashbourne, he told Taylor, 'I shall readily do it.' But the school governors apparently thought otherwise; rumours of his ill success at Bosworth may have reached them, or some lewd comment from Sir Wolstan Dixie, whose malice was capable of carrying over considerable distances. Whatever the reason, they did not grant him an interview and the post was filled by a youthful applicant as unqualified as himself. It seemed as though nothing more could be done: he must make up his mind to earn his keep in the shop.

And then, when the future seemed closed to every kind of promise, a spark of hope appeared in the shape of a letter from Edmund Hector in Birmingham. This best and most affectionate of Johnson's friends had for some time been practising as a surgeon in the busy manufacturing town, lodging with one of its first booksellers in the High Street, and he now proposed that Johnson should join him there for a while as his guest. The bookseller, one Warren, had recently started a small weekly newspaper, *The Birmingham Journal*, and this, Hector imagined, might lead to something. At all events it was better for Johnson in his present depressed state to be in the stir and company of a great town rather than brooding over his books in the stagnation of Lichfield. Hector was well aware of Johnson's neurotic tendencies and was afraid that his friend's fears for the balance of his mind might even come true. 'I was apprehensive', he told Hawkins many years later, 'of something wrong in his constitution, which might either impair his intellect or endanger his life, but, thanks to Almighty God, my fears have proved false.'

Hector's judgment was sound: a change of scene and good company was the best medicine. What he could not forsee was that the visit to Birmingham would have bizarre consequences, and that Johnson would plunge head over heels into the greatest emotional adventure of his life.

4

Johnson Married

ECTOR'S circle of acquaintance in Birmingham was nothing out of the ordinary, but agreeable enough. There was another John Taylor, fast becoming rich in that metallic city through his genius in the gilding and japanning trade; a Huguenot refugee, a Monsieur Desmoulins, now writing-master in the local grammar school, who would presently marry Dr Swinfen's daughter Elizabeth; and the family of Harry Porter, the mercer across the High Street, from whom Hector bought his clothes. With all of these, and more, Johnson was soon on comfortable visiting terms, when he was not sitting at home with Hector and Warren or passing an evening with either in the local tavern. At twenty-three he had a good head for drink, and in later life was apt to claim that no man had ever seen him drunk. This was not strictly true, though very nearly so. There had been one memorable occasion at the Swan Inn when he and Hector had both passed out after an evening with one of Johnson's hard-drinking Ford relations. 'This fellow will make us both drunk,' said Johnson, who knew the man's habits. 'Let us take him by turns and get rid of him.' Hector took the first shift and had drunk three bottles of port with Ford by the time Johnson arrived, already well primed by drinking at Harry Porter's 'instead of saving himself'. Hector was apparently too far gone to stagger next door to his lodging, so went to bed at the Swan and next morning found Johnson 'had been his bedfellow' and had been 'very drunk'. Johnson, Hector told Boswell, had tried to deny this. '*Literally* speaking Hector had not *seen* him drunk, though he was *sure* of the fact.'[1]

The only other person who ever claimed to have seen Johnson the worse for drink was Sir Joshua Reynolds, who remembered that one night in Devonshire, when he had drunk three bottles of wine after supper, Johnson found his speech so much affected that 'he was unable to articulate a hard word which occurred in the course of his conversation'.[2] Certainly an excellent record for any man in that drunken age, and especially for one who liked his wine and the enlivening effects of it as much as Johnson did. But then, even in his twenties and long before he had dreamed of becoming a teetotaller, he managed his social drinking with common sense. 'Drinking may be practised with great prudence,' he told Boswell; 'a man who exposes himself when he is intoxicated has not the art of getting drunk . . . I used to slink home when I had drunk too much.'[3] His only imprudence in the Swan Inn episode had been in drinking quietly with Harry Porter before undertaking the serious business with Ford.

Johnson's cider mug

Harry and Elizabeth Porter were modestly hospitable and he found a tranquil domestic pleasure in their company. Both were in their early forties, both came of solid middle-class families of Warwickshire and Leicestershire small landowners and squires. They were not well off, however, and it was Harry Porter's elder brother, a wealthy Leghorn merchant, who was paying for the education of their two sons. Their seventeen-year-old daughter, Lucy, was living at home when Johnson first appeared among them, and vividly remembered the young man's stark appearance. 'He was then lean and lank, so that his immense structure of bones was hideously striking to the eye, and the scars of the scrofula were deeply visible. He also wore his hair, which was straight and stiff, and separated behind; and he often had, seemingly, convulsive starts and odd gesticulations, which tended to excite at once surprise and ridicule.'[4] He must, at this period, have been in the most unattractive stage of his growing-up; later, when he had filled out and his manner had become less farouche, his countenance, according to Bishop Percy, 'when in a good humour, was not disagreeable. His face clear, his complexion good, and his features not ill-formed; many ladies have thought they might not be unattractive when he was young. Much misrepresentation', Dr Percy added, 'has prevailed on this subject among such as did not personally know him.'[5]

Mrs Porter at least, who was intelligent and well read, was so much struck by his conversation as to discount his peculiarities of appearance and manner, and told her daughter after this first visit, 'This is the most sensible man that I ever saw in my life.'[6] Thus was begun a habit of visiting the Porters, either with Hector or alone, and it is probable that even at this early stage Johnson and Mrs Porter felt some mutual attraction. She was almost exactly twenty years older than he, and therefore a reassuring and maternal figure to whom he could talk without shyness. She was a spirited talker herself, with a shrewd wit and enough experience of life to realize that young Johnson's energy of mind was something extraordinary. How good-looking or otherwise she was at this time it is difficult to say, since David Garrick's cruel descriptions of her in her late fifties and his outrageous mimicries of the two of them have survived, whereas Mrs Porter's appearance at the age of forty-four has not. The only known portrait of her is as a young woman, and in it she certainly appears both lively and attractive. William Shaw, a friend of Johnson's later years, described her as 'still young and handsome' when Johnson first met her, and 'so shrewd and cultivated that in the earlier part of their connection he was very fond of consulting her in all his literary pursuits'.[7] In the first two years of their acquaintance there was no question of a more romantic approach, for Harry Porter was still very much alive and Johnson seems to have been fond of the company of them both. It is more likely than not, however, that a stirring of attraction was felt between them even in these early days, for Johnson was confessedly a man of strong sexual feeling who considered that 'unless a woman has amorous heat she is a dull companion', and 'Tetty' had a coquettish manner, which is not usually a foible of the unresponsive. According to Hector, who lived with him 'in the utmost intimacy and social freedom', Johnson's sexual morals at this time were irreproachable. 'He drank freely, particularly "Bishop" with a roasted orange in it,'[8] but 'never was given to women'. He was attracted by them, but never yet seriously in love, and Boswell, relying on Hector's information, was certain that even at this 'ardent season' of his life he 'formed no criminal connection whatsoever'.

It is all the more probable, then, as the months passed in Birmingham without any notable change in Johnson's situation, that an unexpressed attraction towards Elizabeth Porter may have kept his attention from straying in other directions. Her company was a comfort, but it could be nothing more, and this obscure frustration may well have deepened the lethargy and depression into which he still frequently fell, in spite of Hector's devoted and unselfish efforts. Hector, indeed, spared no pains to get Johnson launched into the literary world, on no matter how modest a level: he supported him for six months in Warren's house, and encouraged him to contribute to *The Birmingham Journal*. A few essays were written and published which have not survived, only one copy of the *Journal* of that early period having ever come to light.

Presently, depressed and irritable and probably unwilling to put Hector to further expense, Johnson moved into lodgings of his own, where the young surgeon, increasingly anxious over his friend's obstinate and mysterious neurasthenia, continued to visit him and offer encouragement. Johnson had once at Warren's table mentioned that a book he had read at Oxford, a French translation of a Portuguese missionary's travels in Abyssinia, might make, if re-translated, an attractive proposition for an English publisher. Warren was interested, and Hector now pressed his friend to undertake it. More, he borrowed a copy of the book from Oxford, and when Johnson was too languid to write or even to leave his bed, wrote down the work chapter by chapter from dictation, the book meanwhile propped on Johnson's knees among the bedclothes. If Hector had not been a medical man as well as a friend he might well at this point have given up the struggle. He was, however, shrewd enough to realize that Johnson was sick, and therefore spared no effort to urge him into any stimulating mental activity which would take him out of himself. In this he to some extent succeeded: Johnson's translation of Lobo's *Voyage to Abyssinia* was eventually published, earning him the sum of five pounds, and though not of itself a remarkable piece of writing (Johnson himself never thought highly of it) shows traces here and there of the Johnsonian gentle irony and rhythmic cadences. He commends, for instance, the Jesuit father's 'modest and unaffected narration' of a journey through an exotic and largely undiscovered land. The priest has 'consulted his senses, not his imagination. He meets with no basilisks that destroy with their eyes, his crocodiles devour their prey without tears, and his cataracts fall from the rocks without deafening the neighbouring inhabitants.'

The book was tolerably well received (one literary magazine's review ran to fifteen pages) but it made no real stir, and Johnson now faced the problem of what to do next. A translation of the Latin poems of Politian, a late Renaissance writer, was his next idea, his mind apparently running on translations. It could be published by subscription, a popular method of the time, and issued from the family bookshop by his brother Nathaniel. The volume of poems was borrowed from the Pembroke library, and printed proposals for the scheme sent out, quoting the price of five shillings for the unbound volume; but apparently nobody wanted to know about Politian and the scheme was abandoned. (The borrowed volume, incidentally, was found in Johnson's bookshelves after his death, which suggests that in the matter of returning books he was no better than the rest of us.)

Nothing else of any promise suggested itself, and since Warren's weekly was too small to offer regular employment Johnson returned to Lichfield in the early spring of 1734, having passed more than eighteen fruitless months in Birmingham. The summer was spent in reading for the proposed translation of Politian and mooning about the bookshop when this, too, came to nothing. And then suddenly, in September, news reached Lichfield that Harry Porter had unexpectedly died, and almost in a matter of hours Johnson was back in Birmingham.

There seems no doubt that what he had in mind was the possibility of marrying Mrs Porter; certainly from his point of view the idea, though eccentric, had much to recommend it. He was strongly attracted to her, and although he had nothing to offer but himself, and Harry Porter had died insolvent, Tetty herself still had her marriage portion of several hundred pounds; enough, at least, to make a practical basis for their life together. The fact that she had an eighteen-year-old daughter, a son of sixteen and another of ten years old, seems not to have deterred him. Jervis was training for the navy at the expense of his rich uncle, and the younger boy was to be brought up in his uncle's trade as a Leghorn merchant. Lucy would presumably stay with her mother; girls were domestically useful and not expensive. He must have known that he would meet with some response from Mrs Porter, or he would hardly have pressed his suit so soon after her husband's death. Some time was allowed to elapse for the sake of decorum while Johnson went backwards and forwards between Lichfield and Birmingham and Harry Porter's chaotic financial affairs were settled. Then, some three months after the funeral, Tetty privately accepted her young lover's proposal, and Johnson formally applied for his mother's permission to get married.

What perhaps neither of them was wholly prepared for was the scream of derision with which almost everyone concerned greeted the news. Mrs Johnson, indeed, behaved better than might have been expected: 'she knew too well the ardour of her son's temper, and was too tender a parent to oppose his inclinations.'9 Whatever she may have felt, if she were not prepared to lose her son she was helpless in the matter. Anna Seward, the Canon of Lichfield's daughter who became known as the 'Swan of Lichfield', wrote Boswell an account of their interview which, since she was not born until eight years after the event, is certainly suspect, but which is sufficiently true to the characters of all concerned to have become famous. (She no doubt had the anecdote from her mother, who was the daughter of Johnson's schoolmaster, John Hunter.) 'No, Sam,' Mrs Johnson is supposed to have said, 'my willing consent you will never have to so preposterous a union. You are not twenty-five and she is turned fifty.' (She was actually forty-six.) 'If she had any prudence, this request had never been made to me. Where are your means of subsistence? Porter has died poor, in consequence of his wife's expensive habits. You have great talents, but as yet have turned them into no profitable channel.' 'Mother,' replied Sam, 'I have not deceived Mrs Porter: I have told her the worst of me; that I am of mean extraction; that I have no money; and that I have had an uncle hanged. She replied that she valued no one more or less for his descent; that she had no more money than myself; and that, though she had not had a relation hanged, she had fifty who deserved hanging.' (There is no evidence of Johnson's ever having had an uncle hanged, so this finishing touch may well have been Anna Seward's.)

Tetty's own family were angry and disgusted. Her elder son was so indignant that he told his mother that if the marriage took place he would never see her again, a promise he implacably kept. The younger boy was not old enough to be so ruthless; he remained passively with his uncle and made no move towards a reconciliation with Johnson until long after his mother's death. Neither of the boys, in fact, ever saw her again. Lucy Porter was the only one of the three who remained loyal, and one supposes she had little choice.

Birmingham and Lichfield being both full of disapproval and gossip, they decided to be married privately in Derby, and also to wait until the late summer, no doubt for propriety's sake. Johnson meanwhile began to make serious efforts to find employment. The best of the monthly periodicals of the day was *The Gentleman's Magazine*, an entertaining pocket-size publication started four years before by Edward Cave and published from St John's Gate, Clerkenwell. Cave was later to become an important figure in Johnson's life, but in 1735 they were still unknown to one another, and Johnson's not over-tactful letter, suggesting himself as a contributor who could improve the quality of the magazine, went unanswered. Having drawn a blank in this direction he next, no doubt after serious discussion with Tetty, began making plans for starting his own school, 'a private boarding school for young gentlemen,' he wrote to a friend, 'whom I shall endeavour to instruct in a method somewhat more rational than those commonly practised'. It was Tetty's money, of course, which made the scheme possible. Although he had no degree, once a suitable house had been found, advertisements published and friends persuaded to help with recommendations, he would surely find pupils. Buoyed up with this hope and in a mood of unusual happiness and confidence, he sent for the books which he had left with Taylor at Oxford five years before, and after a brief interlude of private tutoring near Lichfield applied for a marriage licence at Derby. On July 7th 1735 Johnson and 'the widow Porter' set out from Lichfield on horseback on the Derby road for an excursion of twenty-five miles which was to end in marriage.

It seems not to have been a particularly idyllic journey, for Tetty was inclined to scold and Johnson, always more inclined to common sense than to vagaries, grew tired of being obliging. 'She had read the old romances, and had got into her head the fantastical notion that a woman of spirit should use her lover like a dog. So, Sir, at first she told me that I rode too fast, and she could not keep up with me; and when I rode a little slower, she passed me, and complained that I lagged behind. I was not to be made the

'Tetty' Johnson's wedding-ring, which after
her death Johnson preserved, Boswell tells us, 'as long as he lived, with affectionate care,
in a little round wooden box'

slave of caprice; and I resolved to begin as I meant to end. I therefore pushed on briskly, till I was fairly out of her sight. The road lay between two hedges, so I was sure she could not miss it; and I contrived that she should soon come up with me. When she did, I observed her to be in tears.'[10] This reaction was typical of Johnson, even when most deeply in love and on his wedding journey. His attitude towards women, even to those to whom he was most tenderly drawn, was always the traditional one of dominant male, offering protection and love in return for full authority. He could be tender, playful, coaxing, engaging even to the point of gallantry, but he would not be made a fool of – as even on her bridal day his adored Tetty had better realize. He had, as his friends admitted, an 'uncommon desire to be always in the right', and since he preferred intelligent and spirited women to insipid ones his ascendancy was best preserved by an authoritative manner which could often terrify. Tetty's tears may have been real or they may have been diplomatic: in the day-to-day sparring of married life she was already an experienced contender.

Where they lived at first we do not know: probably at Lichfield, where there was room enough and expenses would be minimal. The scheme of the private academy hung fire; Johnson was soon diverted from it by hearing that the school at Solihull, a village near Birmingham, was in need of a headmaster. The post would make no demands on Tetty's capital and Gilbert Walmesley was at once petitioned to use his influence. Obliging as ever, he wrote a letter of recommendation to the governors, who were cautious enough to make inquiries before sending a reply. Mr Johnson's achievements as a scholar, they eventually wrote to Walmesley with some embarrassment, were all that could be wished, 'but then he has the character of being a very haughty, ill-natured gent., and that he has such a way of distorting his face (which though he can't help) the gent. think it may affect some young lads; for these two reasons he is not approved on. . . .'[11] His physical oddities, as so often before and after in Johnson's life, had inspired dislike, and indeed they unfitted him to a marked degree for the career of schoolmaster. It is strange that he himself seemed unaware of this; his own experience of schoolboys should have warned him; but he was still convinced that his best chance of a steady and respectable living lay in teaching, and returned to the scheme of his own academy as the better plan.

Once again Walmesley was applied to for advice and help and proved himself as beneficent as ever. He pointed out a suitable house to let at Edial near Lichfield, and while the necessary alterations were in progress canvassed among his friends for likely pupils. He succeeded in finding three – his own favourite *protégé* David Garrick, now nineteen and certainly too old for such an establishment if he had not been admittedly backward in his studies, his younger brother George, and one Lawrence Offley, a relation of the Aston family from Cheshire, into which Walmesley, weary at fifty-six of being a bachelor, had decided to marry. It seems probable that these three, in spite of an advertisement in *The Gentleman's Magazine* ('Young gentlemen . . . boarded and taught the Latin and Greek languages by Samuel Johnson') represented the whole catch: even if, as Hawkins later supposed, there were one or two day-boys as well, it was a poor beginning, and the situation did not improve. The truth began gradually to emerge that Johnson's intellectual gifts, remarkable though they were, by no means fitted him to be a schoolmaster. His own precocious learning had been achieved by solitary and irregular methods, and was not of the sort that could be conventionally transmitted. He did his best, forcing himself to rise early, to establish the accepted curriculum of learning by heart, translating, and weekly examinations, but it was all no use. While he laboured doggedly at the uncongenial task and Tetty and her daughter struggled with the house-keeping, the boys, led by the incorrigible David Garrick, were secretly enjoying what they saw as a comic pantomime.

Garrick had not yet fully discovered himself as an actor; he was supposed to be preparing for one of the gentlemanly professions, ostensibly the Bar; but his genius for mimicry was already prodigious, and though Johnson had no idea of this it was being furtively employed to his schoolmaster's undoing. Not only were Johnson's tics and grimaces heaven-sent material for a young comedian; there was also the uproarious joke of his being in love, and with a woman old enough to be his mother. The horrid boys were in the habit of stealing to his bedroom door and watching through the keyhole for a view of his 'tumultous and awkward' love-making, which Garrick would after-wards mimic until they were helpless with laughter. Even many years later, when he was a famous actor, he would still in male company perform this favourite set-piece, representing the lady as alone in bed, complaining of delay, while Johnson puffed and stumbled round the bed, crying, 'I'm coming, my Tetsie, I'm coming!'[12] There was a variation, too, which was equally popular. In this the lady would still be solitary among the pillows while Johnson (as in fact he was to do during the Edial period) struggled to compose the verses of a classical tragedy, responding to her hints by reciting ponderous couplets from the manuscript and absent-mindedly, in mistake for his shirt-tails, stuffing a corner of the sheet into his breeches.

If Johnson had any idea of what was going on it would explain the resentment and jealousy which, in spite of their lifelong friendship, he so often unaccountably displayed towards David Garrick. There were only seven years between them, they had been boys together, and now Johnson was in the role of authority and had been made a joke. He had a poor opinion of David's intellect, which was the reverse of academic and rather of that intuitive and visually interpretative sort which Johnson (perhaps owing to his poor eyesight) did not appreciate. He himself had a gift for mimicry, as Mrs Thrale, who came to know him more intimately even than Boswell, delightedly observed: 'He was incomparable at buffoonery. With better eyesight, and a form less inflexible, he would have made an admirable mimic.'[13] Johnson exhibited this gift in conversation but considered it a paltry one, and was therefore grudging in praise of actors in general and of Garrick in particular. Garrick's huge success and the vast fortune that he made were a cause of jealousy, as David himself was aware. 'Is it not to be expected he should be angry,' he once said to Hannah More, who had wondered that Johnson could say such sharp things both to and about him, 'that I, who have so much less merit than he, should have had so much greater success?'[14] Their relationship was, in the main, one of enduring friendship, though acerbity on Johnson's side gave it a sharp edge. He was notably critical of Garrick, though he would let no one else be so – 'I will allow no man to speak ill of David that he does not deserve.'[15] This rancour is difficult to account for in so generous a nature unless it were that, repressed but still obscurely painful, there

LEFT Anna Seward, the 'Swan of Lichfield'. Her grandfather, the Reverend John Hunter, had been Johnson's headmaster at the Grammar School. RIGHT Hannah More, an eminent Bluestocking and writer on educational and religious subjects, who became a warm friend and admirer of Johnson

was a memory of scuffling at the keyhole and of Davy's laughter. It was, after all, an outrageous indelicacy, difficult to forgive. Garrick, said Johnson once with meaning, 'can represent all modes of life, but that of an easy fine-bred gentleman'.[16] Whatever the truth, it was Garrick, unfairly enough, who had the last word, describing Mrs Johnson to Boswell as 'very fat, with a bosom of more than ordinary protruberance, with swelled cheeks, of a florid red, produced by thick painting, and increased by the liberal use of cordials; flaring and fantastic in her dress, and affected both in her speech and in her general behaviour' –[17] an exaggerated piece of comedy, as Boswell was the first to admit, and belonging to a later stage of Tetty's history.

Since no new pupils were forthcoming it became apparent that the school must come to an end. Offley was going to Cambridge, the younger Garrick had been transferred to another school and David, whose progress under Johnson had been meagre, was to be sent for coaching to a headmaster in Rochester to prepare him for his studies for the Bar. It was impossible to maintain much interest in teaching during these final months, and Johnson solaced himself with sketching out an ambitious classical tragedy which he hoped, when the school was finally given up, would make his fame and fortune in the theatre. It was to be called *Irene*, and concerned a Turkish sultan who, to prove that his manhood had not been compromised by love, savagely murdered the beautiful Greek slave who was his favourite. It is a cruel theme, and seems in every way a curious choice, but classical tragedy and the Oriental tale were equally popular conventions of the time, and would have been considered suitable for an ambitious beginner. Teaching by day and toiling at his play by night (Garrick at least had not made up that circumstance), Johnson was in a more than usually serious mood, reflected in a prayer recorded in his diary: 'I have this day entered upon my twenty-eighth year. Mayest thou, O God, enable me for Jesus Christ's sake, to spend this in such a manner that I may receive comfort from it at the hour of death and in the day of judgment. Amen. I intend tomorrow to review the rules I have at any time laid down, in order to practise them.'[18] One of these rules, which he seems to have rigorously kept for the next twenty years, was to give up wine and all fermented liquors. Drink, he had come to believe, much as he loved it, tended to exacerbate his melancholy; he could not be moderate; his only hope, therefore, was to abstain. 'I can't drink a *little*, child,' he told Hannah More many years later, 'therefore I never touch it.'[19] There was to be a period in middle life when he would go back to drinking and again leave off, but on the whole he kept to his resolution, and this early period at Edial, when he was still in his twenties, saw the beginning of his equally immoderate obsession with tea-drinking.

What was to be the next move? Garrick, on his way to Rochester, would be passing through London, and the thought of that legendary capital, which Johnson had never visited since he had been carried there as a child, was irresistible. In London was the literary life he longed to share, the theatre where budding dramatists might make their name, the taverns and coffee-houses where daily gathered the best intellectual company in the world. If he were to go with Davy Garrick it would be company for both of them and would relieve the tedium of the three-day journey. (They decided, as the cheapest method, to go on horseback, and Garrick later claimed that they had had but one horse between them and 'rode and tied', taking it in turns to ride.) For Johnson such a venture would mean the strictest economy, for Tetty's money had been sunk in the Edial venture and there was little left. There was no question at present of taking his wife and Lucy to London; when their furniture and belongings had been cleared from the schoolhouse they could live with Mrs Johnson over the bookshop, which Nathaniel had recently left to establish a branch of the business at Burton-on-Trent. This was the first but by no means the last time that Tetty was to be left behind: since money was so short there was no alternative, but she must have had misgivings at finding herself with no home of her own, most of her money gone and only her daughter and Mrs Johnson for company. Perhaps it was in this period of boredom that she first privately resorted to that more 'liberal use of cordials' that Garrick suspected, and which gradually did such disservice to her complexion. As to Johnson himself, he was not dismayed by the idea of arriving in London with empty pockets. Years later he and Garrick joked one night in company, pretending that Davy had travelled with three-halfpence in his pocket and Johnson with twopence-halfpenny: certainly they had little enough, and must have slept rough on the journey. Garrick would be well looked after as soon as he reached Rochester, and Johnson was not discouraged by the prospect of cheese-paring in London, having absorbed much practical advice from a hard-up Irish painter whom he had known in Birmingham, and who told him that 'thirty pounds a year was enough to enable a man to live there without being contemptible. He allowed ten pounds for clothes and

63

linen. . . . He said a man might live in a garret at eighteen-pence a week. . . . By spending threepence in a coffee-house, he might be for some hours every day in very good company; he might dine for sixpence, breakfast on bread and milk for a penny, and do without supper.'[20]

As soon as they reached their destination – 'Three days I was upon the road, and on the fourth morning my heart danced at the sight of London'[21] – Johnson followed these instructions almost to the letter, finding himself cheap lodgings with a staymaker just off the Strand, with a congenial tavern near by 'with very good company'. 'I dined', he told Boswell, 'very well for eightpence. . . . It used to cost the rest a shilling, for they drank wine; but I had a cut of meat for sixpence, and bread for a penny, and gave the waiter a penny; so that I was quite well served, nay, better than the rest, for they gave the waiter nothing.' The excitement of the arrival was soon spoiled for both of them by the bad news which followed fast from Lichfield. Before David had even had time to set out again for Rochester word had come that his father, Captain Peter Garrick, had suddenly died, and this shock followed close on a message even more unexpected – Johnson's brother Nathaniel was dead too, and already buried.

Nathaniel Johnson is a mysterious figure, and there is no evidence to tell us why, at the age of twenty-four, he should have died in this sudden manner and been buried so hastily. It has been suggested that he committed suicide, and it seems certain that in his business dealings at Burton-on-Trent he had been found guilty of some fraud or other; some disgrace, at all events, for which he had written to ask his mother's forgiveness for 'these crimes . . . which have given both you and me so much trouble. . . . I know not nor do I much care in what way of life I shall hereafter live,' he wrote, 'but this I know, that it shall be an honest one.'[22] He proposed to 'go to Georgia in about a fortnight' – that ill-starred American colony which General Oglethorpe was optimistically settling with bankrupts, debtors, penitent prostitutes and other graduates of the gaols, and where the Wesleys and Whitefield, inspired by the spiritual possibilities of such a population of sinners, were to have some disillusioning experiences. But Nathaniel did not emigrate to Georgia: he died and was buried within three days of Johnson's departure for London, leaving his brother with an uneasy conscience over the lack of affection there had always been between them. 'As to my brother's assisting me,' Nathaniel had written, 'I had but little reason to expect it when he would scarce ever use me with common civility.' Nathaniel was dead in Lichfield and Johnson was alone in London, and any thought of amendment was too late.

OPPOSITE Mrs Elizabeth Porter, who later married Samuel Johnson and became his 'Tetty', his 'dear Girl', his 'charming Love'

5

London with Tetty

HE London in which Johnson and Garrick now found themselves provincial strangers was both beautiful and hideous, alluring and terrifying, a hodge-podge of elegance and filth, luxury and misery, deafening with the din of cobbled streets and dangerous to the pedestrian at night. It was a city of not more than half a million inhabitants, and still, by modern standards, extremely small; yet its crowds were amply big enough to throng the streets, to load the solitary London Bridge with traffic, to swarm in the squalid rookeries and alleys. From the roof of any good building in the City or West End one could see green fields and open country to the north and west, the Thames with its marshes and market gardens to the south, and to the east the river again with docks and wharves and the spreading fertile fields of Kent and Essex.

Ever since the Restoration the fashionable areas had been moving westward as the nobility and gentry built on desirable sites adjoining St James's, leaving the City and its ancient surroundings to commerce and the law. St James's Square was still clean and new, a marvellously open cobbled space with a railed parterre and stone-rimmed pool round which carriages rolled and sedan chairs were carried, and where even ordinary citizens could walk in comfort, the pavements being well protected by stout posts. Here Frederick, Prince of Wales for the moment had his town-house, since being turned out of St James's Palace by his father, and almost every other was owned and inhabited by a duke or lord. The great Lord Chesterfield had been born in the Palladian-fronted mansion on the corner of King Street, and had only on his marriage left it for Grosvenor Square, a few minutes' walk away and almost equally splendid. (It was round these squares, and particularly St James's, that Johnson always remembered walking all night with the disreputable poet Savage, when neither had money enough for a tavern, or even a 'night-cellar'.) The West End, Whitehall and St James's were spacious, elegant and impressive, with open squares and parks where it was agreeable to stroll in the daytime, where ladies took the air in closed carriages and gentlemen took exercise on horseback; even cows were to be found in St James's and the Green Park with their attendant milkmaids, ready to supply a drink of milk for a penny. The comfort and

OPPOSITE St James's Park and the Mall in the 1740s

St James's Square about 1725. Lord Chesterfield was born in the house on the corner of King Street
belonging to his grandfather, Lord Halifax, and lived in the square until 1733. Here Johnson
and Savage, when their pockets were empty, strolled and talked all night.

cleanliness of these superior neighbourhoods, however, were not to be relied on, despite
the vast population of servants on which the standards of the upper class depended.
Roads were not always cobbled or sidewalks paved, and in bad weather could be dangerous or impassable. No civic body provided for the cleaning of the streets: as in provincial
Lichfield, the pavement before his door was the householder's responsibility, and
nothing much could be done if he chose to ignore it. There was no organized clearance
of refuse: garbage and slops of all kinds were thrown out at night by those who did not
choose to employ a scavenger. There was as yet no sewage system; even the grandest
houses had their close-stools and cesspits, visited in the dark hours by the night-soil

man, who, according to his elaborately engraved trade card, 'decently performs what he undertakes, being always at the work himself, empties vaults and cesspools, unstops funnels and cleans drains at the very lowest prices'.

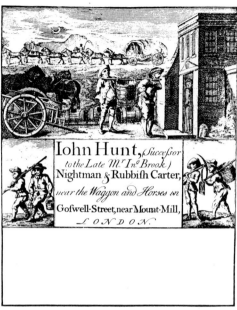

The trade card of a night-soil man whose work was
carried out by lantern-light and moonlight

If conditions in the fashionable quarters of London were less safe and salubrious than they seemed, this was nothing compared with the more plebeian areas to which Johnson gravitated. The streets off the Strand were narrow, dirty, and on moonless nights dangerously dark: street lighting, apart from the lamps over private doors, was still a dream of the future. Beggars, thieves and prostitutes abounded: what is now called 'mugging' was so common as to be hardly worth mentioning, except as it affected trade. Shopkeepers and coffee-houses constantly complained to the City Marshal 'that their customers are afraid when it is dark to come to their houses and shops for fear that their hats and wigs should be snitched from their heads or their swords taken from their sides, or that they may be blinded, knocked down, cut or stabbed';[1] those resolute to avoid such misfortunes either stayed indoors at night or went abroad well armed. ('I don't make a visit without a blunderbuss,' wrote Horace Walpole.)[2] There was no appealing to the police, since no such body existed: only in another ten years would the Fielding brothers, Bow Street magistrates, begin their campaign for a paid and professional police force to replace the unpaid parish constable and the night-watchman. Meanwhile in the suburbs and outlying districts highwaymen plied a fairly profitable trade; Dick Turpin was in his heyday (a commonplace criminal, disappointingly unlike his later romantic image), while pickpockets and felons of all sorts made a nefarious living out of a population which took violence for granted. There was much accidental disaster, too, in those crowded streets, for no rule of the road had yet been agreed upon and coaches, wagons and horsemen moved as and where they pleased, often coming to blows as to precedence in some narrow passage and providing the newspapers with grisly items – skulls crushed under wheels, brains scattered on pavements, bulls run mad on the way to Smithfield and disembowelling pedestrians. Only gradually, through a mixture of habit and convenience, did horsemen and vehicles begin to observe a custom of keeping to the left, and the practice became a rule later sanctified by law. In the same way, purely by chance, the custom of walking on the right was gradually accepted, so that those arguments in narrow or muddy places, which Johnson's mother had seen in her youth, now rarely happened. 'When I returned to Lichfield after having been in London,' Johnson remembered, 'my mother asked me, whether I was one of those who gave the wall, or those who took it. . . . Now' – nearly forty years later – 'it is fixed that every man keeps to the right; or, if one is taking the wall, another yields it; and it is never a dispute.'[3]

Johnson's first lodging in Exeter Street, a turning off the north side of the Strand, was in one of the liveliest areas of London, where never a day passed without news or incident. The Temple, that legal sanctum whose blackened walls he must have viewed with respect, had recently suffered a disastrous fire 'which continued burning until five o'clock in the morning, having consumed the Inner Temple kitchen, buttery and great staircase leading to the hall, and above thirty sets of chambers, before it was completely got under, as in the first instance no water could be procured'.[4] Building repairs had begun, but the place was in chaos. Even nearer at hand, and on the very day of Johnson's arrival, a disgraceful riot had taken place in Drury Lane Theatre, a crowd of footmen with 'offensive weapons' having broken down the doors and forced their way as far as the stage, to the great terror of the audience, among whom were the Prince and Princess of Wales. The reason for this uproar, in which a number of persons were wounded, was that the footmen considered free use of the upper gallery as their privilege, and chose this means of protest when they found the doors of the gallery locked against them. The Pineapple Tavern in New Street, where Johnson dined, would be full of this local sensation the following day, by which time the ringleaders were already cooling their heels in Newgate. It was such breaches of public order, and the growing danger of the streets at night, that caused Parliament a few weeks later to pass a Bill for 'punishing persons going armed and in disguise', and for regulating and strengthening the 'watch' – at that time a futilely inadequate body of men who were supposed to maintain some sort of public order.

Johnson was not likely to be often molested by footpads, his size and strength being obvious; we know of only one occasion when he 'was attacked in the street by four men, to whom he would not yield, but kept them all at bay, until the watch came up'.[5] He wandered about at all hours, observing the night-life of the streets, their cruel contrasts between elegance and squalor, with a mixture of curiosity and compassion. The daytime hours saw him often in local coffee-houses and taverns, spending a few pence in order to read the newspapers or profit from an hour of conversation: he does not seem to have

OPPOSITE TOP The pillory at Charing Cross, still in regular use during the early 19th century.
BOTTOM Charing Cross, which, according to Johnson, saw 'the full tide of human existence'

Tyburn Turnpike, on the Oxford Road, now Oxford Street

worked very resolutely on his tragedy, or to have made more than a half-hearted effort to find work. There is a story that in the early days, while Garrick was still procrastinating in London, the two of them borrowed five pounds from a friendly bookseller in the Strand, one Wilcox, who, hearing that the bigger of the two intended to earn his living in London by his literary labours, kindly advised him, 'Young man, you had better buy a porter's knot.' It was impossible to shut himself in his threadbare room to compose blank verse when the stream of London life was all about him, busy, noisy, challenging, absorbing. After the provincial quiet of Lichfield it must indeed have seemed that 'the full tide of human existence is at Charing Cross'.

And he was not, even in these early days in London, quite bereft of social life of the genteeler sort, since there was at least one private house where he and Garrick were welcome, owing to their old connection with Gilbert Walmesley. Walmesley had now been married for a year to Magdalen Aston, a young woman thirty years his junior, and at the Bishop's Palace Johnson and Garrick had already met two of her delightful sisters – Molly, whom Johnson found particularly enchanting, and Kitty, who had married an aristocratic young rake called Henry Hervey. Harry, as he was known to his friends, was the fourth son of the first Earl of Bristol and a captain of Dragoons. Johnson had first met him several years ago, when his regiment had been garrisoned in Lichfield, and had found him lively and attractive, though he could not conscientiously approve his habits. Harry Hervey was so perfect an example of a certain eighteenth-century type that he might almost be a character in a play – the intelligent and amusing rake-hell (he was nicknamed 'Ha-Ha') who is more often drunk than sober, writes tolerable verse and spends most of his waking hours eluding his creditors. He was the despair of his father, who accused him of having 'given me more anxiety and disquiet than all my other children put together'. [6] He had now taken a house in London, where he entertained Johnson and Garrick and a host of friends, 'revelling and drunkening', to use the Puritan phrase, and spending his money like water. To complete this cheerfully Hogarthian picture, Hervey presently left the army for holy orders, becoming rector of Shotley in Suffolk, a family living; inherited a rich estate through his wife, changing his name to Aston to strengthen his claim; and even preached a few surprisingly good sermons, most of which, as it eventually came out, had been written for him by Johnson. Very little of this career, of course, could Johnson approve, but he was genuinely fond of the man, and not ungrateful. 'He was a vicious man,' he told Boswell, 'but very kind to me. If you call a dog Hervey, I shall love him.'

By mid-July Johnson decided that it was impossible to work amid the distractions of London, and moved into lodgings at Greenwich to finish his tragedy. But even here, in peace and quiet and with the noble park to walk in as he composed, *Irene* obstinately refused to come to life. Johnson was equally obstinate and pressed on, breaking off only long enough to write once more to Cave at *The Gentleman's Magazine*, proposing a new English translation of Sarpi's *History of the Council of Trent*, the oecumenical council which had laid down the lines of Catholic dogma after the Reformation. The idea seems not to have appealed very strongly to Cave, though the letter at least brought Johnson's name to his attention. When Johnson returned to Lichfield at the end of the summer, his play still unfinished, it seems to have been with the intention of fetching Tetty to London and establishing a home there – a step it would have been rash to take if there had been not even a hint of possible employment.

With the house at Edial finally disposed of – a business which, in Johnson's usual dilatory style, took the best part of three months – they packed their belongings and travelled to London together, settling at first in cheap lodgings near Hanover Square, another of those newly built and fashionable precincts which, in contrast to their own elegance, were still surrounded by mean unfinished streets, fields and cottages. The whole area both north and south of the Oxford Road was being rapidly developed, although the road itself (known today as Oxford Street) was still a rough and often dangerous highway running from Newgate through the slums of St Giles to the outlying village of Tyburn, where every few weeks the public hangings took place. Cavendish Square, a little to the north, was still unfinished, standing almost isolated among fields where it was not unknown for foxes to raid the hen-coops during the night. The Johnsons soon moved into a second lodging in this area, perhaps because it was cheaper, and it was at No. 6 Castle Street that the tragedy of *Irene* was at last finished.

Johnson now got in touch with Peter Garrick, David's elder brother, who had started business in London as a vintner and knew one or two influential people in the theatre. Together they repaired to the Fountain Tavern, a house of dubious reputation, for what must have been an unconscionably long session: Garrick drank wine and together they read through the entire tragedy. Impressed, Peter recommended it to Charles Fleetwood, the owner-manager of Drury Lane Theatre, but without success: Fleetwood was chiefly interested in the profits of knockabout pantomime, and since there was no rich patron involved he could not be persuaded even to read the script. So Johnson's one and only tragedy, which had been so laborious to write, was left on his hands – where indeed it was to remain for eleven years, until the manager of Drury Lane was none other than David Garrick.

This bitter disappointment had at least one good result: it drove Johnson to present himself in person to Edward Cave at the offices of *The Gentleman's Magazine* and to start work under that parsimonious and extremely able editor – a beginning in 'Grub Street' which was to lead at last to the success and fame which was his most passionate ambition. Grub Street was a real street in Johnson's day, near the Church of St Giles Cripplegate, inhabited by printers, booksellers and hack writers – an early and extremely impoverished sort of Fleet Street, where journeymen writers of all sorts lived from hand to mouth, often in the conditions delineated by Hogarth in his *Distrest Poet*. It had been a by-word since the seventeenth century, and when Johnson came to define it in his Dictionary it was (with a certain sly enjoyment) as 'the name of a street in London, much inhabited by writers of small histories, *dictionaries*, and temporary poems; whence any mean production is called *Grub Street*.' The jest had worn thin for the inhabitants by 1829, when at their petition the name was changed to Milton Street.

Here, working at first on such odd jobs as Cave allowed him, Johnson began to meet the professional writers who were constantly in and out of Cave's office and discussing everything under the sun in the neighbouring taverns. Far and away the most attractive was Richard Savage, the poet and playwright who had made a celebrity of himself not

LEFT *The Distrest Poet*: the miseries of Grub Street, in Hogarth's view. RIGHT Edward Cave, printer and publisher, editor of *The Gentleman's Magazine* and Johnson's first regular employer

only by being convicted of murder and then reprieved by the Queen's pardon (he had stabbed and killed a man in a tavern brawl), but by claiming to be the illegitimate son of the Countess of Macclesfield by her lover, Lord Rivers, and therefore a man of noble birth with a just grievance, since his supposed mother had totally disowned him. Whether or not there was any truth in his story we may never know; all that is certain is that, with all his talents and his charm, Savage was a wastrel and a sponge. It is odd that Johnson, by no means a credulous man, should have been convinced, as he most seriously was, by his extraordinary story. (Perhaps one day the missing piece of evidence will come to light, and we shall have to admit that Johnson was right after all and that Savage's claim was not just a cunning fiction.)

Another contributor of a very different type who also became a friend was Dr Thomas Birch, scholarly, busy and amusing, constantly trotting in and out of St John's Gate with the latest idea or scrap of literary gossip – 'running about', as Horace Walpole said, 'like a young setting dog in quest of anything, new or old'. Then there was Mark Akenside, the physician-poet, and – most unexpectedly – a young woman of twenty, Miss Elizabeth Carter, who had been contributing verses to the magazine ever since she was seventeen and who was something of a prodigy – fluent in Latin, Greek, Hebrew, Arabic and several modern languages, not to mention history, geography and astronomy. With her, too, Johnson was soon on affectionately friendly terms, though she was usually wary of men and somewhat afraid of them. The gentle playfulness of his manner towards women she found reassuring, while Johnson was charmed by the combination of modesty and learning in the girl who was soon to be known as the most scholarly of the Bluestockings.

It did not take Cave long to discover that the clumsy young man whom he was rather casually employing was a scholar with remarkable powers of literary judgment; a writer, moreover, who could turn his hand to almost anything. A Latin epigram, a translation from the French, a set of verses – once he had actually set about it he seemed able to produce all or any of them with a minimum of trouble. But it was not until the publication of his first long poem, *London*, that Cave fully realized his possibilities and took him on the staff as a regular contributor and sub-editor.

At first glance *London* may seem a curious production from the pen of a man long known to us as the city's most ardent lover, for the picture it paints is of a place corrupt, squalid and dangerous. So, of course, it was; but the explanation of Johnson's censorious attitude is that it was not altogether his own: he was following a literary fashion by imitating Juvenal's *Third Satire* on the follies and rottenness of Roman life. Any educated man would be already familiar with Juvenal, and so that the parallel could be better enjoyed, the relevant Latin lines were printed at the foot of each page. It is not a very great poem, but it has many memorable lines and passes an illuminating ray over the London that Johnson was beginning to know and would eventually love.

This London is a sinister place, where fawning favourites and corrupt ministers are destroying the country's greatness and making English honour 'a standing jest'. Opposition to Walpole's administration was at its height, and the Tory rebel in Johnson was happy to join in the anti-Establishment hue and cry. London is also a place of danger, where the ordinary citizen daily risks disaster.

Here malice, rapine, accident conspire,
And now a rabble rages, now a fire;
Their ambush here relentless ruffians lay,
And here the fell attorney prowls for prey;
Here falling houses thunder on your head,
And here a female atheist talks you dead.

No such female atheist has been identified, but falling houses were certainly a reality, jerry-building being as common then as now. Lady Wentworth, recommending a house in St James's Square to her son, wrote to him, 'It is a noble house and fit for you, and strong. No danger of its falling by great winds. . . . Abundance of the new buildings fall.'

The risks at night in the dark streets are hideously real.

Prepare for death, if here at night you roam,
And sign your will before you sup from home . . .
Some frolic drunkard, reeling from a feast,
Provokes a broil, and stabs you for a jest.

(It was in just such a drunken rumpus that Savage had killed his man.)

Yet ev'n these heroes, mischievously gay,
Lords of the street, and terrors of the way;
Flush'd as they are with folly, youth and wine,
Their prudent insults to the poor confine;
Afar they mark the flambeau's bright approach,
And shun the shining train, and golden coach.

Notorious among these 'heroes' were the Mohocks, a club of upper-class young men who specialized in drunken outrages. 'One of their favourite amusements, called "tipping the lion", was to squeeze the nose of their victim flat upon his face and to bore out his eyes with their fingers. Among them were the "sweaters", who formed a circle round their prisoner and pricked him with their swords until he sank exhausted to the ground, the "dancing masters", so called from their skill in making men caper by thrusting swords into their legs, the "tumblers", whose favourite amusement was to set women on their heads and commit various indecencies and barbarities on the limbs that were exposed. . . . A bishop's son was said to be one of the gang, and a baronet was among those who were arrested.'[7]

The poor are always victims, as Johnson, toiling shabbily in Grub Street and haunting 'the dungeons of the Strand', was resentfully aware:

This mournful truth is ev'rywhere confess'd,
SLOW RISES WORTH, BY POVERTY DEPRESS'D.

Was it wholly their fault if the wretched were driven to crime?

Scarce can our fields, such crowds at Tyburn die,
With hemp the gallows and the fleet supply . . .
All crimes are safe, but hated poverty.

A bitterness tinged with self-pity leaves a mark on the poem which is more personal than a purely imitative satire would produce. He knew his own capabilities, had married Tetty on the strength of them, and risked disaster by bringing her to London: now he found that, as a means of escape from poverty, they seemed useless. The wire-pullers and the flatterers were the ones to succeed:

> How, when competitors like these contend,
> Can surly virtue hope to fix a friend?

Even young Garrick was doing better than he was, making a tolerable profit now with his brother in the wine business, having verses published and impressing Cave with amateur theatricals at St John's Gate. Is it stretching imagination too far to suspect that at least one couplet in *London* reflects 'surly virtue's' resentment from Edial days, when scuffling and laughter were heard at the bedroom door?

> Of all the griefs that harass the distress'd,
> Sure the most bitter is a scornful jest.

Or was he thinking of Richard Savage, now a boon companion, whose woes, and determination to leave London to escape his creditors, were believed by many to be hidden subjects of the poem? There are points of resemblance between Thales, Johnson's 'imitated' hero, and Savage the man, by whose wit and gentlemanly bearing Johnson was perhaps too innocently impressed. It is tempting to identify the two, for it was about this time that Johnson and Savage spent those 'nights . . . in a perambulation round the squares of Westminster, St James's in particular, when all the money they could both raise was less than sufficient to purchase for them the shelter and sordid comforts of a night-cellar.'[8] It seems an unlikely attachment on both sides, but there is no doubt that Johnson was fascinated by Savage and glad to explore the town, even in this penniless manner, with a man who was equally at home on its highest and lowest levels. Savage's 'vagrant course of life', said Hawkins, 'had made him acquainted with the town and its vices; and though I am not warranted to say, that Johnson was infected with them, I have reason to think, that he reflected with as little approbation on the hours he spent with Savage as on any period of his life'.

This somewhat mysterious period led both Hawkins and Boswell to drop discreet hints of moral lapses on Johnson's part which might account, they thought, for the exaggerated sense of sin which in later life so haunted and distressed him. 'His conduct,' said Boswell, 'after he came to London, and had associated with Savage and others, was not so strictly virtuous, in one respect, as when he was a younger man. It was well known, that his amorous inclinations were uncommonly strong and impetuous. He owned to many of his friends, that he used to take women of the town to taverns, and hear them relate their history.' Boswell had secretly read a good deal of the private diary which Johnson destroyed a few days before his death, and evidently had grounds for believing that, in those early days in London, 'Johnson was sometimes hurried into indulgences which he thought criminal.'[9]

This 'not so strictly virtuous' image of Johnson seems strange when we remember the impetuous young bridegroom of three years before, but the strangeness might fade if we could know more of Tetty's unenviable situation in the interval. For her, the unlikely marriage was proving a fiasco. She had been left behind in Lichfield for more than half a year, her money was gone, and now that they were in London together the months dragged by in a succession of dreary lodgings in which she saw very little of her husband. Her sons were both implacably estranged; now she was deprived of Lucy as well; though she did not yet know it, she would never see her again. London was a strange city which she found lonely and oppressive: a domesticated and even house-proud woman, she had no house of her own and no possessions. Their few treasures had been sold to make ends meet, and even the little silver cup which Johnson's mother had bought for him as a child was, as he sadly recorded, 'one of the last pieces of plate which dear Tetty sold in our distress'. It appears that on occasion Johnson moved into separate lodgings, nearer the centre of town, and there may even have been a more serious, though temporary, rift. His leisure, if the idle hours of a man with little or no money can be called such, was spent in male company or strolling at night with Savage, 'not at all depressed by their situation', as he told Sir Joshua Reynolds, 'but in high spirits and brimful of patriotism'. Such diversions were far more stimulating than spending evenings alone with Tetty in murky lodgings, where she was all too apt to find fault with his slovenly habits or give a tart reply if he grumbled at the food provided. 'I asked him', wrote Mrs Thrale, 'if he ever huffed his wife about his dinner? "So often," replied he, "that at last she called to me, and said, Nay, hold Mr Johnson, and do not make a farce of thanking God for a dinner which in a few minutes you will protest not eatable."'[10]

It is an amusing anecdote, but one also suspects an undercurrent of bitterness. For her it was a life of poverty, solitude and boredom, and although Johnson's manner to her was always respectfully courteous and his affection assured, there were some distressing quarrels. For her it was a life so one-sided and disillusioning, for twelve years moving from one miserable lodging to another, that it is no wonder as health and spirits deteriorated that she turned more and more to romantic reading and the comforts of religion and the bottle. It is more than probable, too, that as Tetty advanced into middle age she may have felt less enthusiasm for that 'tumultuous and awkward' love-making which had made Garrick laugh, and Johnson's ardour being what we are assured it was, it would be surprising if he were never tempted by the coaxing prostitutes whom he himself admitted he sometimes treated in taverns to 'hear them relate their history'. Whatever the 'indulgences' may have been with which he afterwards reproached himself, his knowledge of the actual wretchedness of 'those forlorn creatures, the women of the town' (many being children of twelve years old and less, almost all doomed to destitution and disease), filled him with compassionate anger and led him to utter more than one cry of protest on their behalf. 'How frequently have the gay and thoughtless, in their evening frolicks, seen a band of these miserable females, covered with rags, shivering with cold, and pining with hunger; and, without either pitying their calamities, or reflecting upon the cruelty of those who perhaps first seduced them by caresses of fondness, or magnificence of promises, go on to reduce others to the same wretchedness by the same means?'[11]

The publication of *London* looked like a change of fortune for Johnson and must have encouraged him, but in fact it made little difference and the daily Grub Street grind went on as before. Cave thought well enough of the poem to print it, and persuaded Robert Dodsley, a more eminent publisher, to issue it under his imprint. Johnson for some reason had not admitted his authorship: he had offered it to Cave as the production of a needy friend, and to keep up the pretence the poem was published anonymously. By chance it appeared on the same day as a topical *jeu d'espirit* by Pope, and for this reason was eagerly discussed; the coffee-house public was curious to know who the new satirist could be – some suspected Pope himself – and a second edition was called for within a week. After that the interest died down, and although a third edition was printed before the end of the year this was chiefly because of the poem's appeal as an anti-government pamphlet rather than a work of literature. Johnson's romantic Jacobite leanings and his contempt for the Hanoverian succession made him momentarily popular with the heterogeneous opposition groups who had little in common beyond the fact that they were not in office, and who united only to blame the existing government for the increase in crime, the new moral permissiveness and any other national calamity. All in all, Johnson was richer by the ten guineas which Dodsley paid him for the copyright, and by an anonymous success which raised his hopes and as quickly confounded them again.

Other projects were even more unfortunate. A couple of elaborate political squibs, to which he had given much thought and care, failed to make any noise, and the much-discussed translation of Sarpi's *Council of Trent*, for which Cave had been paying him twenty-five shillings a week for tardy instalments, ran into unexpected trouble – another Johnson, a clergyman, keeper of Archbishop Tenison's library at St Martin-in-the-Fields, was apparently well advanced on the same project, and after an acrimonious exchange of letters the scheme was eventually abandoned by both parties. The bad luck continued. Johnson's next undertaking, on which his agreeable young friend Elizabeth Carter was also employed, was a work by the Swiss theologian Crousaz on Pope's extremely popular, and theologically rather daring, *Essay on Man*. No sooner had Miss Carter finished her share of the work than a rival publisher announced a translation of Crousaz's *Commentary*, the part on which Johnson was working by fits and starts. This time Cave refused to give up the enterprise and published Miss Carter's *Examination* with the promise that Johnson's *Commentary* would follow – as indeed it finally did in three years' time, when even the translator himself had lost interest.

It is a little puzzling that throughout all the years that Johnson worked for Cave he should have been quite as poor as he was, or as he claimed to be. Cave was a skinflint employer, but Johnson worked regularly on his staff for ten years and certainly earned what would have been regarded as a living wage by most professional hack writers. One suspects that he and Tetty were bad managers; Johnson, we know, was often quixotically generous, and like Savage and countless others who lived from hand to mouth in Grub Street, regarded money as something that never lay long in the pocket. 'If you could spare me another guinea,' he wrote at the end of a letter to Cave, '. . . I should take it very kindly tonight, but if you do not shall not think it an injury' – a postscript which shows Johnson as amiably reasonable as well as needy.

From the beginning of his employment on *The Gentleman's Magazine* there had been one regular feature which, apart from the innumerable odd jobs which kept him busy,

79

had a considerable success. In 1738 the House of Commons, hoping to silence the more virulent of Walpole's critics, unanimously resolved it a gross breach of privilege to publish any account of debates in Parliament, which had long been one of the monthlies' most popular features. Cave and his rival, *The London Magazine*, immediately invented almost identical devices for defeating the embargo. *The Gentleman's Magazine* began regularly publishing 'Debates in the Senate of Lilliput', in which the proceedings of Parliament, roughly reported by a spy in the public gallery, were presented under absurd Swiftean pseudonyms which the reader would have no difficulty in translating, 'Walelop' for Walpole, 'Ptit' for Pitt, and so on. The Lilliputian speeches were sketchy and approximate; the writer, one William Guthrie at first, would write what he thought was likely on the information given, and his copy was then passed on to Johnson for sub-editing and polishing. Before long Johnson had supplanted Guthrie altogether, and circumstantial and amusing debates were appearing which sometimes had never been thought of, let alone uttered, in Parliament. The system had its risks, for under this thin disguise members and ministers could be made ridiculous, and the reading public was largely unaware that the Lilliputian speeches were not faithful transcripts of what went on in the House. But no action was taken, perhaps because Walpole had sense enough not to risk looking foolish, and 'Walelop', 'Pulnub' and 'Ptit' continued to debate unchecked in Johnson's exuberantly Swiftean pantomime.

But it was none of it profitable, and the disjointed life of hack-work and lodgings was having a depressing effect on his married life. Perhaps Tetty protested vehemently at last; demanded a change in their life or at least an effort towards one; there may have been quarrels and complaints, and a resurgence of those emotional guilt-feelings which Johnson had so often felt, and for the rest of his life would continue to feel towards Tetty. At all events, when news arrived from Lichfield that a vacancy had occurred at Appleby Grammar School, and that somebody – almost certainly Walmesley – had recommended him for the post, he threw himself with unusual energy into a scheme to make himself eligible.

As before, the lack of a master's degree was the stumbling-block. The job was in every way desirable – near Lichfield and a salary of sixty pounds a year – and Johnson had still not wholly rid himself of the notion that, for him, schoolmastering was a suitable profession. Friends in Staffordshire had put his name forward, and even Pope, who had never met him but admired his talents, wrote a recommendation to Lord Gower, who, being a rich man in the right area, might be supposed to have influence. Oxford was unwilling to confer a degree simply for the asking, but Dean Swift, it was thought, if properly approached, might arrange to do something with Trinity College, Dublin. 'They say', wrote Lord Gower obligingly, 'he is not afraid of the strictest examination, though he is of so long a journey, and will venture it ... choosing rather to die upon the road, *than to be starved to death in translating for booksellers.*'

There was no question either of starving to death or of dying on the road, but that was the sort of thing one said to a patron, and this time Johnson evidently thought there was a chance of success, for leaving Tetty alone again in lodgings (once again 'at Mrs Crow's in Castle Street near Cavendish Square'), and abandoning his work at St John's Gate, he set off without delay on the road to Leicestershire.

6

Bachelor Interlude

HE governors of the school at Appleby were slow to make up their minds, and it soon became clear that they had no intention of appointing Samuel Johnson. Their delays and continued arguments may have encouraged him to hope, and at least gave him some excuse to pass several idle months in and around Lichfield; but he was never given an interview, and at the end of three months a suitable young clergyman was accepted. His disappointment was severe; he seems to have been unable, for another three months at least, to make the effort to return to Tetty and journalism in London.

Or was the charm, perhaps, of being in the midlands again, welcomed and entertained by his old friends in Lichfield, Ashbourne and the neighbourhood, too great to be resisted? Hawkins believed that there was a temporary estrangement from Tetty about this time, which might account for the six months' separation. On the other hand it may equally well have been the delights of idleness and luxury (the friends he visited were all enviably well-off) which, coupled with his own laziness, caused him to linger on in familiar haunts. The comfortless poverty of his London life, as he had so far lived it, held little attraction, and if he and Tetty had in fact reached some crisis in their marriage the remedy of a few months spent apart would seem sensible and the excuse would have soothed his conscience. There is no evidence of any communication between them for about five months – though this, of course, proves nothing.

The time spent in his mother's house was probably comfortable enough, if a little dull. It must have meant much to Sarah Johnson to have her favourite son at home again, and she and Lucy no doubt did their best to make his visit agreeable. But there was no disguising the fact that the bookshop was going downhill; it had already lost most of its interesting customers. Even Gilbert Walmesley was now ordering his books elsewhere, and without Michael Johnson's exertions as buyer and traveller the business was depending more and more on cheap stock, oddments, medicines and stationery. Lucy Porter had become Sarah Johnson's right hand; Anna Seward remembered being told that she 'would make no engagement on market days lest Granny, as she called Mrs Johnson, should catch cold by serving in the shop'. And although by Lichfield standards Lucy was well connected, she thought it no 'disgrace to thank a poor person who purchased from her a penny battledore'.

More enjoyable and certainly more luxurious than his spell at Lichfield was a prolonged visit to his old friend John Taylor at Ashbourne. Taylor was now embarked on the kind of life that most appealed to him, and which presented the greatest conceivable contrast to Johnson's. He had for some years carried on his father's business as an attorney at Ashbourne, and now, being married, had added his wife's fortune to his own and was a rich man. Law practice bored him; his situation and abilities, he felt, would be better suited by an easy and remunerative position in the Church. He accordingly took holy orders and was soon, for a good down payment, appointed to the rectory of Market Bosworth by Johnson's old tormentor, Sir Wolstan Dixie. With a curate to look after the parish he was free to pursue his political and agricultural interests, to be diligent on the Bench, to keep an excellent table and improve his already imposing country mansion. A great believer in pluralism, he collected preferments as another man might have collected marble Venuses, gradually adding to his tally as Prebendary of Westminster, Preacher of Broadway Chapel, Westminster, Rector of Lawford, Essex, Perpetual Curate of St Botolph, Aldersgate, and Rector of St Margaret's, Westminster. From time to time he made a surpliced appearance and delivered a sermon, but his habits, in Johnson's view, were 'by no means sufficiently clerical'. His interest was in country matters, his ambition the breeding of the best herd of dairy cattle in England.[1] Mrs Thrale, who visited him with Johnson in 1774, recorded in her journal that 'everything around him is both elegant and splendid. He has very fine pictures which he does not understand the beauties of, a glorious harpsichord which he sends for a young man out of the town to play upon, a waterfall murmuring at the foot of his garden, deer in his paddock, pheasants in his menagerie, the finest coach horses in the county, the largest horned cattle, I believe, in England, particularly a bull of an enormous size, his table liberally spread, his wines all excellent in their kinds'.[2]

Staying with Taylor in Ashbourne, well fed, waited upon and entertained, with books, conversation and company, was a complex of pleasures impossible to resist. Taylor had a congenial circle of friends among the local gentry who were ready to welcome the young man who could already be described as a character, a versatile talker and a poet. Johnson made an interesting impression, and in later life was fond of describing those of Taylor's friends (particularly the women) who had impressed him in their turn. There was William Fitzherbert, for instance, squire of Tissington, of whose gentlemanly manners he gave an account which could have satisfied Lord Chesterfield. He never knew, he said, 'a man who was so generally acceptable. He made everybody quite easy, overpowered nobody by the superiority of his talents, made no man think worse of himself by being his rival, seemed always to listen, did not oblige you to hear much from him, and did not oppose what you said.'[3] Squire Meynell of Bradley, three miles from Ashbourne, was an equally perfect specimen of another kind – the man whose whole pleasure is in sport and drinking, who has a choleric temper, and is happy only in his stableyard and kennels. Johnson was to remember him all his life for his hyper-British contribution to the conversation – 'For anything I see, foreigners are fools.'[4]

OPPOSITE Selina, Countess of Huntingdon, with two of her children, Elizabeth and Ferdinando, in 1740

82

dy Huntingdon
Eliz: Hastings
rd: Hastings.

With Fitzherbert's young wife, Mary, who was Meynell's daughter, he was temporarily so enchanted as to declare that 'she had the best understanding he ever met with in any human being'. This paragon, whose only fault was that she was almost *too* religious, had an older and intimate friend, Miss Hill Boothby, who was about the same age as Johnson. With her he began a friendship which was later to develop into one of remarkable tenderness: his letters to her, and other evidence, suggest that after the death of Tetty he even considered her as a possible wife. But this was more than twelve years later: at Ashbourne he saw her only as Richard Graves described her – 'a very sensible maiden lady'. At this time she may even have been too much of a Methodist for his entire approval, though there is no doubt that he found her a lively talker, capable of cheerfulness even in theological discussions. When Graves later depicted her as Miss Sainthill in *The Spiritual Quixote*, his comic novel about the Methodists, he made her sound amusing rather than priggish. 'To be sure,' she says, in an argument about praying, 'people might say their prayers in any place, or in any posture, and even in a warm bed'; but she was afraid that 'those who deferred their prayers till they lay down upon their pillows . . . very frequently fell asleep without saying them'.

The midland counties were full of gossip about the Methodists, for while Wesley was busy preaching and travelling between London and Bristol and Whitefield had left on his second missionary voyage to Georgia, an unexpected evangelist was attracting attention at Ashby-de-la-Zouch, only a few miles from Ashbourne. This was the redoubtable Selina, Countess of Huntingdon, wife of the ninth Earl, who now in her early thirties had been converted to Methodism and was inspired with the bizarre notion of bringing the upper classes to salvation. (She had a sharp snub from the Duchess of Buckingham, who wrote to her, 'It is monstrous to be told that you have a heart as sinful as the common wretches that crawl on the earth.') She was sending out her own lay preachers into the fields and villages, while at the great house at Donington Park or in her London house in Downing Street she invited her friends to hear the Methodist movement's most celebrated preachers. It was a social novelty, and the polite world attended largely out of curiosity; even such sophisticated unbelievers as Lord Chesterfield and Lord Bolingbroke found it worth while to frequent her sacred drawing-rooms and to observe the effects of different preachers, as they might compare the merits of rival actors. These same preachers would already, much earlier in the day, have made their appeal to a humbler audience crowded into the stableyard or kitchen, and here there would often be those moving evidences of salvation which were the preacher's best reward – faintings, tears, convulsions, mysterious and thrilling crises of emotion. Not everyone approved of such unorthodox goings-on, particularly in the villages, where there were soon to be outbreaks of violence against the Methodists; at Walsall and Wednesbury men and women were beaten and stoned, preachers thrown into ponds and a number of houses wrecked. Lady Huntingdon herself was mocked and abused in the streets and the windows of her house at Ashby were broken, but since these persecutions were 'for the Word's sake' she rejoiced in them as marks of divine favour and went resolutely on with her mission.

OPPOSITE The Reverend George Whitefield preaching, by John Wollaston, *c.* 1742

Most of the late autumn and winter of that year Johnson spent probably at Lichfield, where again he enjoyed good company with Walmesley and found additional delights, since his host was now happily married and his wife's attractive sister, Molly Aston, was often at the Bishop's Palace. Johnson was always, according to Anna Seward, 'fancying himself in love with some princess or other', and his relationship with Molly was certainly one of unalloyed pleasure. He told Mr Thrale she 'was a beauty and a scholar, and a wit and a Whig; and she talked all in praise of liberty. . . . She was the loveliest creature I ever saw!' The happiest period of his whole life, he said, had been that in which he had spent one whole evening talking to Molly Aston – 'That indeed was not happiness, it was rapture; but the thoughts of it sweetened the whole year.'[5]

There is no portrait of Molly Aston which does justice to Johnson's conception of her beauty, but she was evidently a fascinator, possessed of just those qualities which he found irresistible – a combination of good looks, wit, charm and high intelligence. Johnson's manners towards women were generally affectionate, flattering and playful, but he was never, said Hawkins, 'in any other sense a lover, than as he was the author of amorous verses. If ever he was in danger of becoming one in reality, it was of a young woman whom he used to call Molly Aston, of whose wit, and of the delight he enjoyed in conversing with her, he would speak with rapture.' But this, Hawkins was scrupulous to add, 'was in the lifetime of Mrs Johnson, and he was a man too strict in his morals to give any reasonable cause of jealousy to a wife'.[6]

LEFT Dr John Taylor, the worldly and bucolic clergyman who remained Johnson's close friend from his schooldays to his death. RIGHT Molly Aston, who so enchanted Johnson as a young man that he ever after remembered her as 'a beauty and a scholar, and a wit and a Whig . . . She was the loveliest creature I ever saw!'

Poor Tetty, left alone through the long months of what Johnson himself called 'the dreadful winter of Forty', had sufficient grounds for complaint, without adding to them, as she certainly did, the miseries of jealousy. A phenomenal frost set in at Christmas; snow fell in the Midlands and lay for almost three months. In London the Thames froze over, so that crowds walked from bank to bank, stalls were erected for food and amusements and the wretched watermen, deprived of their living, marched into the City carrying a boat in protest. The watermen were not the only ones to suffer: the damage sustained by shipping in the Thames below London Bridge was estimated at a hundred thousand pounds, the equivalent of a million or more today; stocks of coal were quickly used up and the shortage of water became so acute, and its price so high, that many poor families could not afford it. The phenomenal cold spread across almost the whole of Europe, and as the bitter weeks dragged by it was small comfort to shivering Londoners to read that in Poland and Lithuania the intense cold had 'forced bears and wolves from the woods to ravage the open country, and many people thereby lost their lives'.[7]

To add to her discomfort, Tetty had had some accident and injured her leg. She evidently wrote to Johnson to tell him this, perhaps also complaining of rumours that he was enjoying himself too well. His letter of reply is full of tenderness: 'I shall be very uneasy till I know that you are recovered, and beg that you will omit nothing that can contribute to it, nor deny yourself anything that may make confinement less melancholy.' She is to spare no expense on surgeons, since two or three visits from the best man available can be had for a guinea, 'which you need not fear to part from on so pressing an occasion'. He begs for a letter to relieve his mind, 'for I hope you do not think so unkindly of me as to imagine that I can be at rest while I believe my dear Tetty to be in pain'. She is his 'dear girl', his 'charming love', 'the most amiable woman in the world', and he hopes to be with her soon.[8] But still he lingered on in Lichfield.

The final reason for the long delay was that he and his mother, both desperately short of money, had decided to mortgage the house. On the very day on which he had written to Tetty the mortgage agreement was signed and the town clerk handed over the sum of eighty pounds at four and a half per cent. Twenty pounds of this was Johnson's share, and he promises to send the money, 'which I have received this night', the following Monday. As to the immediate future, there is news from David Garrick that Fleetwood at Drury Lane is now showing a little interest in *Irene*, which has at last 'become a kind of favourite among the players. . . . I hope it will reward me for my perplexities'.

It was not until the spring of 1740 that he seems finally to have returned to London, and by that time Fleetwood was playing fast-and-loose again, and it was Garrick, still nominally working with his brother as a wine merchant, who was busy with a light-hearted piece which Fleetwood had accepted and which was soon to go into production. Loyal to his old friend, Garrick commissioned Johnson to write the Prologue, which he contrived to do in a sufficiently amusing manner, deploring the 'Prodigious madness of the writing race' and the foolhardiness of the author.

> Oft has he seen the poignant orange fly,
> And heard th'ill-omened catcall's direful cry:
> Yet dares to venture on the dangerous stage,
> And weakly hopes to 'scape the critick's rage.

87

He would gladly have risked the dangerous stage himself, but no chance was offered. If he was present at Garrick's first night, and saw the delectable Kitty Clive in the lead – 'the best player I ever saw' – and heard the warm applause, it was as near as he got to the realization of his own dream. When the excitement was over he returned to the old routine at St John's Gate. Though he did not know it, he was not to return to Lichfield for twenty years, nor would he ever see his mother again.

Cave was glad to have him back; so versatile an assistant was invaluable, and for the next three years he kept him steadily at work. Johnson and Tetty had now moved into lodgings in the Strand to be nearer the magazine offices, and were soon shifting restlessly about as before, changing to Bow Street, Fetter Lane, Holborn, then back again into the Strand area. What their domestic life was like we have no idea; Johnson hardly ever saw his friends at home; the place for talk and enjoyment, in his view, was the coffee-house or tavern, and these delights it would have been highly unconventional for his wife to share, even if she had wished to. 'In contradiction to those', said Hawkins, 'who, having a wife and children, prefer domestic enjoyments to those which a tavern affords, I have heard him assert, that a tavern chair was the throne of human felicity.'

This was the period when he first met John Hawkins, a serious and intelligent young man of twenty-one, a carpenter's son who had done well at school and was now articled to an attorney in Bishopsgate. Music and literature were his chief interests; he was already a frequent contributor to *The Gentleman's Magazine* when he and Johnson met at St John's Gate and drifted into a friendship which was to last for forty-five years and bring Hawkins a certain fame as Johnson's first real biographer. Two men less alike in temperament it is difficult to imagine. Hawkins was staid, precise, lacking in humour and, as he rose in the world, disagreeably rough in manner to inferiors. Yet he had good qualities, and is perhaps unfortunate in being remembered chiefly by Johnson's description of him as 'a most unclubable man', and by the comically exaggerated account Johnson once gave at Mrs Thrale's of his old friend's shortcomings. 'Why, really,' he said, 'I believe him to be an honest man at the bottom: but to be sure he is penurious, and he is mean, and it must be owned he has a degree of brutality, and a tendency to savageness, that cannot easily be defended.' 'We all laughed,' Fanny Burney added in her diary, '*as he meant we should.*' He was by no means entirely serious, but the joke has survived and Hawkins has suffered for it. When, some forty-five years after their first meeting, his life of Johnson was published, it was so soon eclipsed by Boswell's master-piece that comparatively few people since have bothered to read it, which is a pity: limited though he was, Hawkins had a certain shrewdness, and knew Johnson on terms of equality and for a much longer period than Boswell.

He was undoubtedly one of the more prudent and respectable frequenters of Cave's office. The most outrageously improvident of them all was the Irish poet, Samuel Boyse, a man impossible to help and equally impossible not to pity. 'After squandering away in a dirty manner any money which he acquired,' Johnson related, 'he has been known to pawn all his apparel.' When Johnson had patiently collected the money to redeem his clothes they were back in the pawnshop within two days, and 'This was when my acquaintances were few, and most of them as poor as myself. The money was collected by shillings.' After this second stripping the naked poet 'sat up in bed with a blanket wrapped about him, through which he had cut a hole large enough to admit his arm, and placing the paper upon his knee, scribbled, in the best manner he could, the verses he was obliged to make'. In spite of his 'low vices, among which were gluttony and extravagance', Johnson felt a certain sympathy for Boyse. The frugal Hawkins was less inclined to make allowances: 'He was intoxicated whenever he had the means to avoid starving, and was voluptuous, luxurious, and boundlessly expensive.'

Another eccentric, working at this time as an index-maker for Cave, was the man who called himself George Psalmanazar and who had been the most successful hoaxer of his age. A Frenchman of humble birth, quick-witted and with intellectual leanings, he had learned something of the geography of China and Japan from the missionary Jesuits who educated him, and on these slender foundations constructed a highly profitable fraud. Wandering through Europe as a mendicant student he attracted notoriety by passing himself off as a native of Japan, and was so successful (knowledge of the Far East in those days being almost non-existent) that he was encouraged to invent Oriental religious ceremonies and a spoken and written language which he described as 'Formosan'. (Here he was a little off the mark, not having realized that Formosa was a part of China.) His imposture was detected by an astute Scottish army chaplain, who saw in it a means of profit to them both, and publicly baptized him into the Protestant Church.

Mr George Psalmanazar.

The only known portrait of the reformed imposter who
called himself George Psalmanazar

Psalmanazar was now represented as a victim of the Jesuits, who, he said, had abducted him from Formosa and had used great brutality to force him to accept the Catholic faith. He had bravely defied the Inquisition, and now, being a convinced Protestant, was sure of a sympathetic reception in England. Here, as he had expected, he was a wild success, his cleverness and effrontery carrying all before him. Bishops and ministers were equally deceived, impressed by his fluent gabble in the Formosan tongue, which was 'sufficiently original, copious and regular to impose on men of very extensive learning'. Bishop Compton even financed him for six months at Oxford, where he was given rooms in Christ Church and the Bishop set about raising funds for him 'to teach the Formosan language to a set of gentlemen, who were afterwards to go with him to convert these people to Christianity'. While at Oxford he wrote an invented history of Formosa and continued to enjoy a profitable celebrity until the army chaplain who had sponsored him was promoted, in recognition of his Christian services, to be Chaplain-General of the English forces in Portugal; without his moral support the illusion imposed on the public soon collapsed. Psalmanazar now had to suffer much ridicule and abuse, and lived a life of miserable poverty until, like Johnson and Wesley in their turn, he came upon William Law's *Serious Call* and was apparently converted. He confessed his imposture, declared repentance, and from then on earned a meagre livelihood in Grub Street, writing for twelve hours a day, impressing the world with the sanctity of his demeanour and comforting himself when the day's work was done with a pint of strong punch laced with opium. He was in his sixties when Johnson first met him in the Old Street alehouse where Psalmanazar spent his evenings, and was so deeply impressed by the old man's piety and learning that he never allowed himself to refer to the past, and treated the reformed humbug with sincere reverence. Whether or not Psalmanazar in his old age was playing a part as convincingly as he had once acted the 'Prince of Formosa' we are unlikely to discover; certainly Johnson, who as Reynolds said, 'appeared to have little suspicion of hypocrisy in religion', accepted him as a kind of latter-day saint. Many years later, when Mrs Thrale curiously asked him who was the *best* man he had ever known, he surprised her with the reply – 'Psalmanazar'.

Garrick still occasionally came to St John's Gate, and once, to amuse Cave, put on an impromptu performance of Fielding's *The Mock Doctor* in the big room over the archway, with printers and apprentices reading the supporting parts. He was coming to the end, now, of the frustrating period when he was trying to be a wine merchant: the lure of the theatre was too strong, and with the success of his farce and encouragement from Drury Lane he was waiting for a chance to escape from family pressures and prove himself as an actor. It soon came. Henry Giffard, manager of the theatre at Goodman's Fields near Aldgate, had tried him in one or two trifling parts on tour, and now was prepared to risk giving him the lead in *Richard III*. It was a difficult time for the smaller theatres, for since the restrictive Act of 1737, designed to control indecency and discourage attacks on the government, only Drury Lane and Covent Garden were licensed, and Goodman's Fields and others of its kind were nominally closed. The Act, however, was not strictly enforced, and Giffard had reopened with public concerts, which required

OPPOSITE The Theatre Royal, Drury Lane, in 1776

no licence, a play being thrown in as an extra, 'free of charge'. It was in this fashion, with the drama disguised as an interlude between the halves of a concert, that Garrick first had a chance to show his powers. His success was immediate. Within a year he was topping the bills at Drury Lane, earning five hundred guineas a year and causing a pleasant flutter of scandal by setting up house with his 'Pretty Peggy', the celebrated actress Peg Woffington.

Johnson's life, by contrast, was depressingly drab, but he, too, was maturing and developing his powers, especially under the journalistic disciplines (by no means always contemptible) imposed on him as a writer. He was now entirely responsible for the mock-debates which had originally been written by Guthrie, and was to pour out half a million words of this strange confidence trick over the next three years. It is difficult today to understand how these contrived speeches could be accepted, as they certainly were, as the genuine article; it can only have been due to the absence of actual parliamentary reporting for comparison. The speeches, for safety's sake, were not even topical; months sometimes passed before a particular debate appeared in the magazine, the subjects of discussion and the names of the speakers having been supplied by door-keepers in the House of Commons who were bribed by Cave. Johnson told Boswell that he sometimes 'had nothing more communicated to him than the names of the several speakers, and the part which they had taken in the debate'; sometimes he had only 'scanty notes furnished by persons employed to attend in both Houses of Parliament'. The debates, he admitted, were written from very slender materials, often from none at all – 'the mere coinage of his own imagination'. He aimed to copy the known styles of the various speakers, irony and wit for Chesterfield,[9] eloquence for Pitt, and so on – but in spite of some lively characterization the manner remained indubitably his own, and the matter was dashed off at a speed that suggests a deliberately induced state of imaginative excitement. Hawkins, who saw him frequently at this time, believed that 'he was able to raise his imagination to such a pitch of fervour as bordered upon enthusiasm, which, that he might the better do, his practice was to shut himself up in a room assigned to him at St John's Gate, to which he would not suffer anyone to approach, except the compositor or Cave's boy for matter, which, as fast as he composed it, he tumbled out at the door'.

The fundamental reason for the success of the debates was the growing antagonism towards Walpole as Prime Minister. The political hunt was up, his enemies were pressing to the kill, and the situation (as has happened in the United States in our own day) sharpened the public appetite for political news, however unreliable. When, in 1743, Walpole finally resigned, interest in the debates rapidly dwindled and they were soon discontinued. Johnson himself had given them up by this time, bored at last and perhaps also a little uncomfortable about the deception. They had, however, greatly enlarged his knowledge of the political scene, so that, while remaining a conservative with romantic Jacobite leanings, he was no longer the naïve Tory who had battled with Walmesley. As far as Cave was concerned, the debates had been an unparalleled success, sending up the magazine's circulation from ten to fifteen thousand. He 'manifested his good fortune', Hawkins wryly observed, 'by buying an old coach and a pair of older horses; and, that he might avoid the suspicion of pride in setting up an equipage, he displayed to the world the source of his affluence, by a representation of St John's Gate, instead of his arms, on the door panel'.

In the little room assigned to him Johnson was now at work on a new and more congenial project – a series of brief biographies of famous men, which were to attract more general readers to the magazine. It was a favourable moment, with biography as a genre becoming increasingly popular, and in a new, more intimate style than had been acceptable in the past. The contemporary taste, which Johnson shared, was for describing people as they really were, rather than as monuments for the edification of posterity. The war with Spain, which Walpole had so long opposed and which was now being waged to the public's satisfaction, chiefly on the high seas, made the lives of famous admirals a topical choice, and Johnson's studies of Blake and Sir Francis Drake made exciting reading, appearing, as he put it, 'at a time when a nation is engaged in a war with an enemy, whose insults, ravages and barbarities have long called for vengeance'. He undertook no original research, but like the experienced journalist he now was, extracted the meat from archaic accounts and published histories and presented it afresh in a style which would hold the reader's interest. Here, for instance, is a passage from the life of Drake, describing his dealings with the Spaniards at San Domingo:

> Drake, having some intention of treating with the Spaniards, sent to them a negro boy with a flag of truce, which one of the Spaniards so little regarded, that he stabbed him through the body with a lance. The boy, notwithstanding his wound, came back to the general, related the treatment which he had found, and died in his sight. Drake was so incensed at this outrage that he ordered two friars, then his prisoners, to be conveyed with a guard to the place where the crime was committed, and hanged up in the sight of the Spaniards, declaring that two Spanish prisoners should undergo the same death every day, till the offender should be delivered up by them. They were too well acquainted with the character of Drake, not to bring him on the day following, when, to impress the shame of such actions more effectually upon them, he compelled them to execute him with their own hands.

Johnson who, in a very real sense, was to become the father of modern biography – partly on his own, partly through his influence on Boswell – was thus learning his craft in a popular and practical school, studying its techniques, testing the responses of his readers, developing his own biographical philosophy from its first premise: 'We are to consider mankind, not as we wish them but as we find them, frequently corrupt, and always fallible.'

The reason why Johnson worked chiefly at St John's Gate, rather than at home, is clear enough. His slovenly habits were a constant irritation to his wife, who still, even in the cramped quarters of indifferent lodgings, struggled to keep up a respectable appearance, so that there was a good deal of bickering between them. 'She had a particular reverence for cleanliness,' he told Mrs Thrale, 'and desired the praise of neatness in her dress and furniture, as many ladies do, till they become troublesome to their best friends, slaves to their own besoms, and only sigh for the hour of sweeping their husbands out of the house as dirt and useless lumber.' If she had ever tried to convert him to her way of thinking in the matter of personal appearance she must long ago have given it up as hopeless, for by this time even in Grub Street Johnson was remarked as being grubbier than most. For this, Hawkins primly decided, Tetty herself was to blame. 'Her inattention to some, at least, of the duties of a wife, were evident in the person of her husband, whose negligence of dress seemed never to have received the least correction from her, and who, in the sordidness of his apparel, and the complexion of his linen, even shamed her.' Proceeding from this ill-supported theory (he had never met Tetty, nor ever seen the interior of any of their homes) he decided that 'if this fondness of Johnson for his wife was not dissembled, it was a lesson that he had learned by rote, and that, when he practised it, he knew not where to stop till he became ridiculous.' It certainly struck several people besides Garrick that 'there was somewhat crazy in the behaviour of them both; profound respect on his part, and the airs of an antiquated beauty on hers'. But to suggest that this eccentric marriage was not based on an equally eccentric and lasting affection is to ignore all the most moving and intimate passages of Johnson's letters, prayers and diaries. Like most men, he despised the female sex in general, yet at the same time he loved and honoured a surprising number and variety of women. He had 'a degrading opinion of us poor fair sex', as Fanny Burney observed; adding, in fairness, 'I mean, in general; for in particular he does them noble justice.' Whatever her failings and absurdities, Tetty deserves sympathy; and however unsatisfactory Johnson may have been as a husband he valued her as a person, and devoutly did her 'noble justice' in the end.

Sir John Hawkins, a lifelong friend of Johnson and his first real biographer

7

The Stony Road to Fame

ONDON in the seventeen-forties was never without sensational news of one sort or another, to be discussed in all the coffee-houses where newspapers were provided, or to make topics for the humbler street-trade in broadsheets and ballads. Two of the Prince of Wales's children, for instance, the future George III and his sister Augusta, had been stopped by highwaymen as their carriage was being driven across Hounslow Heath, and the armed robbers had made a gallant impression by crying 'God bless them!' as soon as they heard who the children were, and bidding the coachman drive on. This patriotic behaviour, however, had been somewhat spoiled by their stopping the following carriage containing royal servants and luggage, and 'plundering them', as the newspapers reported, 'of a large booty'.

The Spanish war was a continuous and anxious topic; news travelled slowly from the Caribbean, and when it came was too often of ships lost and British crews drowned or captured, although on balance it seemed that the Spanish had lost quite as many and it was reckoned that their financial losses had been even greater. The press gangs were more active than ever, making sudden swoops on all the dockside areas; in the space of thirty-six hours in 1741 no fewer than 2,370 men were seized for the Navy. Such figures were alarming, and did nothing to encourage enlistment, since it was well known that service in a man-o'-war was a more gruelling and brutal experience than a prison sentence. From time to time, however, the news was encouraging to patriotism, as when wagon-loads of Spanish silver, the plunder of British victories at sea, were drawn through the streets of London to the Bank under a strong guard of seamen, with military bands playing and colours flying. Spanish ships made much better prizes than British ones: the captured *Aquapulca* and her treasure were estimated by the Admiralty to be worth £1,600,000.

Such happenings were daily topics for discussion, but in fact the people in general felt comfortably remote from the war. England was an impregnable island and relatively prosperous: campaigns and conquests meant expansion of trade, particularly in the export of woollen cloth, the great British staple. Besides, Europe was always at war from top to bottom: this was something one took for granted, thanking God for the English Channel and only wishing that France and the Netherlands were further off. Even when

The Press Gang: an early 19th-century sketch by Thomas Rowlandson

George II, less interested in his image as King than as Elector of Hanover, decided to embroil himself in the War of the Austrian Succession by personally leading his German troops against the French at Dettingen, the British public were less alarmed by the possibility of a French declaration of war against England (which in fact happened within a few months) than gratified that their monarch had won a difficult victory. Local London news of politics, crime and violence was far more interesting, and then as now there was no lack of variety. If we in the nineteen-seventies are astonished to learn that pickpockets in Italy find it worth while to fly to London for a royal wedding, the London which Johnson traipsed in the seventeen-forties could offer news of hazards and enterprises equally bizarre. 'London is really dangerous at this time,' Shenstone wrote to a friend in 1743; 'the pickpockets, formerly content with mere filching, make no scruple to knock people down with bludgeons in Fleet Street and the Strand, and that at no later hour than eight o'clock at night: but in the Piazzas, Covent Garden, they come in large bodies, armed with couteaus, and attack whole parties, so that the danger of coming out of the playhouses is of some weight in the opposite scale, when I am disposed to go to them oftener than I ought.'

Clement's Inn, the dignified complex of legal buildings which Johnson would pass almost daily on his way through Temple Bar, had been the scene of an outrageous murder which had shocked the legal profession. The senior advocate of the Inn, Mr John Penney, had been missing for twelve days when his body was discovered in the depths of the communal privy, 'with his throat cut and a large hole on one side of his head, from whence his brains protruded'. He had been robbed of diamond rings and a

96

considerable sum of money by his personal servant. The murderer's published confession and public execution provided a satisfying finale to the drama.

Against this murky background, under a sky from which in winter even the snow fell grey with soot, Johnson laboriously extended his repertoire as a ghost-writer. His old schoolfellow Robert James, now a practising physician and not yet, presumably, as continuously drunk as Johnson was later to describe him, had conceived the idea of compiling a vast 'medicinal dictionary', and appealed to Johnson to help him launch the project. This meant, first, publishing 'proposals' to attract subscribers, and then composing a graceful dedication to a fashionable physician, Dr Richard Mead, who in Johnson's words 'lived more in the broad sunshine of life than almost any man'. (Horace Walpole thought this nonsense: in his view, 'Dr Mead had nothing but pretensions.')[1] The work was to appear in fortnightly parts, and when complete could be bound into three large folios. Johnson found the work (he was collaborating now on the text) unexpectedly congenial. Starting with brief biographies of medical men, he had begun to explore the subject of 'physick' itself; reading under James's guidance for such sections as he was commissioned to produce, he discovered a fascination with the subject which was to last him for life. Although James gave him his grounding in chemistry and medicine, Johnson seems never to have thought very highly of his friend's 'compounded medicines', of which the most successful were the 'Dr James's Fever Powders' which made him famous. These were said to have had a disastrous effect on Goldsmith in his final illness, but continued nevertheless to sell as a patent medicine well into the twentieth century.

The spring of 1742 saw the final capitulation of Walpole to his enemies. He resigned, reluctantly, as Prime Minister, and was 'kicked upstairs', as one of his colleagues put it, to the House of Lords. His reign of down-to-earth businesslike government, focused on peace and commercial prosperity, was over; from now on there would be years of foreign wars, internal political struggles and, as climax, the romantic and futile Jacobite Rebellion. But, as before, the life of the ordinary citizen was little affected. Walpole's resignation in February was of less concern to the man in the street than the completion of the great central arch of Westminster Bridge, to which crowds flocked to see the unfinished structure decorated with banners. Soon it would be possible – thanks chiefly to the lotteries which had financed the venture – for pedestrians and vehicles to cross direct from Westminster to Lambeth instead of going the long way round by London Bridge, or taking the horse-ferry. That, at least, was what everyone hoped: in fact it was another eight years before London's spectacular second bridge – three hundred feet wider than London Bridge and boasting fifteen arches – was opened to traffic. For the present, anyone who needed to cross the river at any point outside the neighbourhood of the Tower would have to go by wherry.

Johnson was now immersed in a laborious but fascinating task which was to absorb him for eighteen months or more and considerably enlarge his knowledge of literature and history. Edward Harley, second Earl of Oxford, had died the preceding year, and the huge library which he had inherited from his celebrated father had been bought as a speculation for thirteen thousand pounds by Thomas Osborne, a bookseller of Gray's Inn. This was certainly a bargain, the lump sum for the books being several thousand pounds less than the first Lord Oxford had paid for their sumptuous binding in morocco, turkey and russia leather, not to mention doeskin and velvet. Before they could be re-sold it was necessary to prepare a detailed catalogue of the fifty thousand books and as many pamphlets, and for this Johnson was engaged to work with William Oldys, the antiquary, who for a brief period had been Lord Oxford's literary secretary. The work was as much an education as a university course in bibliography would have been, and it was in this sense that Johnson chiefly profited by a task that was slow, exacting and laborious. In the course of writing the 'proposals' or advertisements of the coming sale, composing a descriptive introduction to the catalogue and collaborating with Oldys in the colossal task of identifying and describing every item in the vast Harleian collection, Johnson must have handled thousands of rare books and profitably browsed in almost as many more. The pamphlets, too, published in weekly instalments as *The Harleian Miscellany*, were introduced by him and also partly edited, so that his absorption in, and intellectual profit from, the project was profound. There is a story that Osborne, a man of little taste or education, abused him in coarse language for spending more time in reading than was strictly profitable, and that in the argument that followed Johnson knocked down his employer with a folio. The story has been embellished in various ways, even to identifying the sixteenth-century Greek Bible with which Johnson is supposed to have silenced his tormentor, but Boswell's simple version is probably the true one. 'The simple truth I had from Johnson himself: "Sir, he was impertinent to me, and I beat him. But it was not in his shop: it was in my own chamber."'

Absorbing though it was to be involved with this vast and extraordinary library, Johnson would much have preferred a more direct emergence into the literary world, staking his claim as a writer. Other men, real founders of the English novel, were causing a sensation with romances as full of life as the London streets themselves. Fielding had published *Joseph Andrews* in 1742 and *Jonathan Wild* the following year; a modest printer, Samuel Richardson, had written an improving but subtly titillating novel, *Pamela*, which was being eagerly read in every boudoir; and a young surgeon's mate, Tobias Smollett, at this time aboard the *Chichester* in the West Indies and going through all the horrors of the siege of Cartagena, was diligently gathering material for a first novel, *Roderick Random*, about a surgeon's mate in the navy. There was no place in the acknowledged literary world, it seemed, for Samuel Johnson, except as an anonymous journalist or ghost-writer, an assistant compiler of dictionaries and catalogues. He was full of imaginative schemes which he called 'designs', was forever jotting down private memoranda of books he might one day write – lives of illustrious persons, a poetical dictionary, 'considerations upon the present state of London', even a poem to be called *The Palace of Nonsense: a Vision*, which, alas, like the rest, was never written. But the sudden death in a Bristol gaol of his enigmatic friend Richard Savage gave him an unexpected opportunity. The news stirred up all the magazines and publishers, and Cave instantly commissioned him to write a life of Savage to forestall competitors.

For this, as usual, Johnson wasted no time on original research. A certain amount had already been written about Savage: his own published claims, a few letters and articles in newspapers and a brief anonymous biography of fifteen years before. For the later years Johnson could rely largely on his own knowledge and recollection, since he

Tobias Smollett, who as a young surgeon's mate
in the navy drew on his own experience for his first
novel, *Roderick Random*

had been intimate with at least one aspect of his equivocal character, and with these fairly meagre materials he set energetically to work. What nobody seemed to know much about were the last four years, which Savage had idled away between Swansea and Bristol, irregularly supported by contributions from friends who were willing to subscribe a modest pension if he would stay away from London. Each instalment, of course, had been spent as soon as received, the gifts being acknowledged only by self-pitying or vituperative letters. Now, four years after parting from Johnson 'with tears in his eyes', he had been arrested for debt in Bristol, had lain some while in comparative comfort in the city Newgate, where the gaoler was kind, then suddenly complained of pain in his side and died within hours. No further help from friends or patrons could have solved his problems; only death could do that, for 'to supply him with money', as Johnson said, 'was a hopeless attempt . . . no sooner did he see himself master of a sum sufficient to set him free from care for a day, than he became profuse and luxurious'.

Johnson had loved Savage in spite of his faults; the man had erratic brilliance, an impressive manner, an appetite for late hours and conversation equal to Johnson's own. Besides, he regarded him as a man suffering a cruel wrong, since he had always believed in the truth of Savage's story. He was not blind to the vicious side of his character, being always, as Boswell said, 'willing to take men as they are, imperfect, and with a mixture of good and bad qualities'. All in all, considering his wasted gifts and his misfortunes, Johnson saw him as a man to be admired as well as blamed, and even pitied.

He set to work at great speed, snatching what time he could from the labours of cataloguing and from his final series of parliamentary debates. Many years later he remembered that he had written 'forty-eight of the printed octavo pages of the life of Savage at a sitting, but then I sat up all night'. [2] He finished it a few days before Christmas 1743 and thankfully received fifteen guineas from Cave as full payment. The little book of under two hundred pages was published a few weeks later, anonymously: nobody yet thought it worth while to put Samuel Johnson's name on a title-page.

Its success, however, was immediate, which is not surprising, for it is still the most absorbing of all Johnson's brief biographies and its news value at the time made it compulsive reading. Joshua Reynolds, coming upon it on his return from Italy, began reading it, he told Boswell, 'standing with his arm leaning against a chimney-piece. It seized his attention so strongly that, not being able to lay down the book till he had finished it, when he attempted to move, he found his arm totally benumbed.' [3] It is not, as we know now, without errors of fact, and Johnson took a more partial view of Savage's poetry than would be possible today; but he had a remarkable insight into the man's exasperating and masochistic personality, and this, colouring the whole sensational story of the noble bastard disowned and persecuted by a fiendish mother, gave his account an attractively human quality. As for the story itself, who will ever know whether Savage was an innocent victim or a criminal liar? The most conscientious modern investigator [4] of his case can go no further than to suppose that Savage either believed, or had made himself believe, his own story. Beyond that, as with so many other mysteries, 'the world', as Boswell put it, 'must vibrate in a state of uncertainty as to what was the truth'.

The success of the *Life of Savage*, however, made Johnson no better known, and put no more than Cave's few guineas in his pocket. His fortunes were at their lowest ebb that winter; he had debts he could not pay and his clothes were so shabby that he was sometimes ashamed to be seen. Dr Harte, the tutor of Lord Chesterfield's illegitimate son, dining with Cave one day, spoke warmly in praise of the anonymous *Life of Savage*. Meeting him again a day or two later, Cave told him, 'You made a man very happy t'other day', and explained to the bewildered clergyman that when 'a plate of victuals' had been sent behind the screen, it was for Johnson, 'dressed so shabbily that he did not choose to appear'. [5]

One of the debts which most persistently worried him was the interest on the mortgage of the house in Lichfield, eighty pounds at four and a half per cent, which neither he nor his mother had been able to pay over the last three years. During the winter he had written to Theophilus Levett, the mortgagee, taking responsibility for his mother's share as well as his own, and begging that he would 'not mention it to my dear Mother'. [6] He hoped, he said, to be able to discharge the whole debt, a matter of twelve pounds, in two months' time, and this, it seems, he was able to do, thanks to opportune help from Harry Hervey. Ha-Ha himself was in a difficulty of a different sort, having been asked, in his new character as the Honourable and Reverend Henry Hervey Aston, to preach a sermon in St Paul's Cathedral on the Anniversary Feast of the Sons of the Clergy. This was to be an important occasion, in the presence of the Archbishop of Canterbury and

OPPOSITE Peg Woffington the actress, with whom David Garrick lived for several years, after their first stage appearance together in May 1742

eight other bishops, as well as the Lord Chief Justice and aldermen of the City; and Hervey, though greatly flattered, felt himself not quite equal to the task. The solution was obviously for Johnson to write the sermon, and this he willingly did, while Hervey came to the rescue in the matter of the mortgage. Ghosting a pulpit address was a job that Johnson was glad to do for as little as two guineas, renouncing all rights as soon as he was paid; at different times he composed no fewer than forty, of which twenty-five were for his old friend Dr Taylor, who was so pleased with them that he arranged for them to be published as his own. Hervey's sermon, too, was published under his own name and warmly praised in the newspapers. The two friends had helped one another, and on both counts observed a discreet silence. Only those in the know (if there were any others) might have recognized certain passages in the solemn oration as expressing Johnson's far from conventional view that charity should not discriminate against the undeserving. 'We are not to refuse any man relief, because he is wicked . . . the crime and the criminal are always to be distinguished, and the detestation which we may properly indulge against the one, ought never to harden our hearts against the other. . . .' Poor Harry Hervey, his career as a preacher was too brief to retrieve his earlier reputation, for he died not very long after. When Lady Betty Germaine heard the news she expressed the general opinion in a letter to Lady Suffolk: 'Thank God, worthless Hervey Aston is dead, which may be a means to save his son and daughters from entire beggary.'

Johnson was now determined to find a project of his own which might liberate him from the tedious ill-paid round of hack-work. His days were spent in writing advance publicity for publishers, composing variations on the endless theme of parliamentary debates, in writing sermons, prefaces and dedications for which others got the credit, revising and improving other people's poetic productions and working long and late as a sub-editor at St John's Gate. What he longed to do – and it was an idea for which the public was more than ready – was to edit a new edition of Shakespeare in about ten small volumes, which would be easy to read and convenient for the pocket. No one had yet produced an entirely satisfactory edition of the plays; texts were corrupt and the popular stage abounded in mangled versions. A carefully studied critical edition, such as he envisaged, was sure of a good reception because one was so badly needed, and this 'design' appealed to Johnson all the more since he had been under the spell of Shakespeare since his childhood. He was barely nine years old, he told Mrs Thrale, 'when having got the play of *Hamlet* to read in his father's kitchen, he read on very quietly till he came to the ghost scene, when he hurried upstairs to the shop door that he might see folks about him. . . .'[7] This *frisson* of the supernatural, when Shakespeare chose to evoke it, had haunted him ever since. 'He that peruses Shakespeare looks round alarmed, and starts to find himself alone.'[8] The emotional power of the plays, which he had devoured in solitude and never yet seen acted, profoundly disturbed him. 'I was many years ago', he confessed, 'so shocked by Cordelia's death that I know not whether I ever endured to read again the last scenes of the play till I undertook to revise them as an editor.'[9]

OPPOSITE Samuel Johnson in 1769: a portrait by Reynolds that gives a striking impression of the Doctor's odd gesticulations

103

This, then, was his project, and Cave responded to the proposal with enthusiasm. To test public response and display his method Johnson set to work on an introductory pamphlet, *Miscellaneous Observations on the Tragedy of Macbeth*, with added proposals for his new edition. All seemed to be going well when an expensive new set of Shakespeare was unexpectedly published, edited by Sir Thomas Hanmer. This was a setback, though not a sufficiently serious one to discourage either Cave or Johnson. They pressed on towards the publication of *Miscellaneous Observations,* Johnson inserting a few disparaging references to the Hanmer edition ('Such harmless industry may surely be forgiven, if it cannot be praised'), and the pamphlet came out in the first week of April. Within three days Cave received a minatory letter from Jacob Tonson, the head of an already celebrated bookselling business in the Strand, pointing out that he and his partners held the copyright of Shakespeare's works, and threatening a Chancery suit if Cave went on with his project.

It seems incredible today, but in the eighteenth century the law relating to copyright was crude and confused, and Tonson's great-uncle, the first of the name, had acquired the rights of Shakespeare's plays in 1709, when he brought out the first complete edition since the original four folios. He had since published two further editions, one edited by Pope and the other by Theobald, had another in preparation under the editorship of the learned Dr Warburton, and can be fairly said to have cornered the Shakespeare market. It is conceivable that Cave might have won his case if the matter had gone to court, since the Act of 1709 entitled Tonson's firm to exclusive rights for only twenty-one years, and this period had expired; but possession being nine points of the law and Tonson a powerful publisher, Cave thought it better to climb down than risk defeat, and the scheme was abandoned. It was to be another eleven years before Johnson was allowed to proceed with his cherished plan, this time under the aegis of Jacob Tonson himself, the publishing world's most powerful Shakespeare operator.

Frustrated and discouraged, Johnson about this time made a last attempt to get out of Grub Street and into a profession which would earn him a decent living and professional respect. This time it was the law on which he set his hopes, slender as he must have known such hopes to be. He had always been drawn to the study of law, was fond of the company of lawyers and jurists and knew that if he had been able to qualify in the subject he would have made a formidable exponent. As with schoolmastering, his lack of a degree was the great obstacle. If he had only had the money to study law, he told Boswell many years later, he would have preferred it to tragic poetry – a provocative statement containing an element of truth. (One quails to think of being cross-examined by Johnson.) He now applied to his old mentor, Dr Adams of Pembroke, asking him to discover from Doctors' Commons 'whether a person might be permitted to practise there, without a doctor's degree in civil law'. It is extraordinary that he should ever have supposed it possible; but even if it had been, his arguments would hardly have recommended themselves to the legal profession. 'I am a total stranger to these studies,' he told Dr Adams; 'but whatever is a profession, and maintains numbers, must be within the reach of common abilities, and some degree of industry.' The answer, as he might have expected, was a decided No.

Few men's lives have been as well documented as Johnson's, and it therefore seems strange that from the moment of this last disappointment nothing is known about him for almost a year. No letters have survived; apart from a few slight verses in *The Gentleman's Magazine* there is no evidence that he wrote, composed, translated or edited anything. How and where was he living, what was he doing, between the summer of 1745 and the following spring? This mysterious gap in his history has inspired, both in his own time and ours, a romantic theory that he was somehow involved in the disastrous Jacobite Rebellion, and was obliged to go into hiding for a while until the witch-hunt after the rebels had subsided. Johnson's often-expressed partiality for the Stuarts, his contempt for the Hanoverians and his general anti-Whiggery have certainly fed the rumour, but there is not a shred of evidence, and the story, diverting as it is, must be discarded as a myth. Boswell, though he would have loved to believe in such an adventure, was entirely sceptical, being shrewd enough to see that for reasons of argument Johnson professed 'an affectation of more Jacobitism than he really had'. He had even heard him declare 'that if holding up his right hand would have secured victory at Culloden to Prince Charles's army, he was not sure he would have held it up; so little confidence had he in the right claimed by the house of Stuart, and so fearful was he of the consequences of another revolution on the throne of Great Britain'.

Wherever he was – and he and Tetty were almost certainly in London, whether or not 'shuddering, half-famished, in an author's garret', as Anna Seward put it – the Young Pretender's landing on the west coast of Scotland on July 24th was electrifying news. The King was away in Hanover and a large part of the British army was occupied in the Low Countries; the Highland chiefs and their clansmen must have imagined it a God-

LEFT Prince Charles Edward Stuart, the Young Pretender, at the time of the '45 Rebellion.
RIGHT The Battle of Culloden, April 16th 1746, at which the Young Pretender's hopes were crushed by the Duke of Cumberland

given moment to strike. Yet, although the general in command of the available British army proved incompetent beyond belief, and the people watched with a strange apathy as Prince Charles's forces, after a victory at Prestonpans, advanced over the border into Cumberland, there was more than enough folly, recklessness and indiscipline on the rebels' side to cancel out their strategical advantages. The Prince was charming and brave, but sadly lacking in experience and common sense. He had been innocent enough to bring with him from France a number of Irish advisers, who, 'drawn into Scotland', as one of his senior officers commented, 'by the allurement which the enterprise held out to them of making their fortune, were extremely injurious to the interests of the Prince, from the bad advice they gave him; and unfortunately they enjoyed his full confidence'.[10] Then, many of the brave clansmen who had mustered in the glens under his standard, often armed with nothing better than scythes and bludgeons, proved, after the first victory, to be more interested in loot than in the progress of the campaign, so that half the army deserted as soon as they had seized as much plunder as they could carry. The Prince, too, misled by his own poor judgment and ignoring the advice of his best commander, Lord George Murray, lingered on in Derby when it would have been better tactics to retreat, thus giving the Duke of Cumberland time to march north and get dangerously close with an army reinforced with Dutch mercenaries.

The news from Johnson's own midland area was alarming. The rebels were quartered in Ashbourne; the Duke of Cumberland and his troops were in Lichfield itself, preparing to pursue the Pretender's forces on their unwisely delayed retreat towards the Scottish border. (The Empress of Russia at this point entered the diplomatic arena, declaring her abhorrence of the Jacobites and her readiness to send supporting troops to Britain, a suggestion which was judiciously ignored.) From this stage in the emergency, once the rebels and their pursuers had reached Scotland, the English northern towns, which on the whole had shown a non-committal passivity, returned with relief to their normal concerns, while in Scotland the Pretender's forces dwindled as he fled northwards and more and more of his Highland followers judged it expedient to vanish into the heather.

The end came on April 16th 1746, when the Duke, earning his title of 'Butcher' Cumberland in the space of a half-hour's battle at Culloden, in which over a thousand men, including wounded and prisoners, were slaughtered, destroyed the hopes of the Jacobites for ever. Prince Charles Edward fled from the field to hide in mountain glens and eventually the Hebrides, disappearing into a mist of legendary subterfuges and adventures until his escape to France. One of his *aides de camp*, the Chevalier de Johnstone, who had parted from him with tears, bitterly recalled that after their defeat 'the scaffolds of England were, for a long time, deluged every day with the blood of Scottish gentlemen and peers, whose executions served as a spectacle for the amusement of the English populace, *naturally of a cruel and barbarous disposition. . . .*'

The newspapers had not for years had such a feast of melodrama, but even the public executions of the rebels began to lose a little of their charm after a few days, and other wonders, equally dear to popular taste, began to displace them. Only twelve days after Culloden, the public was regaled with a more domestic story. 'The wife of one Richard Haynes, of Chelsea, aged 35, and mother of 16 fine children, was delivered of a monster

After the disastrous rebellion of '45, 'the scaffolds of England were, for a long time, deluged every day with the blood of Scottish gentlemen and peers . . .'

with nose and eyes like a lion, no palate to its mouth, having hair on its shoulders, claws like a lion instead of fingers, no breast bone, something extraordinary protruding from the navel, as big as an egg, and one foot longer than the other. During her pregnancy she had been to see the lions in the Tower, and had been much terrified with the old lion's roaring.'[11]

Two days after the lion-child had made the front pages Samuel Johnson, not hiding in a cellar in the midlands or in any way involved with the rebels beyond following with absorption what he read in the public prints, completed the first draft of *The Plan of a Dictionary* – an ambitious undertaking in which several important publishers were concerned and on which he had brooded at intervals for several years. Boswell, it seems, was right in his conjecture after all – that during these blank months Johnson was in fact 'sketching the outlines of his great philological work'. The idea had occurred to him some years before, when, sitting in Dodsley's bookshop, he had overheard a remark that a scholarly and detailed dictionary of the English language was a thing much needed. He had done nothing about it at the time, but the suggestion had started a train of thought which seemed more promising and congenial each time he turned his mind to it. He told Boswell that it was no sudden inspiration or decision; it had 'grown up in his mind insensibly'; he had 'long thought of it'.

Now, with a consortium of publishers, headed by Robert Dodsley, offering him a £1,575 contract for the work, he was preparing his scheme of such a dictionary as he believed would standardize and illustrate the English language. He was at last, after nine laborious and depressing years in London – 'No place cured a man's vanity or arrogance so well as London' – embarked on the course which would make him in a few years more, not rich, but famous.

8

Dictionary Johnson

HE undertaking to which Johnson had committed himself was formidable, and he believed himself to be under no illusion as to the magnitude of the task. French and Italian dictionaries, admittedly much better than existing English ones, were compiled by whole bodies of lexicographers working together as academies over several decades. Yet Johnson, who had had no training in lexicography, was agreeing to do the same thing single-handed within three years, and expressing a quite astonishing self-confidence. When Dr Adams of Pembroke, understandably alarmed, reminded him that the French Academy of forty members had taken forty years to compile their dictionary, he replied, 'Sir, I have no doubt that I can do it in three years',[1] and turned the matter aside with a little joke, pretending to calculate how many Frenchmen could be said to equal one Englishman.

He must, however, have known that the task was infinitely greater than he pretended; his air of confidence may well have been self-defence. He wanted the job; he saw it as an opportunity for the display of his powers; was full of ideas for the Dictionary as a form of creative expression, and was not to be daunted by any limitations of time imposed by publishers. (Compiling the Dictionary, in fact, took him more than eight years.) Even at the beginning, once the work was started, he confessed that he was 'frighted at its extent, and like the soldiers of Caesar, look on Britain as a new world, which it is almost madness to invade'.

It was not that there was no reputable English dictionary to use as a starting-point. There had been several published earlier in the century, notably Nathan Bailey's *Universal Etymological English Dictionary*, which had first been published in 1721 and then reissued in 1736, impressively enlarged into a huge folio. There had been others, less ambitious and less satisfactory: even John Wesley, earnest in his belief that literacy must be part of the salvation of the labouring class, was compiling a pocket-size volume for the working man, in which hard words were explained in simple terms, as though for children. Bailey's Dictionary suffered to some extent from this same simplicity of approach: words were 'explained' without being classified as parts of speech, without even the humblest etymology, or quotations to illustrate their usage. Johnson himself was not deeply interested in etymology, or indeed particularly well versed in the Germanic as opposed to the classical origins of the language; but he had a clear idea of what a dictionary at that particular period was required to do, and set about designing his plan on a grand scale.

He wished, primarily, to 'fix the English language', which through slang, ignorance and lack of accepted standards was falling into a chaotic state. But can language ever be fixed? It is, after all, 'the work of man, of a being from whom permanence and stability cannot be derived'. It 'did not descend to us in a state of uniformity and perfection, but was produced by necessity, and enlarged by accident'.[2] Nevertheless, by giving the direct derivations of words, and without exploring the remoter marshes of etymology, it should be possible, he thought, to clear the language of those current vulgarities, catch-phrases and slang ('cant' as it was called) which debased the purity and vigour of the English idiom. He aimed to 'secure our language from being over-run with cant, from being crowded with low terms, the spawn of folly or affectation. . . .'[3] What would he have thought of the cant of the twentieth century, now embalmed by the zeal of scholars in its own dictionaries?

So the great work was begun. Johnson and Tetty at this time were living in lodgings in Holborn, in conditions which must have become insufferably crowded by day, since he was soon obliged to employ five or six assistants to do the copying and other mechanical details of compilation. In the first months, however, he was principally absorbed in reading and marking what he read, making 'fortuitous and unguided excursions into books', laboriously charting his course through the 'boundless chaos of a living speech'.[4] Tetty was in poor health and glad to escape into quiet lodgings in the village of Hampstead, where the air was clean and she could be free from the squalor and confusion of small rooms littered with hundreds of dusty volumes which must not be tidied or touched. Johnson was not over-particular in his handling of the books he used, as Hawkins, who may have lent him some, remembered. 'The books he used for this purpose were what he had in his own collection, a copious but a miserably ragged one, and all such as he could borrow; which latter, if ever they came back to those that lent them, were so defaced as to be scarce worth owning.'[5]

It was not only the discomfort of their living conditions which made Tetty occasionally thankful to get away. Johnson was now in his late thirties, while she was only two years short of sixty, and the 'tumultuous and awkward fondness' which Garrick had laughed at was something she could no longer endure. She was already, it seems, in the early stages of some terminal illness which was causing discomfort, and had for some time past put a ban on their sexual relations. Since Johnson's 'amorous propensities' made him uxorious, the problem was easier to evade when they were living apart; so, making her illness her excuse, Mrs Johnson removed to Hampstead whenever the money could be scraped together, sometimes taking Dr Swinfen's daughter with her for company. The lodgings there were miserable enough, and may even have been a sort of primitive nursing-home, for Johnson once told Fanny Burney, 'not without apparent secret anguish', that when Tetty first arrived there 'she complained that the staircase was in very bad condition, for the plaster was beaten off the walls in many places. "Oh," said the man of the house, "that's nothing but by the knocks against it of the coffins of the poor souls that have died in the lodgings."'[6] It is from Dr Swinfen's daughter, who was presently to marry her Huguenot writing-master and become Mrs Desmoulins, that we know something of the problems of the marriage at this time, since after Johnson's death she gave Boswell an account of these periods at Hampstead, with some intimate details which he privately recorded, knowing well enough that he could never use them.[7] Tetty, it seems, having only one room, would occasionally allow a visiting female friend to share her bed, but only on promise of secrecy, since she had long insisted that her illness made it impossible for her to bear a bedfellow, and if Johnson knew that she ever broke this rule he might renew his pleading. That he suffered from this deprivation Mrs Desmoulins also knew only too well, for when he occasionally came out to Hampstead and had a room in the same house, it was one of her duties to sit up for him and warm his solitary bed with a pan of coals; and it was on these late-night occasions, with Tetty asleep in the next room, that he would draw her down on the bed and fondle her as she lay with her head on the pillow. There was always a moment, she told Boswell, when his feelings became too much for him and he would thrust her away, crying out in anguish. The bounds of propriety, she made it quite clear, were never exceeded, but she was fully aware of the agony of his struggle.

After a year of work on the Dictionary, when the daily presence of his staff of assistants had become a necessity, the Johnsons moved into a house in Gough Square, a small secluded court hidden behind Fleet Street, where he would be within easy reach of his printer, William Strahan. This was, and still is, a handsome early eighteenth-century house of four storeys and a basement, such as might have served a prosperous lawyer or City merchant. The rent was thirty pounds a year. Here, for the first time since her marriage thirteen years before, Tetty had a home of her own, of which she might be proud; but what little we know of these last four years of her life suggests that she was past caring for domestic niceties. She had aged, she was ailing, and when she was not comforting herself with drams or a soothing half-grain of opium she was more concerned with religious matters than with looking after the meals or receiving company.

With Tetty's more or less secret drinking Johnson undoubtedly had a kind of sorrowful sympathy; his own abstinence over many years may have been practised partly to help her by example. As an admirer of Dr George Cheyne, whose books on health he strongly recommended to Boswell, he could hardly have missed his observation that women 'of the most elegant parts, and the strictest virtue otherwise . . . who are in all other respects blameless, are taking to secret drinking': and knew only too well – since even medicinal 'cordials' were often heavily laced with alcohol – how fatally easy it was to become addicted. 'A little lowness', said Dr Cheyne, 'requires drops, which pass readily down under the notion of physic; drops beget drams, and drams beget more drams, till they come to be without weight and without measure; so that at last the miserable creature suffers a true martyrdom, between its natural modesty, the great necessity of concealing its cravings, and the still greater one of getting them satisfied *somehow*.'[8]

Tetty had always been a sincere Christian, and now, as often happens, was more concerned with the state of her soul, and with her husband's spiritual future, than with more mundane affairs. We know from Johnson's prayers that she was anxious about him, exhorted him to make greater spiritual efforts and received his promises of amendment. It seems, indeed, as though serious religious conviction took hold of him afresh in this period, and was partly due to the influence of Tetty. For the rest, she made life tolerable for herself by spending much of her time in bed, avoiding that part of the house which was given over to the Dictionary, and indulging a feminine taste for novel-reading. (What those romances were which so absorbed her we do not know, but it would be interesting to discover whether they included John Cleland's *Fanny Hill*, one of the notorious and outstanding best-sellers of the seventeen-fifties.)

It was here in Gough Square, in her upstairs room, according to her friend Anna Williams, that the maid knocked and announced that her elder son, Captain Jervis Porter of the Royal Navy, from whom she had heard no word for many years, had come to the door and asked if she were at home. She was sick, the maid had told him, and in bed. '"Oh," says he, "if it is so, tell her that her son Jervis called to know how she did", and was going away. The maid begged she might run up to tell her mistress, and without attending his answer, left him. Mrs Johnson, enraptured to hear that her son was below, desired the maid to tell him she longed to embrace him. When the maid descended, the gentleman was gone. . . . It was the only time he made an effort to see her.' 'Her son is uniformly undutiful,' Johnson told Anna Williams, after doing his best to comfort Tetty; 'so I conclude, like many other sober men, he might once in his life be drunk, and in that fit nature got the better of his pride.'[9]

The house served Johnson's purpose extremely well, since there was room for everything, even for his team of amanuenses in the daytime and a servant in the basement. The ground floor comprised a dining-room and a small parlour, both of a comfortable size without being pretentious; a tea-table, a few straight-backed chairs, a corner cupboard and a rug for the floor would be all they would require. The drawing-room on the first floor, looking down on the little square, was oak-panelled and of pleasant proportions; across the landing was a small bedroom. Two more spacious bedrooms occupied the second floor and above these was a long attic which had probably once been servants' or children's quarters but which now, with a long wooden table like a shop counter and a few stools and a chair, served as the Dictionary workshop. The servant whom the Johnsons had at this time evidently slept in the basement, which ran under the whole of the house and had several arched recesses as well as an open hearth where the cooking was done, besides ample space for a practical if somewhat dark kitchen. (Coal and wood would be kept in the railed basement area, or in the small patch of garden at the back.) The five floors were connected by a stout central staircase with pinewood balustrade which, like most of the house, still exists in its original respectable condition, having survived neglect, decay and air-raids with the help of unobtrusive restoration. This was the house which was presently to shelter Johnson's ill-assorted household of dependents, but in the early years, while Tetty still nominally presided, probably only Robert Levett, that strange creature, had made his nest there – whether in the attic or down below among the pots and pans, nobody knows. Later, when the Dictionary was finished, he slept in the garret, but long before then he seems to have occupied some crevice or other, from which he had many discreet or accidental glimpses of Tetty, whom he described with disgust as 'always drunk and reading romances in her bed, where she killed herself by taking opium'.[10]

'Doctor' Levett, as he was called, mean and even grotesque in appearance but respectable both in talents and in character, had become one of Johnson's intimates by accident, through meeting him in Old Slaughter's Coffee House in St Martin's Lane, a favourite resort both of French *émigrés* and chess-players. Johnson occasionally went there to improve his French; Levett, who was bilingual, was already an *habitué*. He had worked in his early youth as a waiter in Paris, where his intelligence had impressed a group of surgeons among his customers, and these had somehow contrived to give him a smattering of medical education. On the strength of this he had returned to London, where he practised on a simple level among the very poor, accepting their pitiful payment in whatever form it was offered and living from hand to mouth in the most wretched circumstances. Johnson, admiring his 'unwearied diligence in his profession', and finding also a certain comfort in his silent presence, allowed him 'house-room, his share in a penny loaf at breakfast, and now and then a dinner on a Sunday'.[11] In return, Levett was more or less on call whenever needed, especially at breakfast, which in Johnson's case was usually about midday. Hawkins at this hour 'found him and Levett at breakfast, Johnson, in deshabille, as just risen from bed, and Levett filling out tea for himself and his patron alternately, no conversation passing between them'. (The lateness of the hour was not quite as peculiar as it seems, for though Johnson was a notoriously late riser, breakfast to most people was more in the nature of a mid-morning break – tea or coffee with a roll at ten or eleven, with half the morning's activity behind them.)

It is curious that Johnson's besetting sin should have been idleness, with which in his prayers and meditations he reproached himself all his life, when in fact the sum of his achievement at this time – even rising from bed at midday and spending half the night in conversation – is so prodigious. As well as the colossal labour of the Dictionary he was continuing to turn out prologues, prefaces and sermons as and when required, and during one of his Hampstead visits composed the greater part of his second and most celebrated poem, *The Vanity of Human Wishes*. This serious, sober, pessimistic work reflects clearly enough his state of mind at the time, which is one of total disenchantment with life. The statesman, soldier, scholar are alike victims of delusion and disappointment; nothing is permanent or safe; even the rich man and the virtuous are doomed, and the poet, the dedicated writer, is no exception.

> Yet hope not life from grief and danger free,
> Nor think the doom of man revers'd for thee:
> Deign on the passing world to turn thine eyes,
> And pause awhile from letters, to be wise;
> There mark what ills the scholar's life assail,
> Toil, envy, want, the garret and the jail.

Even the good and honest man, to whom life has been kind and whose conscience is mercifully clear, faces the slow *dégringolade* of age.

OPPOSITE Johnson's house in Gough Square, Fleet Street, where the Dictionary
was compiled, and 'Tetty' died

Year chases year, decay pursues decay,
Still drops some joy from with'ring life away.

The poem marches sombrely on, offering in the end, as the only hope, religion and resignation.

With these celestial wisdom calms the mind,
And makes the happiness she does not find.

A theme so stoical and gloomy, so sternly expounded, was not likely to be popular with the public, and the poem, for which Dodsley paid Johnson fifteen guineas, sold less well than his *London*, which had run through several editions. Garrick, though anxious to praise his friend's new work, the first to carry his name on the title-page, found it heavy going: 'When Johnson lived much with the Herveys, and saw a good deal of what was passing in life, he wrote his *London*, which is lively and easy. When he became more retired, he gave us his *Vanity of Human Wishes*, which is as hard as Greek.'[12]

Garrick had a project in hand which was more to his liking. From the moment of becoming manager of Drury Lane he had promised Johnson that he would produce *Irene*, and now, in February 1749, the play was actually in rehearsal, with Mrs Pritchard in the name part and Garrick himself playing not Mahomet, but Demetrius. It is difficult for any reader today to imagine that he can have felt much enthusiasm for the production, so heavy and lifeless does it seem in print. It eventually ran for nine nights – a respectable run in those days – but made no very favourable impression on the public, and was never revived: nevertheless, Garrick did his best to make a success of it, forcefully arguing with Johnson in favour of certain alterations to make it 'fit for the stage'. One of these was to alter the title to *Mahomet and Irene*, which was more suggestive: another, which proved too much for the lively first-night audience, was to have the heroine put to death on stage. Dr Adams, who attended the first performance, told Boswell that before the curtain went up there were catcalls and whistling, 'which alarmed Johnson's friends. . . . The Prologue, which was written by himself in a manly strain, soothed the audience, and the play went off tolerably, till it came to the conclusion, when Mrs Pritchard, the heroine of the piece, was to be strangled upon the stage, and was to speak two lines with the bow-string round her neck. The audience cried out "*Murder! Murder!*" She several times attempted to speak; but in vain. At last she was obliged to go off the stage alive.' Could any play have a more disastrous opening? Johnson himself was in the wings, dressed in the fancy scarlet waistcoat and gold-laced hat which he had thought proper for the occasion, and can have missed no detail of the disaster. He appeared outwardly unmoved, however, and when some tactless acquaintance asked him how he felt 'upon the ill success of his tragedy', impassively replied, 'Like the Monument.' He believed then, as he did later, that it was unprofessional and absurd for a writer to rail against adverse opinions of his work, and therefore, as Boswell put it, 'instead of peevishly complaining of the bad taste of the town, submitted to its decision without a murmur'. He must at least have been pleased with the financial takings, for his share of the house profits was nearly two hundred pounds, and for the text of the play, which was published, Dodsley paid him another hundred.

It was during the run of *Irene*, in spite of his apparent composure, that Johnson decided that the lively and raffish back-stage scene was too dangerously disturbing. According to Boswell he told Garrick, 'I'll come no more behind your scenes, David; for the silk stockings and white bosoms of your actresses excite my amorous propensities.' In the version given by John Wilkes – who had the story from Garrick – what Johnson had actually said was that 'the white bosoms of your actresses do make my genitals to quiver', a vivid phrase which may have been Wilkes's improvement, or may equally well have been Johnson's. There is no reason to believe that he was always prudish in speech in male company, however inwardly exigent his moral convictions.

What Tetty thought of all these excitements we do not know. It is unlikely that she saw any of the nine performances, for this was in the early period in Gough Square, when she was often ill and often unpresentable. No doubt she heard all about it from Johnson himself, and commended and sympathized in private. With his next work – for he had launched yet another literary project to add to the formidable burden of the Dictionary – she was impressed, and told him so; which suggests that her critical faculties at least had not deteriorated. This new undertaking was no less than a series of periodical essays, to be published every Tuesday and Saturday at twopence a copy. Cave and his partners were to publish it, Johnson receiving two guineas for each paper. What he had in mind was a continuous and personal communication with the public, in form not unrelated to Addison's *Spectator* (which had come to an end nearly forty years before) though in content both more serious and more personal. His admiration for Addison was great; for the ease and purity of his style, even more for the intimate, communicative tone of his writing. Johnson had long thought of attempting something of the kind, but with this difference, that the moral content, rather than entertainment, was to be the chief consideration. To this end he had for a long time carried a little notebook about with him in which he jotted down ideas for possible essays: he now had so many themes that it was difficult to know where to begin, and with Cave waiting to announce the series there was the problem of deciding on a suitable title. Nothing particularly apt suggested itself, and time pressed. 'When I was to begin publishing that paper,' he told Reynolds, 'I was at a loss how to name it. I sat down at night upon my bedside, and resolved that I would not go to sleep till I had fixed its title. *The Rambler* seemed the best that occurred, and I took it.' Had he perhaps been thinking of Savage, and his *Wanderer*? His mood was a solemn one, as though he sensed the importance of the undertaking, and hesitated to begin without first setting down a humble appeal to God, 'that in this undertaking thy Holy Spirit may not be withheld from me, but that I may promote thy glory, and the salvation of myself and others'.

The appearance of the first few essays caused little stir, but Tetty, to whom he showed them, considered them a great advance on anything he had yet done. 'I thought very well of you before,' she told him, 'but I did not imagine you could have written anything equal to this.' She was not flattering him. Gradually, although sales never rose above five hundred, this continuous distillation of Johnson's experience of life, his thought, his moral precepts and his philosophy, began to reach a public far wider than this figure suggests, and to build up an anonymous reputation long before his name was in everyone's mouth as the larger-than-life compiler of the Dictionary. The essays appeared twice a week without a break for two years, often written in haste, even late at night within a few hours of publication; and yet, so extensive had been his subconscious preparation, that they manifested a range of thought and quality of reflection 'unexceeded', as a modern critic[13] puts it, 'by any other writer of English prose since Francis Bacon'. Other periodicals noticed the new phenomenon at once and began reprinting long passages, sometimes even whole essays, for their moral teaching and (what was no less attractive) their value as entertainment – a combination which justified ten collected editions in Johnson's lifetime. His anonymity was not the publishers' decision, but his own. There was too painful a contrast, he felt, between the moral teaching of his lay sermons and the facts of his own life – 'For many reasons a man writes much better than he lives.' It was better 'for a writer, who apprehends that he shall not inforce his own maxims by his domestic character', to remain concealed. He was even prepared to admit that 'very often . . . those who raise admiration by their books, disgust by their company'.[14] But the disguise was a thin one, and in the small London literary world of the time it was soon common knowledge that the Johnson who was toiling away on the great Dictionary was also the versatile author of *The Rambler*. Richardson, an immediate devotee of the essays, guessed his identity at once and demanded confirmation from Cave, who complacently told him that, yes, 'Mr Johnson is the *Great Rambler*, being, as you observe, the only man who can furnish two such papers in a week, besides his other great business.' There were, besides, such intimates as 'Mr Garrick and others', who, Cave admitted, had recognized the author's style from the first, and 'unadvisedly asserting their suspicions, overturned the scheme of secrecy'.

Appearing now for the first time as an admired writer, Johnson set about improving the quality of his life by the regular enjoyment of good company. To do this at home, in the circumstances, was out of the question; besides, as he had told Hawkins and others more than once, to one of his temperament 'a tavern chair was the throne of human felicity'. He therefore rounded up a group of congenial acquaintances and with them formed a 'club', which was to meet every Tuesday evening at the King's Head, a famous beefsteak house in Ivy Lane near St Paul's. There seem to have been ten of them, including Johnson, and their different avocations suggest the variety of company that he most enjoyed. Three of them were physicians, his favourite being Richard Bathurst, son of a West Indian planter and a young man for whom he had a particular affection, sympathizing with his ill success in his profession, which had never brought him a higher fee than a guinea. There was one clergyman, and another destined for the dissenting ministry; a merchant; a bookseller (John Payne, one of Cave's partners in publishing *The Rambler*); an attorney (Hawkins); and Dr John Hawkesworth, a fellow writer. What this weekly gathering meant to Johnson, no one understood better than the more reserved Hawkins: 'The great delight of his life was conversation and mental intercourse. That he might indulge himself in this he had, in the winter of 1749, formed a club that met weekly at the King's Head. . . . Thither he constantly resorted, and with a disposition to please and be pleased, would pass those hours in a free and unrestrained interchange of sentiments, which otherwise had been spent at home in painful reflection.' (Most of his friends were aware that his home life was fairly unhappy.) He came to the club straight from his work, and usually hungry, 'for our conversations seldom began until after a supper so very solid and substantial as led us to think, that with him it was a dinner. By the help of this refection, and no other incentive to hilarity than lemonade, Johnson was . . . transformed into a new creature; his habitual melancholy and lassitude of spirit gave way; his countenance brightened; . . . he told us excellent stories, and . . . both instructed and delighted us.'[15]

A Wedgwood portrait of Johnson
made by John Flaxman

The Dictionary by this time had been going steadily forward for two years, and the importance of the work had been well publicized by an elaborate pamphlet or *Plan*, which had been dedicated to Lord Chesterfield. This dedication, not of the Dictionary itself but of the preliminary brochure, was Dodsley's idea, not Johnson's. It was still the age of patronage, when an obsequious dedication to a bishop or nobleman increased an author's chances of being noticed in the right quarters. What more prestigious patron could be found for the Dictionary than Lord Chesterfield, whom Dodsley knew? Apart from being a distinguished peer he was rich and famous, a diplomat and elder statesman who had been Viceroy of Ireland and was now one of the King's principal Secretaries of State. Almost equally important, he was a wit, a scholar and a man of letters, deeply interested in the English language and a skilled practitioner. His correspondence, his occasional published essays and stylish journalism were appreciated everywhere in the political and polite world; he was known to be a man of liberal views and civilized behaviour.

Johnson received the suggestion without enthusiasm. The very notion of a noble patron, whom he must address in flattering terms, aroused his antagonism. The Dictionary would undoubtedly profit from the publicity of a great man's approval, but as Hawkins said, 'The pride of independence was most strong in Johnson at those periods of his life when his wants were greatest', and he accepted the idea of the dedication grudgingly. His only reason for agreeing, he told Boswell, was that it would give him

117

more time for completing the *Plan*, which, as usual, he had left to the last minute. 'I laid hold of this as a pretext for delay, that it might be better done, and let Dodsley have his desire.'

Chesterfield accordingly was approached, and having already heard something of the Dictionary and been shown a draft of the proposals, to which he added a number of intelligent suggestions, agreed to lend his name to Johnson's *Plan*. He was himself quite indifferent to compliments of this sort – 'The truth is, that the several situations I have been in having made me long the *plastron* of dedications, I am become as callous to flattery as some people are to abuse'[16] – but he was interested in the scheme of the Dictionary and impressed, so far as he could judge, by Johnson's abilities. He received him in a private interview, let Johnson do most of the talking, responded in his usual agreeable manner and afterwards sent him a present of ten pounds, a gift which would be more like a hundred pounds today. It did not occur to him that he would be expected to do more, and indeed the idea that a busy minister, daily besieged by petitioners of every description, should be supposed to repeat what he had already done, seems optimistic. Johnson went away, apparently satisfied, and Chesterfield heard nothing more of him for seven years.

In that long interval Chesterfield, now in his sixties, had retired from office, was in poor health and growing increasingly deaf, consoling himself by writing a series of incomparable letters to his natural son, and astonishing his friends by building himself the most magnificent private palace in London. The area he had chosen has long been a by-word for elegance, but in the mid-eighteenth century Mayfair was on the very outskirts of London: Chesterfield cheerfully described his new house as 'situated among a parcel of thieves and murderers'.[17] The imposing façade looked across Tyburn Lane, still muddy and rural, to the open spaces of Hyde Park, where, it was true, Horace Walpole had recently been robbed by the famous highwayman McLean, and where no one in his senses ventured at night, however fashionable its gravelled walks by day. The area was fast developing into an aristocratic enclave, with handsome houses extending the new streets, and Chesterfield House, with its symmetrical porticos and formal gardens, dominated the whole. Was it here, or at the earlier house in Hanover Square, that Johnson claimed that he had been 'repulsed' from the door? The story is still something of a mystery, and has been so variously embroidered that it is unlikely ever to be unravelled. What seems certain is that Johnson felt himself to be neglected, that he made some attempt to see Chesterfield again and was unsuccessful, and that whatever the footman at the door may have said or done, his master knew nothing of the matter. Johnson himself repudiated the story that he had been kept waiting for an hour while Chesterfield talked to Colley Cibber the actor; but whatever it was, there was some unintended slight at which Johnson took offence, and remembered for years with smouldering resentment.

Chesterfield for his part, hearing that the Dictionary was at last nearing completion, bestirred himself and wrote two genial anonymous essays recommending it in *The World*.

OPPOSITE Philip Dormer Stanhope, 4th Earl of Chesterfield, the unlucky patron
of Johnson's *Plan of a Dictionary*

118

The English language, he said, was in a state of anarchy, and 'We must have recourse to the old Roman expedient in times of confusion, and choose a dictator. Upon this principle, I give my vote for Mr Johnson to fill that great and arduous post.' Johnson disliked the faintly facetious tone of the articles, and was outraged when he discovered that Chesterfield had written them. The indignation he had nursed in silence now rushed to the surface in fury. After such neglect, such insolent indifference, was this supercilious courtier to be allowed to strut and pose as the Dictionary's patron? He sat down to compose an annihilating revenge. For this, as he knew, he possessed the perfect weapon, a genius for words; for words of the most perfect smoothness and courtesy can be loaded with venom. So came to be written one of the most famous letters in the English language, one which was to damage Chesterfield's posthumous reputation for ever, since the sting in the tail of each phrase would be remembered, and Chesterfield's not unreasonable behaviour forgotten.

> . . . Seven years, my lord, have now past since I waited in your outward rooms or was repulsed from your door, during which time I have been pushing on my work through difficulties of which it is useless to complain, and have brought it at last to the verge of publication without one act of assistance, one word of encouragement, or one smile of favour. Such treatment I did not expect, for I never had a patron before. . . . Is not a patron, my lord, one who looks with unconcern on a man struggling for life in the water, and when he has reached ground encumbers him with help? The notice which you have been pleased to take of my labours, had it been early, had been kind; but it has been delayed till I am indifferent and cannot enjoy it; till I am solitary and cannot impart it; till I am known and do not want it. . . .[18]

How much, or how little, the letter wounded Chesterfield there is no knowing. True to his concept of civilized behaviour, he left it lying on his table where his friends might read it, and observed to Dodsley, 'This man has great powers', pointing out the severest passages and praising their style. One cannot assume that he was not stung, for Dodsley and others of Johnson's friends had made the letter known all over London; but if he were, he was too old a hand to admit it. 'Join in the laugh against yourself,' he had advised his son, on the subject of malicious witticism; 'acknowledge the hit to be a fair one, and the jest a good one, and play off the whole thing in seeming good humour: but by no means reply in the same way; which only shows that you are hurt, and publishes the victory that you might have concealed.'[19] The published victory was Johnson's, and has become part of his legend, perpetuating his anger and Chesterfield's discredit. Even the Dictionary itself, with caustic humour, took part in the revenge, the word *patron* being defined as 'commonly a wretch who supports with insolence, and is paid with flattery'. And when a new edition of *The Vanity of Human Wishes* was called for, it appeared with a word changed in a significant couplet:

> There mark what ills the scholar's life assail,
> Toil, envy, want, the patron and the jail.

To have a patron was even worse than starving in a garret.

OPPOSITE Topham Beauclerk, descended from Charles II and Nell Gwynn, and himself a considerable rake

121

Johnson did not exaggerate when he described himself as 'solitary'. On the 17th of March 1752, three years before the end of his work on the Dictionary, Tetty had died, and in the cruellest sense of the word he was alone. 'The dreadful shock of separation took place in the night; and he immediately dispatched a letter to his friend, the Reverend Dr Taylor, which . . . expressed grief in the strongest manner he had ever read,'[20] Taylor, who as Prebendary was temporarily in residence in Westminster Cloisters, received the letter about three in the morning: he rose and dressed immediately and went to his friend, whom he found 'in tears and in extreme agitation'. They prayed together, and after a while, as Johnson seemed somewhat calmer, Taylor left, only to be followed in a few hours by another imploring note – 'Let me have your company and instruction. Do not live away from me. My distress is great.' Johnson was, indeed, prostrated with grief and despair, to a degree that his closest friends, who were unanimous in thinking his marriage a disaster, found it difficult to comprehend. They knew his horror of loneliness and his dread of death, but to grieve in this manner for the ageing invalid with whom for so many years he had known quarrelling, separation and discomfort, seemed to them unreasonable.

No doubt there was an element of self-pity in Johnson's grief, and the frightening melancholy which was never far away made the most of every feeling of self-reproach towards his dead wife; but when all this is admitted, and the steady deterioration of their life together, there still remained a basis of grateful affection which their mutual imperfections had failed to destroy. 'Marriage', Johnson had written in one of his *Ramblers*, 'is the strictest tie of perpetual friendship',[21] and so, in spite of all difficulties and frustrations, theirs had remained. In the sermon which, still in considerable distress, he composed for her funeral, he admitted 'That she had no failings, cannot be supposed', and went on to enumerate her virtues – charity, gratitude, willingness to help 'all whom her little power enabled her to benefit'. She had, besides, 'passed through many months of languor, weakness and decay, without a single murmur of impatience'. This sermon was never preached, and it is said that Taylor refused to deliver it because he considered it too fulsome. Perhaps it was; it was the image of Tetty that Johnson presented to the world. In his secret annals, however, written at intervals over many years, the feeling expressed is one of anguished tenderness. In 1764, twelve years after her death, he 'Thought on Tetty, dear poor Tetty, with my eyes full.' Six years later, 'This is the day on which in 1752 I was deprived of poor dear Tetty. . . . When I recollect the time in which we lived together, my grief for her departure is not abated, and I have less pleasure in any good that befalls me, because she does not partake it.' And again, after another eight years, 'Poor Tetty, whatever were our faults and failings, we loved each other. . . . Couldst thou have lived!' Finally, only two years before his own death, 'This is the day on which in 1752 dear Tetty died. I have now uttered a prayer of repentance and contrition; perhaps Tetty knows that I prayed for her. Perhaps Tetty is now praying for me. God help me.'[22]

9

The House in Gough Square

ITHIN a fortnight of Tetty's death the house in Gough Square, now more than ever disorganized and comfortless, began to assume that miscellaneous and slightly freakish character which was to distinguish Johnson's household for the rest of his life. Levett was there already, dark, dusty and silent, attending to his back-street practice by day and at night available as undemanding company if he were not, as sometimes happened, quietly drunk. Johnson's partiality for this odd character was inexplicable to his friends, who found Levett's shabby figure and swarthy corrugated visage repulsive; but Johnson 'thought himself happy in having so near his person one who was to him, not solely a physician, a surgeon, or an apothecary, but all'.[1]

The anonymous maidservant lived her life below stairs, and there is nothing to tell us whether, now that her mistress was gone, she sighed alone by the kitchen fire or occasionally had clandestine company. If any of the five copyists slept in the garret with the Dictionary (as indeed they may have done, since all that Johnson could pay them was twenty-three shillings a week between them) they were sober and needy men who gave little trouble. But the third week after the funeral saw the introduction of a new and surprising inmate, who for the remaining thirty years of Johnson's life was to be both an exasperation and a comfort. This was a Negro boy called Francis Barber, who at the time of his coming under Johnson's wing seems to have been about six or seven years old. In a sense he was a present, of the sort that is hardly welcome, but difficult to refuse. Richard Bathurst's father, the Jamaica planter, had recently gone bankrupt, and had brought this child, the son of one of his slaves, to England with him, apparently intending to give him some education and his freedom. He was sent for a short while to a little school in Yorkshire, and then, on Colonel Bathurst's death, handed over to his son, who was finding it difficult enough to make ends meet and who evidently saw a way out of his difficulty by presenting him to Johnson.

There was no novelty in having a child of this age as a servant: many conversation-pieces of the period include, as an exotic touch, a tiny Negro page in satin waistcoat and turban, a creature more for ornament than use. At a more practical level, children of the very poor were clandestinely bought and sold according to demand; there were paupers' markets in Whitechapel and Spitalfields where they could be hired as unskilled labour,

Hogarth's *Harlot* keeps a Negro page, a status symbol in her early *Progress*.

or to train as beggars, pickpockets and prostitutes. It was not yet a crime even to steal a child, although to purloin its clothing was a felony. The numbers of abandoned, destitute and delinquent children everywhere, especially in the cities, presented an appalling problem, and hundreds were being transported overseas, to the American plantations and the colonies. Fielding, both as writer and magistrate, was campaigning for better legislation; Thomas Coram, old sea-dog turned philanthropist, had established the Foundling Hospital, and Jonas Hanway, most energetic and verbose of reformers, was pouring out millions of words on behalf of the country's vagrant and destitute children. Johnson's motive in accepting the child must, then, have been at least partly charity. Mrs Thrale believed that it was also for Richard Bathurst's sake that he took the boy, cherishing him as a living link with his unfortunate friend, whom ill success in his profession had driven into the Navy, and who later died at sea during the siege of Havana.

The ways in which the boy was supposed to be useful to Johnson were, as Hawkins remarked, 'not very apparent, for Diogenes himself never wanted a servant less than he seemed to do'. His wig was never combed, his clothes were habitually dusty and rarely brushed. 'In short,' said the more fastidious Hawkins, who by this time had known him well for at least ten years, 'his garb and the whole of his external appearance was, not to say negligent, but slovenly, and even squalid; to all which, and the necessary consequences of it, he appeared as insensible as if he had been nurtured at the Cape of Good Hope.' He was not interested in training the boy as a valet, and would be equally indifferent to the idea of a Negro page to impress the neighbours. He was made use of, therefore, chiefly to answer the door, run errands and carry letters. What was important about 'the Child', or 'my Boy', as Johnson called him, was that he should be cared for and brought up properly, and his soul saved. He had been born a slave, which was enough to arouse his new master's indignation, since Jamaica, in Johnson's view, was 'a place of great wealth and dreadful wickedness, a den of tyrants and a dungeon of slaves'. He took care to teach him to pray, and from time to time gave him religious instruction. All this the boy accepted meekly enough during the first four years, but when he was eleven or twelve the boredom of life became too much, and he ran away and took service with an apothecary in Cheapside, so that Gough Square saw no more of him for almost a year. Then he was back again for two years, growing fast and apparently 'of a delicate frame, and particularly subject to a malady in his throat', which caused Johnson much distress when Francis absconded again (he was now thirteen) and went to sea in the crew of a naval frigate. This time he was away for rather longer, and Johnson's alarm over the dangers of the escapade was very real, so much so that he made application to the Admiralty for the boy's release, and Francis was eventually discharged, 'without any wish of his own', after two years' service in the Navy, which no doubt had modified his ideas. After this, there were no more escapes or rebellions, and he settled down as a fairly steady member of what Johnson in his private journal called his 'family'.

Another inmate of a very different sort had also joined the household after Tetty's death. This was Miss Anna Williams, the middle-aged daughter of a Welsh physician who had ruined himself through scientific experiments which never quite came off. The Government had offered a reward of twenty thousand pounds to anyone who could work out a method of ascertaining longitude at sea, and Zachariah Williams had done just this, on the variation of the magnetic compass-needle. In his results, however, there was too great a margin of error, and he did not win the prize. (The problem remained unsolved until ten years later, when John Harrison perfected the chronometer.) Anna Williams, being highly intelligent, had done what she could to ease her father's poverty by translations and various miscellaneous writings. Unfortunately her sight had begun to fail while she was still young, and by the time of her visits to Tetty in Gough Square her eyes were opaque with cataract. Johnson persuaded her to undergo the operation in his house, as being more comfortable than lodgings, and this she did, though with unhappy results, for the operation failed and she became blind.

Now that Tetty was gone Johnson at once offered her a room, and she was duly installed. She had a minute income of her own – the interest on two or three hundred pounds invested in the stocks – which would hardly have kept her alive without this help, since now that she was blind there was no longer any hope of earning a living. She refused, however, to be either despondent or idle; took over the management of the domestic expenses, such as they were, and even embarked – how, it is impossible to imagine – on compiling a philosophical dictionary. This project, not surprisingly, came to nothing, but she busied herself for a number of years with collecting a volume of 'Miscellanies', and was always on hand to pour out Johnson's tea, to give him advice, or join in conversation. As the years went by she became somewhat difficult and peevish, but to Johnson her presence was, and remained, a comfort. His behaviour to her, wrote Mrs Chapone, 'was like that of a fond father to his daughter', and Hawkins, too, was

125

touched by 'this intimacy, which began with compassion, and terminated in a friendship that subsisted till death dissolved it'.

It was not until nearly three more years had passed that the Dictionary was finished. The huge labour was at last complete, 'with little assistance of the learned, and without any patronage of the great . . . amidst inconvenience and distraction, in sickness and in sorrow'.[2] There was, of course, no dedication to Chesterfield, no mention of him in the splendid Preface in which Johnson reviewed his aims and difficulties and explained his ambitious and innovatory method. This was the first dictionary which, as well as defining words, illustrated their use by copious quotation, and it had been Johnson's cherished plan to make this part of the work a compendium of knowledge, pleasure and moral instruction. 'I was desirous that every quotation should be useful to some other end than the illustration of the word; I therefore extracted from philosophers principles of science; from historians remarkable facts; from chemists complete processes; and from poets beautiful descriptions.' The scheme was vast, and he had soon found that the scale on which he had envisaged it was impracticable. 'I could not visit caverns to learn the miner's language', and the happy visions of exploring the whole of literature and science were 'the dreams of a poet doomed at last to wake a lexicographer'. Nevertheless, the work was designed to offer an epitome of education. Facts about plants, for instance, must be included. 'Had Shakespeare had a dictionary of this kind, he had not made the woodbine entwine the honeysuckle'[3] – a sly reference to Titania's botanical slip in *A Midsummer Night's Dream*, which later editors have usually ascribed to a printer's error.

There cannot be many dictionaries in the world in which the beliefs, prejudices and character of the lexicographer are so apparent as in Johnson's. He refuses in the Preface to shelter behind any intimidating scholarly image – 'Some words there are which I cannot explain, because I do not understand them' – and he likewise refuses in the text to brush his personal convictions out of sight. So there are some errors in the first edition which his detractors pounced on, and which have survived in favourite anecdotes ever since. 'Ignorance, madam, pure ignorance,' he answered the lady who demanded to know why he had defined 'pastern' as 'the knee of a horse'; and there are other definitions which, in his struggle to be precise over even the simplest word, have become famous for their complexity. 'Network' is a celebrated example: 'Anything reticulated or decussated, at equal distances, with interstices between the intersections.' But then, how *is* it to be defined, for the enlightenment of someone who has no very clear idea what network is? A great modern dictionary does better, admittedly, but not so very much better: 'Reticulated, meshed structure or fabric of cord, wire, etc.' The whole problem of definining simple words, without drawing on terms infinitely more elaborate and obscure, is quite outside the ordinary man's experience: no one can begin to imagine the difficulties who has not tried to be a lexicographer. And to cite these two examples, one a mistake and the other an absurdity, is to give a ludicrously unfair impression of Johnson's Dictionary, which was a considerable advance on the English lexicography of his time, and – still more remarkable – is the only dictionary that can be read solidly for pleasure.

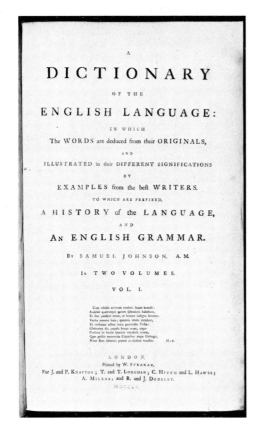

2. A mixed metal.

Change silver plate or veſſel into the compound ſtuff, being a kind of ſilver *electre*, and turn the reſt into coin. *Bacon.*

ELE'CTRICAL. ⎱ *adj.* [from *electrum.* See ELECTRE.]
ELE'CTRICK. ⎰

1. Attractive without magnetiſm; attractive by a peculiar property, ſuppoſed once to belong chiefly to amber.

By *electrick* bodies do I conceive not ſuch only as take up light bodies, in which number the ancients only placed jett and amber; but ſuch as, conveniently placed, attract all bodies palpable. *Brown's Vulgar Errours, b. ii. c. 4.*

An *electrick* body can by friction emit an exhalation ſo ſubtile, and yet ſo potent, as by its emiſſion to cauſe no ſenſible diminution of the weight of the *electrick* body, and to be expanded through a ſphere, whoſe diameter is above two feet, and yet to be able to carry up lead, copper, or leaf-gold, at the diſtance of above a foot from the *electrick* body. *Newton.*

2. Produced by an electrick body.

If that attraction were not rather *electrical* than magnetical, it was wonderous what Helmont delivereth concerning a glaſs, wherein the magiſtery of loadſtone was prepared, which retained an attractive quality. *Brown's Vulgar Errours.*

If a piece of white paper, or a white cloath, or the end of one's finger, be held at about a quarter of an inch from the glaſs, the *electrick* vapour, excited by friction, will, by daſhing againſt the white paper, cloth, or finger, be put into ſuch an agitation as to emit light. *Newton's Opt.*

ELECTRI'CITY. *n. ſ.* [from *electrick.* See ELECTRE.] A property in ſome bodies, whereby, when rubbed ſo as to grow warm, they draw little bits of paper, or ſuch like ſubſtances, to them. *Quincy.*

Such was the account given a few years ago of electricity; but the induſtry of the preſent age, firſt excited by the experiments of *Gray,* has diſcovered in electricity a multitude of philoſophical wonders. Bodies electrified by a ſphere of glaſs, turned nimbly round, not only emit flame, but may be fitted with ſuch a quantity of the electrical vapour, as, if diſcharged at once upon a human body, would endanger life. The force of this vapour has hitherto appeared inſtantaneous, perſons at both ends of a long chain ſeeming to be ſtruck at once. The philoſophers are now endeavouring to intercept the ſtrokes of lightning.

ELE'CTUARY. *n. ſ.* [*electarium, Col'in's Aurel.* which is now

Johnson's *Dictionary of the English Language,* 1755: LEFT the title-page of the first edition, and RIGHT some definitions

The element of pleasure was deliberate, a part of Johnson's plan; the quotations were generous and imaginatively chosen, covering a wide range both in period and subject. There was, besides, a personal tone in some of the definitions, intended to startle, irritate or amuse. Thus, the word 'Tory' is first defined as 'a cant term, derived, I suppose, from an Irish word signifying a savage' – which shows how far he had come since the old Lichfield days of battling against Walmesley; and of 'pension' he outrageously adds, 'In England it is generally understood to mean pay given to a state hireling for treason to his country' – a piece of exuberance which was to cause him embarrassment some seventeen years later. His fondness for affecting scorn of Scotsmen inspired a joke probably intended to tease, among others, his copyists, five of whom were Scottish: 'Oats. A grain, which in England is given to horses, but in Scotland supports the people' – a jest as private as his definition of 'lexicographer' as 'A writer of dictionaries, a harmless drudge . . .'

These lexicographical pranks, which nowadays would be unthinkable, must, as Boswell said, 'be placed to the account of capricious and humorous indulgence'. One of them, indeed, brought Johnson perilously near to prosecution, for an old resentment over his father's indictment by the Excise Board, for failing to pay the new tax on parchment, led him to define 'excise' as 'A hateful tax levied upon commodities, and adjudged not by the common judges of property, but wretches hired by those to whom excise is paid.' The Commissioners of Excise were sufficiently affronted to consult the Attorney General as to whether this were a libel, and therefore actionable. It might indeed, the Attorney General decided, be so considered; but, he added, it would be 'more prudent in the Board not to prosecute' – thus saving His Majesty's Excise from making themselves ridiculous.

The years absorbed by this 'long and painful voyage round the world of the English language' had seen Johnson often weary, sick, discouraged, miserable and lonely. He must now, he knew, be prepared for the final ordeal: the publication which might mean praise and fame, or, more probably, the blast of critical censure and attack. In some moods he felt himself curiously numb, as though he no longer cared: with Tetty gone, who was there to share in his achievement, remembering the pains of the voyage as he remembered them himself? He concluded his Preface at last on a dispassionate note: 'I may surely be contented without the praise of perfection, which, if I could obtain it, what would it avail me? I have protracted my work till most of those whom I wished to please have sunk into the grave, and success and miscarriage are empty sounds: I therefore dismiss it with frigid tranquillity, having little to fear or hope from censure or from praise.'

Yet even in the Preface the mood fluctuates: there are moments, he admits, when 'I look with pleasure on my book, however defective, and deliver it to the world with the spirit of a man that has endeavoured well.' One thing at least the Dictionary had procured, even before publication: recognition from the University of Oxford. In the summer of 1754, when the great work was within a few months of completion, he had written to his friend Thomas Warton, Fellow of Trinity, that he could not finish it to his liking 'without visiting the libraries of Oxford, which I therefore hope to see in about a fortnight'. He accordingly spent five weeks in the University, staying in Kettel Hall in Broad Street, visiting his old college, going for long walks with Warton and supping with him afterwards, but not, apparently, collecting any fresh material for the Dictionary. The visit may, indeed, have had an ulterior motive, for by the autumn he and Warton were corresponding on a topic which they had evidently discussed – the possibility of the University's bestowing on Johnson the degree of Master of Arts. If this could be done in time for the publication of the Dictionary it would add greatly to his prestige on the title-page, and Thomas Warton, himself a poet and a man of learning (he was soon to become Professor of Poetry and, later, Poet Laureate) busied himself with proposals in the right quarters. The Chancellor was approached, and in turn wrote to the Vice-Chancellor and Convocation, recommending Johnson on the strength not only of the Dictionary, but also of the *Rambler* essays, 'in which the cause of religion and morality is everywhere maintained by the strongest powers of argument and language'. This time there was no rebuff, as in the days when he had hoped to be a schoolmaster: now he had proved himself and the degree was obligingly conferred, the diploma being carried to London by Dr King, principal of one of the colleges. So the five weeks spent walking and talking about Oxford had not, after all, been wasted, and the coveted letters A.M. were set up by the printers preparing the title-page of the folio

Kettel Hall, Broad Street, Oxford, where Johnson spent five summer weeks in 1754, when he was approaching the end of his work on the *Dictionary*

Dictionary. His mind at rest on this important point, Johnson suddenly remembered some oddments he had forgotten. 'As you are soon to come to town,' he wrote to one of his Oxford friends, 'I shall be glad if you will pay my barber, whom I forgot, for a week's shaving, etc., and call at Mrs Simpson's for a box of pills which I left behind me, and am loath to lose.'

All was now complete; the last sheets had gone to the printer; the long years of drudgery and delay, of impatience and exasperation on the publishers' part and laborious struggle on his own, were finally over. 'When the messenger who carried the last sheet to Mr Millar returned, Johnson asked him, "Well, what did he say?" "Sir," answered the messenger, "he said, Thank God I have done with him." "I am glad", replied Johnson with a smile, "that he thanks God for anything."'

The money he had been paid for the Dictionary was already spent; he was neither richer nor poorer than when he had begun; but in a sense he had become a different person, and in the space of a few weeks he would be famous. The Dictionary made no sensational impact, it is true: reviews were cautious and there was at first little of the

Johnson in 1756, by Reynolds. Boswell thought it a perfect evocation of his presence, 'sitting in his easy chair in deep meditation'.

hostile criticism he had expected; his only opponents were 'the critics of the coffee-house, whose outcries are soon dispersed into the air, and are thought on no more'.[4] But gradually, even though a year later he must still admit that 'praise has been very scarce', the whole of London had become aware of the great Dictionary, and through London and Oxford the whole of the literary and academic world. It was discussed, criticized, admired and quoted wherever discriminating company was to be found. The ubiquitous Thomas Tyers hardly exaggerated when he claimed that Johnson's reputation was 'as great for compiling, digesting and ascertaining the English language, as if he had invented it'.

LEFT Arthur Murphy, author and actor, Johnson's 'dear Mur', who introduced him to the Thrales. RIGHT An early self-portrait by Reynolds. In later life he wore spectacles, and eventually lost the sight of one eye while still at the height of his powers.

The chief pleasure of this new celebrity was that it brought friends. Though Johnson was still too poor to be idle, he at least had more leisure now that the Dictionary was done, and eagerly welcomed fresh contacts, delighted to find (since he was now forty-five) that most of his new admirers were both talented and young. Arthur Murphy, for instance, a writer and actor, was still in his twenties, and first presented himself to Johnson to aplogize for an embarrassing mistake. He had been producing a small periodical, *The Gray's Inn Journal*, and being one day in the country and at a loss for a subject, had picked up a French magazine and decided to translate 'a very pretty oriental tale' which he found in it. On returning to town he was disconcerted to have this same story pointed out to him in *The Rambler*, from which the French magazine had lifted it without acknowledgment. His interview with Johnson might have been extremely awkward, but fortunately they liked one another on sight, and Murphy's literary *faux pas* was the beginning of a lifelong friendship.

The musician Charles Burney, too, was still in his twenties when he wrote to Johnson from Norfolk, praising the Dictionary in such terms as gave enormous pleasure, especially since, as Johnson confessed, 'Yours is the only letter of good-will that I have received.' In due course Burney called on him in Gough Square, where he dined and drank tea, Miss Williams presiding at the tea-table. After dinner, Burney remembered, 'Mr Johnson proposed . . . to go up with him to his garret, which being accepted, he there found about five or six Greek folios, a deal writing-desk, and a chair and a half. Johnson giving to his guest the entire seat, tottered himself on one with only three legs and one arm.' This crippled chair in the bare attic, where Johnson continued to do all his writing, astonished the young Joshua Reynolds in his turn, observing that when he got up 'Mr Johnson never forgot its defect, but would either hold it in his hand, or place it with great composure against some support, taking no notice of its imperfection to his visitor.' Reynolds, newly returned from Italy and enjoying his first fashionable success as a portrait-painter, became, like Burney and Murphy, a friend at once and for life, exchanging visits to and fro between Gough Square and Great Newport Street, where he had his studio. Johnson, he acknowledged candidly, 'may be said to have formed my mind, and to have brushed from it a great deal of rubbish'.

Then there was young Bennet Langton, son of a well-to-do Lincolnshire squire, who cannot have been more than seventeen when, as a great admirer of *The Rambler*, he contrived, through the landlady of his London lodgings, who knew Levett, to get himself introduced to Johnson. He had no idea what Johnson looked like, and from his writings had imagined a decent, well-dressed, decorous philosopher. 'Instead of which, down from his bed-chamber, about noon, came, as newly risen, a huge uncouth figure, with a little dark wig which scarcely covered his head, and his clothes hanging loose about him.' But his conversation was so stimulting that Langton fell completely under his spell, while Johnson for his part conceived an immediate affection for this sober, scholarly, almost freakishly tall and lanky youth, whom someone described as a 'very tall, meagre, long-visaged man, much resembling a stork standing on one leg'. After this

Bennet Langton, who, at only seventeen, was an admirer of *The Rambler*, had made himself known to Johnson, and remained his devoted friend for life. He was one of 'the young dogs of this age' whom Johnson loved.

meeting they began a long and congenial correspondence, in which from time to time Johnson delighted to offer the younger man advice. 'Do you take notice of my example,' he wrote in 1759, when Langton had become Warton's pupil at Oxford, 'and learn the danger of delay. When I was as you are now, towering in confidence of twenty-one, little did I suspect that I should be at forty-nine, what I now am.' What Johnson was, however, was something Langton respectfully admired; so much so that, observing his poverty, he persuaded his father to offer Johnson a Lincolnshire rectory which was in his gift, and which would provide a comfortable living once his friend had taken holy orders. If the suggestion had come twenty years earlier, perhaps Johnson might have considered it, but now he knew himself too well; the faulty creature he acknowledged himself to be was not fit to harangue villagers from a pulpit. His moral teaching was better done from behind the mask of the *Rambler* or *Adventurer*, or at least from the privacy of his own garret. Besides, how could he live among the fens of Lincolnshire, and relinquish London?

So the offer was gratefully declined, and Johnson went on to make friends with one of Langton's even younger Oxford cronies, the charming and sophisticated Topham Beauclerk, who, besides being everything a young man could desire – good-looking, intelligent, rich and moreover the grandson of a duke – had inherited the additional charm of being directly descended from Charles II and Nell Gwyn. The only thing against him from Johnson's point of view was that, as one might expect of a youth living up to such an ancestry, Beauclerk had an impudent wit and was a considerable rake. 'What a coalition!' said Garrick with mock dismay, when he heard that 'the moral, pious Johnson and the gay, dissipated Beauclerk' had become companions. It was not so strange as he pretended, for Johnson loved gaiety and youth, and Beauclerk had too much sense to behave in his company as shamelessly as he often did elsewhere. With such young 'dogs' Johnson could escape from his serious preoccupations and enjoy high spirits and absurdity with the best. One night, when he had known them a little while, Beauclerk and Langton found themselves very merry after a late supper in a tavern, and about three in the morning decided to knock up Johnson and take him for a spree. They rapped violently on his door until at last 'he appeared in his shirt, with his little black wig on top of his head, instead of a night-cap, and a poker in his hand, imagining, probably, that some ruffians were coming to attack him. When he discovered who they were, and was told their errand, he smiled, and with great good humour agreed to their proposal: "What, is it you, you dogs! I'll have a frisk with you."' He quickly dressed, and they strolled to Covent Garden, which was already busy with the carts and hampers of vegetables come in from the country. For a while Johnson made a pretence of helping the porters, 'but they stared so at his figure and manner, and odd interference, that he soon saw that his services were not relished', and the trio wandered on. The Piazza taverns were already open, and they went into one for a bowl of 'Bishop', a mixture of wine, sugar and orange juice of which Johnson was particularly fond. Then they strolled down to the Thames, hired a boat and were rowed as far as Billingsgate. It was now getting light, with small craft stirring on the river and the streets showing signs of life, by which time Johnson and Beauclerk were in such spirits that 'they resolved to persevere in dissipation for the rest of the day'. Langton, however, being engaged to breakfast with some young ladies, deserted them at this point, vigorously scolded by Johnson for leaving them 'to go and sit with a set of wretched *un-idea'd* girls'. Such a manner of spending the night would have astonished his more sedate friends; but to Johnson, to exchange the melancholy night hours for the streets, the river and the dawn, in the company of these two enchanting young men, was nothing less than rapture.

Another all-night revel, this time at 'the Club', was recorded by Hawkins, whose own enjoyment had been marred by toothache and an uneasy feeling about 'the resemblance it bore to a debauch'. The occasion, or excuse, was the publication of Charlotte Lennox's 'first literary child', a novel, for which Johnson hoped great things, since Mrs Lennox was not only clever but poor – a combination which never failed to arouse his sympathy. Her history, in fact, had been singularly unfortunate. Born a daughter of the Lieutenant-General of New York, she had been sent to England at the age of fifteen to the house of a rich aunt who had offered to adopt her, but who proved to be not only incompetent but insane. Charlotte's father dying soon after without making any provision for her, she was left destitute, and for a while tried to make a living on the stage. For this she had little talent – Horace Walpole described her as 'a deplorable actress' – and she turned for support to literature. In this she was modestly successful, and at least earned the reputation of a minor bluestocking.

'Our supper was elegant,' Hawkins remembered, 'and Johnson had directed that a magnificent hot apple-pie should make a part of it, and this he would have stuck with bay-leaves, because, forsooth, Mrs Lennox was an authoress . . . and further, he had prepared for her a crown of laurel, with which (but not till he had invoked the muses by some ceremonies of his own invention) he encircled her brows. The night passed, as must be imagined, in pleasant conversation and harmless mirth, intermingled at different periods with the refreshments of coffee and tea. About five Johnson's face shone with meridian splendour, though his drink had been only lemonade; but the far greater part of us . . . were with difficulty rallied to partake of a second refreshment of coffee, which was scarcely ended when the day began to dawn . . . and it was not till near eight that the creaking of the street door gave the signal for our departure.' Charlotte Lennox was one of the very few living people to whom Johnson paid a hidden compliment in his Dictionary, quoting from her novel, *The Female Quixote*, to illustrate the use of the word 'talent'. (He had one or two hidden jokes besides, such as quoting himself under 'important', and Garrick, whose comic genius never failed him, under 'giggle'.)

To GI'GGLE. *v. n.* [*gichgelen*, Dutch.] To laugh idly; to titter; to grin with merry levity. It is retained in Scotland.

GI'GGLER. *n. f.* [from *giggle*.] A laugher; a titterer; one idly and foolishly merry.

A sad wise valour is the brave complexion,
That leads the van, and swallows up the cities:
The *giggler* is a milk-maid, whom infection,
Or the fir'd beacon, frighteth from his ditties.   *Herbert*.
We shew our present, joking, *giggling* race;
True joy consists in gravity and grace.   *Garrick's Epilogue*.

In contrast to such occasional gaieties, Johnson's routine of life was cheerless enough: his health had deteriorated, and he was still wretchedly poor. Even with the Dictionary behind him he was still writing articles to order for a guinea apiece, and more than once was arrested for debt, to be bailed out by one or other of his booksellers. It was nothing unusual for him to have to send out a letter by hand to a friend, begging for the loan of a guinea to tide him over, and these constant difficulties made it more difficult than ever for him to work. 'A man doubtful of his dinner,' he wrote, 'or trembling at a creditor, is not much disposed to abstract meditation, or remote inquiries.' He had not yet escaped from the treadmill of the shiftless hack, whose experience of life, in Macaulay's words, was 'to lodge in a garret up four pairs of stairs, to dine in a cellar among footmen out of place, to translate ten hours a day for the wages of a ditcher, to be hunted by bailiffs from one haunt of beggary and pestilence to another, from Grub Street to St George's Fields, and from St George's Fields to the alleys behind St Martin's Church, to sleep on a bulk in June and amidst the ashes of a glass-house in December, to die in an hospital, and to be buried in a parish vault'.

The deterioration of his health at this period is somewhat mysterious; one of the troubles seems to have been constant colds, which settled on his chest and wrecked his days and nights with painful coughing. 'I am often, very often ill', he excused himself for delaying to answer a letter. On other occasions he speaks of 'a cough so violent that I once fainted under its convulsions', and of himself as 'a poor helpless being reduced by a blast of wind to weakness and misery'.[5] The winters in Gough Square could be appallingly cold, and little heat could be coaxed from the draughty fireplace in Johnson's garret. These were the years, besides, when a new disease had made its appearance in England, brought, it is said, from Italy, which may have been responsible: the *London Magazine* gave 'news from Rome of a contagious distemper raging there, called the *Influenza*' – a name meaning, quite simply, 'the influence', since nobody could either control or understand it.

He suffered periodically, too, from an inflammation in his 'good' eye, which, since the other was practically blind, for days together prevented him from reading. But his great enemy, now as always, was that mysterious melancholy which threatened his sleepless nights and gave him a morbid terror of being alone. 'From that kind of melancholy indisposition', he wrote to his old friend Edmund Hector, 'which I had when we lived together at Birmingham, I have never been free, but have always had it operating against my health and my life with more or less violence.'[6] And to Warton, hearing that the poet William Collins had had to be put into a madhouse, 'Poor dear Collins . . . I have often been near his state, and therefore have it in great commiseration.'[7]

He had not yet recovered, and could not, from the loss of Tetty. With all their disparities they had to the end kept something of the old affection, which poor blind Anna Williams could never replace. His growing fame would have pleased Tetty; it would have justified her good opinion. There was a feeling of emptiness still, since there was no one to care for his achievement as she had cared. 'I have ever since', he told Warton, 'seemed to myself broken off from mankind . . . a gloomy gazer on a world to which I have little relation';[8] and when Dodsley the bookseller lost his wife, 'I hope he will not suffer so much as I yet suffer for the loss of mine.'

His best solution, perhaps, would have been to marry again, and this he did at one time consider, a little more than a year after Tetty's death. On Easter Sunday 1753 he wrote in his diary, 'As I purpose to try on Monday to seek a new wife, without any derogation from dear Tetty's memory, I purpose at sacrament in the morning to take my leave of Tetty in a solemn commendation of her soul to God': and the following day added, 'During the whole service I was never once distracted by any thoughts of any other woman, or with my design of a new wife, which freedom of mind I remembered with gladness in the garden. God guide me.'[9]

What 'other woman' he may have had in mind remains a mystery. We know of his intention only through Boswell's sharpness, for Johnson destroyed that part of the diary before his death; not knowing, perhaps, that Boswell had quickly transcribed one or two passages when he had allowed him to look through its pages in 1776. After twenty-three years Johnson may not clearly have remembered what he had written, and Boswell for various reasons considered the matter too delicate to be included in his biography. In any case nothing came of it, either through Johnson's procrastination or the lack of a suitable candidate. It is tempting to wonder if his thoughts turned to that 'very sensible maiden lady', Miss Hill Boothby, whom he had met and liked thirteen years before, when visiting among Taylor's friends at Ashbourne. His letters to her at this period have not survived, which may or may not be significant: those which he wrote nearly three years later, and which *have* survived, are of a most moving tenderness. 'Dearest Madam', 'Dearest dear', 'My Sweet Angel' some of them begin; but then, as Johnson was miserably aware, by this time Hill Boothby was dying, and he was writing anxiously and often, with undisguised affection. 'I love and honour you, and am very unwilling to lose you.' 'None but you on whom my heart reposes.' 'Dear Angel, do not forget me. My heart is full of tenderness . . .'.[10]

If he had actually proposed to Hill Boothby it is doubtful if she would have accepted him, for her friend Mary Meynell had died, and she was fulfilling a promise by taking over the running of her friend's household and the care of her six children. And three years after Johnson's 'design of a new wife' Hill Boothby herself was dead, and he had reached the point of accepting his celibacy and his loneliness, though with what bitter anguish his prayers are sufficient witness.

In these lonely years, since the Dictionary had brought no profit and it was a perpetual struggle to keep the roof of Gough Square over his head, Johnson worked hard, if sporadically. It was all very well for Boswell to joke about the Dictionary having been written by 'the most indolent man in Britain'; those who knew him at the time were aware that he often toiled late into the night, however inactive he appeared to be at other times of day. He did not love work, but when once he could no longer postpone the essay, review, preface or other literary task to which he was committed, his concentration was so intense that he wrote rapidly, and the thing was soon done. His friend Hawkesworth had started a periodical called *The Adventurer*, which was simply a series of self-contained essays published anonymously and contributed by Hawkesworth, Warton, Bathurst, Johnson and others. The secret of their individual authorship was on the whole well kept, and there has been a good deal of argument, from Boswell onward, as to which were Johnson's essays and which were not. Twenty-nine are nowadays accepted as being his, but Johnson himself, when pressed to be precise on the subject, 'smiled, and said nothing'.

As well as *The Adventurer*, and before he began his much livelier series of 'Idler' essays for the weekly *Universal Chronicle*, he accepted commissions for reviews and prefaces, some of which can be read with entertainment today. It is unexpected, for instance, to find him prefacing a book on the game of draughts, but we learn from it that he considered himself no mean player, and the game itself, in some respects, 'even equal with that of chess'.[11] He had, in fact, played draughts a good deal at Oxford, though never for money; and once even lamented to Boswell that he had never learned to play at cards, which were 'very useful in life', since they generated kindness and consolidated society. (His written views on card-playing disagree, and one cannot imagine him spending silent and concentrated hours at the card-table. Besides, as Boswell – who himself had 'a rage of gaming' – observed elsewhere, playing at cards brings one into company that one would not otherwise choose.)

Johnson's love of tea-drinking, which by now had become excessive – compensation, perhaps, for his abstinence, and also as a means of making other people sit up late with him – had a splendid chance of expression when he came to review a long-winded travelogue by Jonas Hanway, to which the author, never at a loss for something to reform, had appended *An Essay on Tea: Considered as Pernicious to Health, obstructing Industry, and Impoverishing the Nation.* Hanway was not alone in believing that tea was second only to gin as a threat to health and a demoralizer of the poor. It was expensive, certainly, and many took the view (as they might of cannabis today) that it was also the cause of innumerable disorders. Lord Hervey's delicate health had been wholly blamed by his father on 'that detestable and poisonous plant, tea, which had once brought him to death's door, and if persisted in would carry him through it'. John Wesley, many years before Hanway, had been surprised by 'some symptoms of a paralytic disorder' after drinking tea at breakfast, and had exhorted his followers to give it up altogether, which many of them did; never dreaming that in the next generation tea would be the temperance reformer's most useful weapon. Johnson was aware of all this, and delighted to describe himself in his review as 'a hardened and shameless tea-drinker, who has, for twenty years, diluted his meals with only the infusion of this fascinating plant; whose kettle has scarcely time to cool; who with tea amuses the evening, with tea solaces the midnight, and, with tea, welcomes the morning'. He admitted on reflection that tea was 'a liquor not proper to the lower classes of the people', thus partially agreeing with Wesley, who had convinced the Methodists that 'it would prevent great expense, as well of health as of time and money, if the poorer people of our society could be persuaded to leave off drinking tea'.[12] Happily for the domestic comforts of the nation, no one paid much attention to Hanway's diatribe, and the tea-table with its silver urn and fine china remained one of the social pleasures of the eighteenth century.

All this, however, was only small stuff, bringing in a few guineas. What he needed was a solid enterprise for which he could write proposals and raise subscriptions, following the laborious practice of the time, which obliged an author to solicit his friends for advance payment on a book before it was written. He now felt sufficiently confident to revive the idea of his annotated edition of Shakespeare, and sketched out conventional 'Proposals' which were to bring in subscriptions, the price being two guineas, 'one to be paid at subscribing, the other on the delivery of the book in sheets'. The work was to be published by the end of the following year, 'on or before Christmas 1757', and, as with the Dictionary, Johnson absurdly believed he could finish it in this short time. 'It is all work,' he told Hawkins, 'and my inducement to it is not love or desire of fame, but the want of money, which is the only motive to writing that I know of.' Once the contract was signed, however, his fatal tendency to procrastinate seemed to paralyse him, and he did nothing. 'It was provoking to all his friends', said Hawkins, 'to see him waste his days, his weeks and his months so long, that they feared a mental lethargy had seized him, out of which he would never recover.' And when finally he roused himself it was not to steady progress on his Shakespeare, but to writing an entertaining weekly essay, 'The Idler', for *The Universal Chronicle*; and this naturally delayed the Shakespeare even more. 'The Idler' regularly brought in a small sum, and as one of his medical friends[13] remarked, 'He never thinks of working if he has a couple of guineas in his pocket.' In the end, to the exasperation of subscribers and the despair of his publishers, Johnson lingered over his Shakespeare for nine years.

In the January of 1759 news arrived from Lichfield which he had long been dreading: Sarah Johnson, now in her ninetieth year, was dying. This was a calamity which he

Johnson's tea-service, inherited and preserved by his Negro servant, Francis Barber, and now in the Birthplace Museum, Lichfield

knew to be natural and inevitable, and therefore to be faced without too much grief; but his feelings for his mother had always been both complex and deep, and now his conscience pressed home the fact that he had not been home to see her for almost twenty years.

For this there were many reasons which were sufficient excuse from a practical point of view: he was always pressed for money and either working or promising to work on something new. The Dictionary and *Rambler* years in particular had been a long hard grind, and in those days of appalling roads the journey from London to Lichfield was not something to be lightly undertaken. Even thirteen years later, travelling by stage-coach, the journey took him twenty-six hours, and the return was often a hazardous business, with the coaches already full of passengers from the north. But the real reason, as he knew, had been his own incorrigible tendency to delay, and his self-reproach on this score made him unduly apprehensive whenever he asked for, or received, news from Lichfield. 'I have a mother more than eighty years old', he wrote to Langton the month after the Dictionary had been published, 'who has counted the days to the publication of my book, in hopes of seeing me; and to her, if I can disengage myself, I resolve to go.' But he did not, or could not, disengage himself, and a little later wrote, 'I fully persuade myself that I shall pass some of the winter months with my mother; I would have come sooner, but could not break my shackles.' He wrote to Lucy for news and sent money whenever possible, but remained where he was. 'You frighted me, you little

Anna Williams's silver teaspoons, which she bequeathed to the Ladies' Charitable Trust in 1783, and which are now in Johnson's House, Gough Square

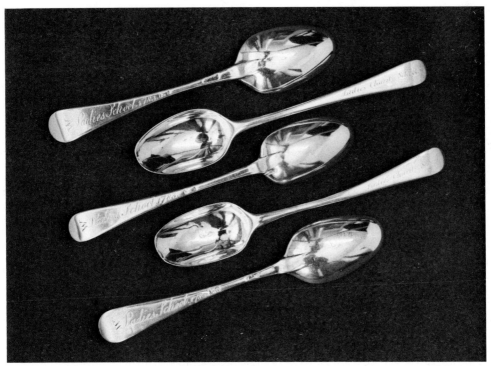

gypsy, with your black wafer', he wrote to Lucy on one occasion, forgetting that she had recently lost an uncle, 'for I had forgot you were in mourning and was afraid your letter had brought me ill news of my mother, whose death is one of the few calamities on which I think with terror.'

Now the calamity was approaching, and as he prepared to leave London he sent off a series of poignant notes to his mother, with six guineas scraped together and another six borrowed. 'Pray, send me your blessing, and forgive all that I have done amiss to you. And whatever you would have done, and what debts you would have paid first, or anything else that you would direct, let Miss put it down; and I shall endeavour to obey you.' 'Dear honoured Mother, Your weakness afflicts me beyond what I am willing to communicate to you. I do not think you unfit to face death, but I know not how to bear the thought of losing you.' 'Dear honoured Mother, Neither your condition nor your character make it fit for me to say much. You have been the best mother, and I believe the best woman in the world. I thank you for your indulgence to me, and beg forgiveness of all that I have done ill, and all that I have omitted to do well. God grant you his Holy Spirit, and receive you to everlasting happiness, for Jesus Christ's sake. Amen. Lord Jesus receive your spirit. Amen. I am, dear Mother, your dutiful son, Sam. Johnson.'

By the time he was ready for the journey it was too late, and to his old regrets he must add the final one that at the last he had failed to reach her. What he could do now, he did, writing to Lucy with anxious promises of money, hoping that she and Kitty (Catherine Chambers, his mother's maid) would continue to live together in the old house. 'If you and Kitty will keep the house, I think I shall like it best. . . . My mother's debts, dear Mother, I suppose I may pay with little difficulty; and the little trade may go silently forward. I fancy Kitty can do nothing better; and I shall not want to put her out of a house where she has lived so long, and with so much virtue.'

The 'little difficulty' was something of a euphemism, since Johnson's own affairs had reached the point where he could no longer possibly afford to live in Gough Square. After ten momentous years he must give it up and return to rented rooms. Frank, the Negro boy, had run away to sea; Miss Williams was found lodgings, and Levett presumably was prepared to shift for himself as he had done before. Johnson moved first to rooms in Staple Inn, then to Gray's Inn and finally to chambers in Inner Temple Lane, where he followed his own characteristic pattern of life, according to Murphy, 'in poverty, total idleness, and the pride of literature'.

10

'At last, on Monday the 16th of May...'

LITTLE while before his mother's death the idea had occurred to Johnson that a simple story, following the fashionable form of the oriental tale, would be an excellent means of conveying the conclusions he had come to concerning the 'choice of life'. Was there, in fact, a recipe for happiness? Supposing a man could choose, was there any deliberate plan of life which offered a reasonable hope of escaping misery? The idea of a dangerous and enigmatic choice had long been a theme of fairy-tales, and the *Arabian Nights*, now accessible to Johnson's generation in English and French translation, had created a taste for mysterious eastern scenes and philosophical adventures. A 'little story book', as he described it to Lucy, which had the simplicity of an eastern tale and yet carried a moral message, might possibly sell well. He discussed it with his friend William Strahan, the printer, agreed on one hundred pounds for a first edition, and set to work with an unusual sense of urgency, knowing that his mother's death would mean debts to pay, as well as the necessary expense of a decent funeral. *Rasselas, Prince of Abyssinia* – a name that had lingered in memory since the days of translating Lobo's voyage to that almost mythical county – was written, he told Reynolds, in the evenings (and no doubt the nights) of one week, and sent off to the printer in handfuls as fast as it was written. Though it did not please everybody, its success was immediate. Johnson's literary celebrity was already such that any new work of his would attract attention, and although the two little volumes were published anonymously he made it clear to Strahan that he expected his authorship to be made known. This was easily achieved, and his deceptively simple *novella* became even more a subject of discussion because, by a strange coincidence, Voltaire's *Candide* was published at almost the same time, and the readers of both were astonished by their similarities. If they had not been published so closely 'that there was not time for imitation', Johnson frankly admitted that everyone would suppose that 'the scheme of that which came latest was taken from the other' – despite the fact that Voltaire's tone is one of ribald cynicism, and that of *Rasselas* a pious and occasionally witty pessimism.

Johnson offers no hope of a remedy for man's discontent, beyond a certain stoic endurance, and that precious vitality of intellect which he calls 'curiosity'. 'Human life is everywhere a state, in which much is to be endured, and little to be enjoyed.' Prince

Rasselas and his sister, the Princess Nekayah, escaping from the Happy Valley in which the Emperor's children are luxuriously immured, learn that the world outside holds even less to satisfy 'that hunger of imagination which preys incessantly upon life', and with Imlac, their philosopher-guide, return at last, sadder and wiser, to the comfortable security of their valley. It is basically a sad story, but told in a style so serene and harmonious, such a cunning blend of adventure and philosophy, that it quickly became, and for a long time remained, extremely popular. Johnson's contemporaries, it may seem to us now, overrated it, accepting it as a sort of gospel of pious rationalism, speaking both for the Age of Reason and for a sombre Christian faith, and this exaggerated veneration produced in time the inevitable reaction, so that *Rasselas* today is no longer so highly regarded or widely read. It is still, however, a rewarding and instructive tale which illuminates for us the landscape of Johnson's vision and imagination, and leaves some memorable passages in the mind. A 'little story book', as he considered it, can hardly be expected to do more.

A portrait of Johnson, by James Barry. Johnson knew Barry
but may not have actually sat for him.

On the strength of this success, and with his mother's small affairs now more or less settled, Johnson decided to indulge himself with a visit to Oxford, and spent seven weeks of the summer in the University. This time he was the proud possessor of a Master's gown, which he wore wherever he went, following the academic custom. It was, he reported, 'at my first coming quite new and handsome', so one supposes that it did not long remain so. He swam three times in the river, a thing he had not done for many years, and on one occasion even challenged a Fellow of All Souls to climb over a wall – a proposal which was not accepted. In the last two years he had taken to wine again, and it was probably during this summer visit that he drank three bottles of port in University College, without, as he seriously assured Boswell, 'being the worse for it'. But drinking, as he was privately aware, was something of a risk, for in spite of his good head he could never be sure of drinking in moderation, and drunkenness was a state that disgusted him both morally and physically. The sparse and sometimes cryptic entries in his diary over the next few years are rarely without resolutions on this subject, and reflect a pattern of repeated resolve and failure.

The diary entries, scanty as they are, give a deeply melancholy impression of Johnson's state of mind, being less concerned with daily happenings than with his religious life, in which he set himself so strenuous a standard that he was perpetually disappointed. That this inner struggle, this commitment to spiritual obligation and discipline, was the secret centre of Johnson's life there is no question; nor can there be any doubt that the neuroses which deepened his endemic melancholy naturally asserted themselves at precisely those times when he was examining his conscience and recording his prayers and resolutions of amendment.

It was his habit to take the sacrament once a year, at Easter, and to prepare himself for the solemn event by fasting, prayer, examining his conduct over the past year, expressing contrition, promising reform. A prayer was always composed and recorded in the diary, where it could be reviewed the following year and his promises compared with his achievement. He usually, too, listed his resolutions to serve as a reminder, a milder and safer discipline than a vow. Vows, in Johnson's view, were in the ordinary course of life extremely dangerous, being broken almost as easily as resolutions and leaving behind a disproportionate guilt.

The sins against which, year after year, he implores God's help with a kind of mounting despair are 'idleness, intemperate sleep, dilatoriness, immethodical life, lust, neglect of worship, vain scruples'. From time to time there is an additional resolve to 'live temperately', 'to drink less strong liquors', 'to go to church every Sunday' or to put his rooms in order; but the two great sins which are never omitted from the calendar are idleness and sensuality. Exactly how Johnson defined all these temptations we cannot always be sure, but the idleness and sensuality present no great problems of interpretation. The 'intemperate sleep', or habit of drowsing in bed until past noon, was an obvious result of the late hours he kept, just as the late hours were due to insomnia and the dread of being alone. It was his almost invariable habit to sit talking in a friend's house or a tavern until the small hours; he then usually ambled homewards about two o'clock, stopping to take tea with Miss Williams in her lodgings if she still had a light showing (she displayed a remarkable fidelity in sitting up for him) and shutting himself at last into his own chambers to spend a further couple of hours reading, prowling about, gloomily brooding and putting off the hour of going to bed until he was thoroughly wretched. The following day, having 'slept ill', he would rise perhaps at two o'clock, or if he had managed to keep his resolution of getting up at eight (one of his most cherished aims and one of the least successful), by the next night he would be complaining in his diary, 'Sleepy all day', or 'In these days every day sleepy.' In this state it was hardly possible to force himself to work, and so once again he would be imploring God in the small hours, 'O Lord, forgive me the time lost in idleness', or making a fresh list of resolves to save himself from despair and self-disgust: 'To rise early. To study Religion. To go to Church. To drink less strong liquors. To keep Journal. To oppose laziness, by doing what is to be done.'

His agonized resolutions against sensuality may seem a strange obsession in a man whose sexual behaviour was as blameless as Johnson's, but an attentive reading of the prayers and diaries leaves the strong impression of a man determined to live chastely, whose powerful sexual urges give him little rest, and who turns for comfort to day-dreaming and fantasy. 'Marriage has many pains,' the Princess Nekayah tells her brother, 'but celibacy has no pleasures'; and now for many years, ever since some in-definite period before his wife's death, he had known no sexual comfort, and his conscience forbade the easy relief which most of his friends would have turned to without a second thought, spending the price of a supper on a wholesome-looking whore. His powers of imagination offered him a tantalizing substitute, always available in idleness and solitude, or during the wretched night hours when he could not sleep. These imaginary indulgences distressed his conscience almost as much as if they had been real; he was aware, too, that day-dreaming at this pitch of intensity has its dangers, especially for the man who believes the balance of his mind to be precarious. 'There is no man', he makes Imlac caution Rasselas, 'whose imagination does not sometimes predominate over his reason.' As the opium of day-dreaming takes effect, 'All other intellectual gratifications are rejected; the mind, in weariness or leisure, recurs con-stantly to the favourite conception, and feasts on the luscious falsehood whenever she is offended with the bitterness of truth. . . . Then fictions begin to operate as realities, false opinions fasten upon the mind, and life passes in dreams of rapture or of anguish.'[1]

These, then, are the sins that in the confessional night hours before Easter lead him to condemn himself as 'depraved with vain imaginations, and entangled in long habits of sin.' Again and again he lists his besetting failings and implores God's help. 'Give me thy grace to break the chain of evil custom. Enable me to shake off idleness and sloth . . . grant me to be chaste in thoughts, words and actions . . . to be diligent in my calling, that I may support myself and relieve others.' And to the snares of idleness and sensuality he frequently adds a third: 'Enable me to break the chain of my sins, to reject sensuality in thought, and to overcome and suppress vain scruples.' What those vain scruples were is not always clear; sometimes they are moments of religious doubt, difficulties of belief. 'Everything which Hume has advanced against Christianity', he told Boswell, 'had passed through my mind long before he wrote.' Such 'scruples' were a threat to faith, and he fought against them. He uses the word, too, in another sense, to mean a futile hesitation over small matters: to spend hours in making up his mind over something unimportant was another reprehensible waste of time. So the sombre rhythm goes on, between confession and resolution, penitence and failure, hope and despair. 'My indolence', he wrote in his diary before Easter 1764, 'since my last re-ception of the Sacrament, has sunk into grosser sluggishness, and my dissipation spread into wilder negligence. My thoughts have been clouded with sensuality, and, except that from the beginning of this year I have in some measure forborn excess of strong drink, my appetites have predominated over my reason. A kind of strange oblivion has overspread me, so that I know not what has become of the last year, and perceive that incidents and intelligence pass over me without leaving any impression. . . .' In another two years his melancholy would drive him to the point of serious breakdown, but in the early seventeen-sixties even his most intimate friends suspected nothing beyond the understandable depression of poverty and sloth. His time-wasting habits and lack of system, Hawkins considered, were the cause of all his troubles: 'All he did was by fits and starts.' Murphy believed that in the years of working on the Dictionary his mind had been 'strained and over-laboured by constant exertion', and had not yet recovered its tone. But from his late-night conversations in good company, or even from his letters, it would have been impossible to guess the depths to which he sometimes sank when alone.

In the autumn of 1760 the old King died, and his grandson George III came to the throne at the age of twenty-two. 'We were so weary of our old King', Johnson wrote to his friend Baretti in Milan, 'that we are much pleased with his successor; of whom we are so much inclined to hope great things, that most of us begin already to believe them.' This Joseph Baretti, to whom he retailed the London gossip, was a teacher of languages and miscellaneous writer who had come to London some years before and been introduced to Johnson by Charlotte Lennox. He was a man of some talent though uncertain temper, and had recently completed an Italian-English dictionary for which Johnson had promised to write a dedication. They had cheered each other on occasions when they had had only a shilling or two between them; Johnson respected Baretti's energy and was genuinely fond of him, ignoring the waspishness of which some other people, with good reason, learned to be wary. Now that Baretti was accompanying one of his well-

Joseph Baretti, who, though a man of uncertain temper, remained a friend of Johnson's for many years

to-do pupils on a European tour Johnson wrote him long letters, giving him his own news and that of their mutual friends. Young Joshua Reynolds was 'without a rival, and continues to add thousands to thousands', his success as a portrait-painter earning him no less than six thousand a year. Levett had got into a scrape by marrying a prostitute, 'not without much suspicion that he has been wretchedly cheated in his match'. The pair had apparently been meeting in a coal-shed in Fetter Lane, and the woman, supposing him to be a respectable doctor with a profitable practice, had passed herself off as a close relation of a man of fortune. Both being under a delusion, they married for advantage, and Levett was quickly undeceived when his wife was arrested for picking pockets at the Old Bailey. At her trial, *The Gentleman's Magazine* reported, 'Her husband was with difficulty prevented from attending the court, in the hope she would be hanged.' He was disappointed: the new Mrs Levett was acquitted, and the pair separated.

As for himself, Johnson admitted, 'He who continues the same course of life in the same place will have little to tell. . . . Miss Williams and I live much as we did.' The only change was that he was going to the theatre oftener than he used; 'but I have gone thither only to escape from myself'. In the preceding winter he had paid a somewhat melancholy visit to Lichfield, where he found the streets 'much narrower and shorter than I thought I had left them, inhabited by a new race of people, to whom I was very little known': his step-daughter, Lucy, too, was disconcertingly changed; less agreeable than formerly. 'My daughter-in-law, from whom I expected most, and whom I met with sincere benevolence, has lost the beauty and gaiety of youth, without having gained much of the wisdom of age. I wandered about for five days, and took the first convenient opportunity of returning.'

The one great piece of news, however, which he might have relayed to Baretti was not mentioned. On the very day when he was writing to Milan he had also written to the Prime Minister, Lord Bute, to thank him for the grant of a pension of three hundred pounds a year. This unexpected mark of favour was one of the early benefits of the young King's coming to the throne. In George II's reign no man of letters had been helped or honoured, and his successor was anxious to make a good impression on the world of literature and learning. 'Dictionary' Johnson was a deserving case; his literary reputation was high and his poverty well known. The only embarrassment was that definition of the word 'pension' which, like 'excise', had been one of the most offensive in the Dictionary. Could the Government offer a pension – 'Pay given to a state hireling for treason to his country' – to the man who had so described it? Could Johnson, whose pride and independence were sufficiently known, accept himself as a pensioner, 'A slave of state hired by a stipend to obey his master'? In fact the problem was resolved quite easily. Johnson consulted Reynolds as to the propriety of accepting, and was tactfully reassured that his definitions could never apply to himself. Murphy, seriously conferred with over a tavern dinner, was of the same opinion, and Johnson was convinced. 'At that meeting he gave up all his scruples.'[2] Courtesies were exchanged with the Prime Minister, who assured him, repeating the words twice, 'It is not given you for anything you are to do, *but for what you have done.*' So the royal bounty was thankfully accepted, and Johnson was freed at once from the necessity of supporting himself, in the sense that he would not starve if he remained idle. His Shakespeare could be finished at leisure, and from then on he could write from choice rather than necessity. Three hundred a year was a reasonable income for a single man; sufficient, at least, to enable him to ignore the jokes which went the rounds on the irony of his becoming a pensioner. People now asked each other behind their hands whether he would change his definitions, but Johnson was not to be trapped into any such absurdity; when the Dictionary went into a new edition the harsh interpretations remained unchanged.

One of the immediate pleasures of his new independence was that he could afford to accompany Reynolds on a six weeks' jaunt into Devon, where they were entertained by Reynolds's family and friends and saw a great deal that was interesting and attractive in the West Country. One of Reynolds's reasons for making the trip had been to visit some of the great houses where a number of his most recent portraits were hung, and accordingly on the journey they made detours to such noble seats as Wilton, Longford Castle and Kingston Lacy, inspecting their galleries of portraits and elegantly land-scaped gardens. But the most rewarding part of the whole ramble was the three weeks spent in Plymouth, where they established a base in the house of the Reverend Dr Mudge, Reynolds's old schoolfriend, and made innumerable expeditions, visiting among other places of interest the naval dockyard and the harbour crowded with vessels preparing for action under Sir Charles Hardy. The war at sea was naturally a great subject of discussion, for although it affected civilian life comparatively little England had been at war with France, on the seas and in America, for the past six years, and had recently declared war on Spain as well, successfully taking Martinique, Havana and Manila. 'The good or ill success of battles or embassies', Johnson had written to

LEFT The naval dockyard at Plymouth, where Johnson found much of interest when he visited Devon with Reynolds in 1762. RIGHT A water-colour of H.M.S. *Deal Castle*, with the officers' goat aboard

Baretti, 'extends itself to a very small part of domestic life', but here he was in the thick of naval activity, inquiring into the technicalities of shipbuilding and evidently greatly impressed by all he saw. It was here that he probably learned for the first time that a she-goat was kept aboard most well-conducted vessels to provide fresh milk for the officers' coffee, a service that he honoured ten years later by composing a Latin couplet to be engraved on the collar of Sir Joseph Banks's circumnavigating goat when she retired. This fortunate animal, Johnson told Mrs Thrale, 'had been on two of his adventurous expeditions with him, and was then, by the humanity of her amiable master, turned out to graze in Kent, as a recompense for her utility and faithful service.' (It was Banks himself, who had accompanied Cook round the world in the *Endeavour*, who enlisted Johnson's aid in honouring her.)[3]

It was not in Plymouth, however, but at Portsmouth on a later occasion, that he disapproved of the roughness of the sailors' language, asking an officer what a certain place on board was called and being told that it was 'where the loplolly man kept his loplolly',[4] which he considered 'disrespectful, gross and ignorant.'[5] The only disappointment at Plymouth was the sea's being too rough for Reynolds and his companion to land on the Eddystone Rock. Johnson had been eager to inspect Smeaton's great engineering achievement of the lighthouse, but the yacht put at their disposal for the purpose was so violently thrown about by the waves that the attempt had to be abandoned.

It was while dining with some of Reynolds's Devonshire friends that Johnson 'devoured so large a quantity of new honey and clouted cream . . . besides drinking large potations of new cider' that his companions became alarmed, knowing what their cider could do to the unwary; but thanks to Johnson's strong head there were no 'unpleasant consequences'.[6] It was on another of these evenings after supper that he drank three bottles of wine and found his speech affected; attempting a difficult word three times, as Reynolds remembered, he finally pronounced, 'I think it is now time to go to bed.'

The only other adventure in this year of the pension was the enthralling affair of the Cock Lane ghost, in which Johnson became involved as a member of the committee formed to investigate the mystery. This 'ghost' was one of that poltergeist-type of phenomenon which seems to occur only where there is a pubescent girl in the house who derives a paranoid satisfaction from frightening people, and who is also mysteriously skilled in fraudulent manifestations. In this humble house in Cock Lane, Smithfield, however, the girl in question had a powerful accomplice in her father, the parish clerk, who had a grudge against a man who had sued him for debt, and whom he hoped to bring to the gallows by accusing him, through the ghost, of poisoning his sister-in-law. The ghost proclaimed itself only when the child Elizabeth was in bed; then mysterious rappings and scratchings would be heard, which seemed not to come from the bed at all but from different parts of the room, from the panelling or wainscot. When questioned the spirit would answer in the traditional manner, one knock for 'yes' and two for 'no', and in this way established the identity of the dead woman and promised that if the vault under St John's Church were opened the truth of the accusation would be proved by loud knocks on the woman's coffin.

148

It all sounds transparent enough today, but in that more credulous age, when serious psychical research was still undreamed of and for many people superstitious terrors were the most potent thrills of existence, the Cock Lane ghost was an immeasurably greater sensation even than our own Talking Mongoose or Borley Rectory. The newspapers were full of it; the whole town seemed to go mad over the supernatural excitement. 'The Methodists have adopted it,' wrote Horace Walpole, 'and the whole town of London think of nothing else. . . . I went to hear it, for it is not an *apparition*, but an *audition*. We set out from the Opera . . . the Duke of York, Lady Northumberland, Lady Mary Coke, Lord Hertford and I, all in one hackney coach, and drove to the spot: it rained torrents; yet the lane was full of mob, and the house so full we could not get in.' At last, however, they squeezed into a wretched room crowded with fifty people and lit with only a single candle, so that they 'tumbled over the bed of the child to whom the ghost comes'. Walpole thought the whole place reeked of fraud, especially as 'they told us, as they would at a puppet show, that it would not come that night till seven in the morning, that is, when there are only 'prentices and old women'.[7] He dismissed the whole thing as a 'pantomime' not worth investigating, but a good many serious people, quite apart from the Methodists, thought otherwise. Johnson himself, though sceptical, was extremely curious.

He neither wholly believed in ghosts, nor disbelieved; but his sense of the importance of the issue was so strong that he would have given a great deal to be convinced either way, if only the truth could be known. 'This is a question', he told Anna Seward many years later, 'which, after five thousand years is yet undecided; a question, whether in theology or philosophy, one of the most important that can come before the human understanding.' So the Cock Lane ghost seemed to him not a puppet show to be treated with levity, but a phenomenon worth examining on the chance that it might contain a vestige of truth, and he was more than willing to join a committee of inquiry into the knockings and scratchings. Led by the Reverend Dr Douglas, who already had the exposure of more than one imposter to his credit, the group met one night about ten o'clock in the room where the child had been put to bed, and waited patiently for manifestations. After more than an hour, when nothing had happened, they went downstairs and questioned the girl's father, who strongly denied any possibility of trickery. 'While they were inquiring and deliberating,' Johnson wrote afterwards in his account of the affair, 'they were summoned into the girl's chamber by some ladies who were near her bed, and who had heard knocks and scratches. When the gentlemen entered, the girl declared that she felt the spirit like a mouse upon her back, and was required to hold her hands out of bed.' From this point, as one might expect, there were no more rappings, and when after midnight the committee went down to the vault to wait again for the ghost's knocking on the coffin, they were equally disappointed. All their questioning failed to extract a confession, and Johnson gave it as a unanimous opinion that 'the child has some art of making or counterfeiting a particular noise, and that there is no agency of any higher cause'.[8] This conclusion was endorsed when the girl's parents and three of their neighbours were arrested and tried at the Guildhall for conspiracy. All were found guilty and given brief prison sentences, John Parsons the parish clerk being sentenced besides to stand three times in the pillory – once at Cock

The Cock Lane 'ghost': a sceptical broadsheet of 1762

Lane, once at the Royal Exchange, and finally at Charing Cross. Each time he was sympathetically treated by the crowd, who were so reluctant to give up their ghost that they took up a collection of money for his benefit.

In January 1763 peace was at last concluded between England, France, Spain and Portugal, and the British people found to their surprise that they were possessed of the beginnings of an empire. All Canada had been ceded by the French, also the Middle West of America up to the Mississippi, and most of Florida. In the West Indies the British had won Tobago, Dominica and St Vincent, and Senegal in West Africa. The rule of the East India Company was now recognized in Bengal, Minorca was restored to the Crown, and with it the command of the western Mediterranean. The British had made no friends in Europe, but at least it was now possible to travel over the whole continent. Canada and India, and virtual command of the seas, had laid the foundations of an expanding complex of colonies and possessions.

London, of course, was to be the hub of this new universe, and now more than ever the ambitious, the talented and the self-seeking made their way by hook or crook to the capital. Among the many who regarded the cities of London and Westminster as the source of all stimulus and pleasure was one James Boswell, of Auchinleck in Ayrshire, a young man of ancient family who had for London 'as violent an affection as the most romantic lover ever had for his mistress'. His father, a Scottish law lord and stern Presbyterian, had no sympathy with his son's ambitions to travel, to mix with famous men, and to have a commission in the Foot Guards; the family had been distinguished for several generations in the law, and it was to the law, as Lord Auchinleck saw it, that his son must apply himself, instead of frittering away his time in London. (Young Boswell's army ambitions, after all, were based on hopes which his father would have considered frivolous: 'I am thinking of the brilliant scenes of happiness which I shall enjoy as an officer of the guards. How I shall be acquainted with all the grandeur of a court, and all the elegance of dress and diversions; become a favourite of ministers of state, and the adoration of ladies of quality, beauty and fortune!') So it was settled (though only after a stern threat of disinheritance) that young Boswell, who was now twenty-two, should study civil law at Utrecht before doing his Grand Tour, in preparation for a sober career as an Edinburgh advocate. He was now, in the spring of 1763, on a very short allowance enjoying a last taste of London before departure.

It was not the first time that he had spent several months there. When he was only twenty he had spent a whole year in London, and one of the things he had tried most eagerly to do was to meet 'Dictionary' Johnson. He had a passion for knowing the famous, not only for the sake of self-aggrandizement (which today would make him a 'name-dropper'), but also because he yearned for intellectual stimulus, for fame, for the recognition of his own qualities, of which he had a high opinion. He knew how to make himself charming – 'I must say indeed that if I excel in anything, it is in address and making myself agreeable' – and indeed, in spite of some weaknesses of character and a good deal of vanity, was so generally good-humoured and accommodating that he was considered a pleasant addition to most company. (David Hume described him later as 'very good-humoured, very agreeable, and very mad'.) He was never shy of presenting himself to strangers, and now, singled out by some indefinable prophetic attraction, Johnson was his target. He had read enough to regard him already with 'a kind of mysterious veneration', and had badgered his friends to arrange an introduction. Nothing had so far come of this, and Boswell had had to content himself with collecting anecdotes and listening to Tom Davies, the actor turned bookseller, who imitated Johnson's voice and manner better than anyone.

But 'at last, on Monday the 16th of May, when I was sitting in Mr Davies's back-parlour, after having drunk tea with him and Mrs Davies, Johnson unexpectedly came into the shop; and Mr Davies having perceived him through the glass-door in the room in which we were sitting, advancing towards us – he announced his aweful approach to me, somewhat in the manner of an actor in the part of Horatio, when he addresses Hamlet on the appearance of his father's ghost, "Look, my lord, *it comes*."'

The apparition could, indeed, be formidable. The great bulk looming through the glass door, the unwieldy gait and alarming appearance as he came into the room, shook even Boswell's composure. 'Johnson's eyes', Mrs Thrale remembered, '. . . were so wild, so piercing, and at times so fierce, that fear was I believe the first emotion in the hearts of all his beholders.' On this occasion, moreover, he was in a sarcastic mood, and Boswell's first nervous civility fell flat. Tom Davies introduced him as a gentleman from Scotland, and Boswell, remembering Johnson's prejudice against the Scots, who were politically unpopular since the '45, anxiously assured him, 'I do indeed come from Scotland but I cannot help it.' He had meant this sally as a 'light pleasantry to soothe and conciliate', but Johnson was not amused. 'That, Sir', he replied, 'I find, is what a very great many of your countrymen cannot help', and Boswell found his manner so brusque that 'this stroke stunned me a good deal'. He had no better luck as the conversation developed, for Johnson dealt him another snub when he ventured an obsequious observation about Garrick. He now felt himself 'much mortified', and afterwards confessed that 'had not my ardour been uncommonly strong, and my resolution uncommonly persevering, so rough a reception might have deterred me for ever from making any further attempts'. He felt bruised, and no wonder; but when he left, the bookseller followed him to the door and reassured him. 'Don't be uneasy,' he told Boswell, who was almost whimpering, 'I can see he likes you very well'.

And so it appeared, for when, encouraged by Davies, he plucked up courage to visit the lion in his den, he found Johnson sitting with some other gentlemen, and was received very courteously. Boswell's gaze took in every detail of the room. 'It must be confessed that his apartment, and furniture, and morning dress, were sufficiently uncouth. His brown suit of clothes looked very rusty; he had on a little old shrivelled unpowdered wig, which was too small for his head; his shirt-neck and knees of his breeches were loose; his black worsted stockings ill drawn up; and he had a pair of unbuckled shoes by way of slippers. But all these slovenly particularities were forgotten the moment that he began to talk.'

The impact of Johnson's conversation was so stunning that at first Boswell could hardly remember what had been said. He had for some years been an obsessive diarist and collector of anecdotes, so that his verbal memory was well developed, but his emotions on finding himself admitted to Johnson's circle were almost too much for him. 'I was so wrapt in admiration of his extraordinary colloquial talents, and so little accustomed to his peculiar mode of expression, that I found it extremely difficult to recollect and record his conversation.' Gradually, however, as Johnson became more friendly, his nervous confusion subsided and he began his system of taking notes as soon as possible after leaving the great man's presence. Each night in his lodgings these notes would be expanded into a coherent narrative, a task which often obliged him to sit up all night. On one occasion he sat up four nights in one week, struggling to recapture what had been said over tavern suppers followed by copious talk and bottles of port. The strain was considerable, but when Boswell complained to a Scottish M.P. of his acquaintance that this sitting up late and drinking port was affecting his nerves ('A bottle of thick English port is a very heavy and a very inflammatory dose'), he was told

OPPOSITE Tom Davies's bookshop in Russell Street, where 'at last on Monday the 16th of May,'
Boswell first encountered Johnson

roundly, 'One had better be palsied at eighteen than not keep company with such a man.'

Johnson for his part found Boswell an increasingly agreeable companion. 'Give me your hand,' he had said after one of their early discussions, in which Boswell had confessed to certain religious difficulties, 'I have taken a liking to you'; and so indeed it seemed. 'I love the acquaintance of young people,' he told him as they supped in a private room at the Turk's Head, 'because in the first place, I don't like to think of myself growing old. In the next place, young acquaintances must last longest, if they do last; and then, Sir, young men have more virtue than old men; they have more generous sentiments in every respect. I love the young dogs of this age.'

There was almost no subject, Boswell found, that he could not discuss with his mentor, so that he was often quite amazed at his own temerity. His difficult relationship with his father, for instance, which had been the source of so much trouble, was rationally disposed of. 'Sir, there must always be a struggle between a father and son, while one aims at power and the other at independence.' His religious difficulties were sympathetically discussed, and a treatment suggested for the melancholy with which even the mercurial Boswell believed himself to be afflicted. 'Against melancholy he recommended constant occupation of mind, a great deal of exercise, moderation in eating and drinking, and especially to shun drinking at night. . . . He observed that labouring men who work hard, and live sparingly, are seldom or never troubled with low spirits.' (So easy is it to give good advice to others.) Even that favourite among Boswell's temptations, an alluring prostitute, led to an exchange of views in which he momentarily believed himself to be of Johnson's opinion. 'As we walked along the Strand tonight, arm in arm, a woman of the town accosted us, in the usual enticing manner. "No, no, my girl," said Johnson, "it won't do." He, however, did not treat her with harshness, and we talked of the wretched life of such women; and agreed, that much more misery than happiness, upon the whole, is produced by illicit commerce between the sexes.'

It was now almost time for Boswell's departure for Holland, and the two of them planned an idyllic outing to Greenwich, during which Johnson would advise his young friend on the best course of study. So on a fine Saturday at the end of July they hired a sculler at Temple Stairs and were rowed smoothly down-river as far as London Bridge, where it was best to go ashore and take another boat from a wharf on the further side, rather than risk the tide-race under the arches. 'We landed at the Old Swan and walked to Billingsgate, where we took oars and moved slowly along the silver Thames. It was a very fine day. We were entertained with the immense number and variety of ships that were lying at anchor, and with the beautiful country on each side of the river.' Landed successfully at Greenwich, they walked in the park, where Johnson gave his promised advice with such a 'blaze of eloquence' that Boswell was too dazzled to remember much of what he said. Besides being dazed he was a little the worse for wear, having sat up all the previous night writing his journal, and on the voyage home shivered uncontrollably in the night air. At the Turk's Head, however, he soon recovered, and they concluded the day very sociably, Boswell giving romantic accounts of his ancestral seat at Auchinleck and Johnson declaring in a burst of affection, when Holland was mentioned, 'I must see thee out of England: I will accompany you to Harwich.'

Accordingly, early in the morning of August 5th they set out together in the stage-coach for Harwich, entertaining themselves for part of the way by conversing with the other passengers, who had no idea of their identity. To the astonishment of everyone but Boswell, who by now was familiar with his habit of taking a perverse line in argument if it suited him, Johnson defended the Spanish Inquisition and even the practice, still legal in Holland, of torturing accused persons to encourage confession. In between these provocative sallies he took a small Latin volume from his pocket and immersed himself in ancient geography.

They spent the night at Colchester and finished their journey next day with ample time for dinner before the mail-boat's departure. It was to be their last meal together for a long time; Boswell's law studies and Grand Tour would keep him abroad for two and a half years at least, and he was discouraged at the prospect of being so long away from the fount of wisdom. At the same time he could not help observing Johnson's extraordinary table manners, which were surprisingly gross even in an age by no means over-nice in its eating behaviour. 'When at table, he was totally absorbed in the business of the moment; his looks seemed rivetted to his plate; nor would he, unless when in very high company, say one word, or even pay the least attention to what was said by others, till he had satisfied his appetite, which was so fierce, and indulged with such intenseness that while in the act of eating, the veins of his forehead swelled, and generally a strong perspiration was visible.' This was unsuitable behaviour in a philosopher, but Boswell had learned by now that his oracle was a man of extremes. 'Johnson, though he could be rigidly *abstemious*, was not a *temperate* man either in eating or drinking. He could refrain, but he could not use moderately.' This reflection, on which he often pondered, was a comfort to Boswell, whose own lack of self-control was his undoing.

At last the time came to depart, and the two men strolled together to the beach – a 'coalition', as Garrick might have put it, containing all the incalculable elements of fame. The atmosphere was pleasantly touched with emotion – Johnson benevolent, Boswell conciliating, afraid of being forgotten. '"Nay, Sir", said Johnson, "it is more likely that you should forget me, than that I should forget you." As the vessel put out to sea, I kept my eyes upon him for a considerable time, while he remained rolling his majestic frame in his usual manner: and at last I perceived him walk back into the town, and he disappeared.'

11

A Dinner in
Dead Man's Place

OSWELL was now out of sight and out of reach, and would remain so for more than two and a half years. The separation affected him less than might be supposed, for although he found himself wretchedly bored in Utrecht, and wrote a first letter so abysmally self-pitying that Johnson considered it 'hardly admitted or deserved an answer', he soon decided that he had had enough of law, and set off on a two-year course of more congenial adventures. (His being banished to Utrecht in the first place was due to the fact that Scottish law, which is somewhat different from English, refers directly to its Roman original, on which the Dutch were the greatest authorities in Europe.)

In spite of the impression which he never ceased to embroider in his *Life of Johnson*, Boswell at this stage had certainly not decided that Johnson was to be his great man *par excellence*, the subject of a glorious biography which would enshrine his hero and – what was far more important – make himself, Boswell, famous. He was soon busy collecting other heroes, of whom General Pasquale Paoli, the Corsican leader, was for a time to be the reigning favourite. He had wandered from Holland to Italy, where he contrived to meet the exiled John Wilkes and to climb Vesuvius in his company; had then fixed his sights on Voltaire, whom he visited at Ferney and inveigled into a discussion on natural religion; and finally, at Motiers, presented himself before Rousseau, whom he characteristically advised beforehand in a letter: 'Open your door, then, Sir, to a man who dares to say that he deserves to enter there. Trust a unique foreigner. You will never repent it.'

It was Rousseau who gave Boswell an introduction to Paoli, and so set him off on an unexpected adventure into that turbulent and little-known island, where the passionate revolt against the domination of Genoa, the farouche and spirited nature of the Corsicans, and above all, the courageous and noble character of Paoli himself, filled Boswell with romantic excitement and put everything else for the time being out of his head. He spent every possible moment in the presence of the great man, sat up night after night with his journal, even had himself dressed in the costume of a Corsican chief, which made the people stare and flattered his self-esteem. He was overwhelmed with admiration for Paoli, and fell at once into the role that suited his temperament better than any other – the disciple at the feet of a mighty master. ('He was always', said Macaulay distastefully, 'laying himself at the feet of some eminent man, and begging to be spit

156

John Wilkes (centre) conferring with two fellow politicians, John Glynn (left) and
John Horne Tooke, in 1768

upon and trampled upon.') 'Never', Boswell wrote in his journal, 'was I so thoroughly
sensible of my own defects as while I was in Corsica. I felt how small were my abilities,
and how little I knew.' Such unusual humility shows the strength of the impression that
Paoli, no less than Johnson, had made upon him. Both were, in contrast to himself,
impressive authority-figures, and his association with them was all the more important
because he had never achieved this relationship with his father. Boswell longed to be
loved and approved by his father above all people, and this was impossible, since Lord
Auchinleck had neither patience nor affection to spare for such a son. A sober, diligent,
hard-headed young attorney at the Scottish Bar was what he would have liked, and this
was something 'Jamie' could never be; such talents as he had seemed to lead to nothing
but frivolous waste of time and money, since nobody at this stage could possibly have
imagined that he had genius.

   This genius, which after his return from his wanderings was to focus his attention
more purposefully upon Johnson, was of a peculiar kind, difficult to define. The copious
journalizing, which from the beginning had shown all the symptoms of obsession, was
by no means confined to encounters with great men, or even to memorable events.
Boswell himself was the specimen under the microscope; one gets the feeling that
nothing that happened to him seemed *real* until he had recorded it. He did not bowdler-
ize; if such and such a thing happened to Boswell, however discreditable, then it was
grist to his mill, and he would afterwards be rapt with fascination over the extraordinary
inconsistencies of his own character. In spite of his self-conceit and apparent confidence
he was emotionally insecure, and this journal of his, with its record of his own doings
and feelings and contacts with the famous, in some curious way proved to him that he

existed, that he possessed identity and significance when, as so often happened in his bouts of 'gloomy distress', he fell into that state 'when the mind is so tender and sore that everything frets it'. Very early in his acquaintance with Johnson he had discussed the whole question of this journal, its extraordinary importance to himself and the danger of its ever falling into alien hands. 'He said that indeed I should keep it private, and that I surely might have a friend who would burn it in case of my death. For my own part,' Boswell added, 'I have at present such an affection for this my journal that it shocks me to think of burning it. I rather encourage the idea of having it carefully laid up among the archives of Auchinleck.'[1]

With this in mind, and also the *Tour of Corsica* which he intended to publish on his return, Boswell methodically developed his skills, both as recorder and writer. He was rapidly becoming more adept in concentrating his attention on precisely what was being said at any moment, and how it was expressed: though he sometimes took a rapid note in company when he thought himself unobserved, he soon learned that this could annoy people, and came to rely more and more on memory alone. 'He came', Paoli himself told Fanny Burney many years later, in his 'blundering, but not unpretty' English, 'to my country, and he fetched me some letter of recommending him; but I was of the belief he might be an impostor, and I supposed, in my minte, he was an espy; for I look away from him, and in a moment I look to him again, and I behold his tablets. Oh! he was to the work of writing down all I say! Indeed I was angry. But soon I discover that he was no imposter and no espy; and I only find I was myself the monster he had come to discern.'[2]

Boswell's visit to Corsica, and his using his journal as material for the book which would bring him his first literary fame, was a valuable rehearsal for the much more arduous task which he would undertake some twenty years later. Paoli himself, by his kindly reception, had done much to reassure him about himself, and the propriety of his passion for hunting the famous. An acknowledged self-conceit had supported him before, but now he felt truly justified. 'I was,' he scribbled in his journal, 'for the rest of my life, set free from a slavish timidity in the presence of great men, for where shall I find a man greater than Paoli?'[3]

Johnson seems not to have missed his young acquaintance particularly, in spite of having found his company agreeable, for after a first long letter of sound advice he wrote no more to Boswell for two years. His need for immediate companionship was exigent, and it was beyond him to keep up a laborious correspondence with someone whom he might never see again. While Boswell was actually with him he had cheerfully referred to their future meetings, even on one occasion suggesting that they might take a jaunt together to the Hebrides, a spirited notion not intended to be taken seriously. Though he could not know it, he was approaching a crisis in his own life which would change his course in an unforeseen direction, and as often happened to him in such a lull, was less concerned with remote acquaintances than with his personal campaign against monotony and melancholy.

After nearly nine years of sporadic labour, his edition of Shakespeare was at last approaching its end, though the impetus with which he had set out on this great task had gradually dwindled, and now, despite despairing cries from his publishers and satirical squibs in the Press –

> He for subscribers baits his hook,
> And takes their cash; but where's the book?[4] –

he refused to be hurried. He had been confident in the beginning that he could achieve the whole colossal performance in eighteen months, relying, perhaps, on the vast amount of Shakespeare that he had digested for the Dictionary; but when this assumption proved illusory he slowed down, obstinately ignoring the anxiety of his friends, who, as Hawkins observed, 'were more concerned for his reputation than himself seemed to be'. There was, however, nothing so very unusual about this behaviour. 'The promises of authors', as Walter Raleigh sensibly pointed out a century and a half later, 'are like the vows of lovers; made in moments of careless rapture, and subject, during the long process of fulfilment, to all kinds of unforeseen dangers and difficulties.'[5] Johnson at least, when he made excursions of pleasure and visited his friends, often took parts of his unfinished Shakespeare with him, annotating the text while he stayed with Reynolds at Twickenham and correcting proofs of *Othello* at Easton Maudit in the rectory of his poetical friend Dr Percy. He did not find it necessary to haunt the theatres, where corrupt texts and frivolous alterations (of which Garrick was famously guilty) would have confused the issue. Besides, like many other people, Johnson greatly preferred reading the plays in private to hearing them mumbled or declaimed by players.

The state of Johnson's mind in the period following Boswell's departure is something of a mystery. On the face of it he seems to have enjoyed more company and variety than

LEFT David Garrick, as Kitely in Ben Jonson's *Every Man in his Humour*; he was eventually admitted into Johnson's club. RIGHT Oliver Goldsmith, by Reynolds: 'the most flattered picture,' said Reynold's sister, that she 'ever knew her brother to have painted'

ABOVE Edmund Burke, of whom Johnson declared: 'If a man were to go by chance at the same time with Burke under a shed to shun a shower, he would say, "This is an extraordinary man."'

he had been able to afford before the pension, yet it appears that he suffered some form of mental or nervous breakdown in the spring of 1764, and again, and to a more distressing degree, in the summer of 1766. It may well have been because he sensed in Johnson some increasing need of help, of comfort or reassurance, that Joshua Reynolds, always a perceptive and considerate friend, suggested in the winter of 1763, as they sat together one night by the fire, that they should form a small club for the sake of company and conversation. Johnson agreed, and together they drew up a list of desirable members. Only a few of their friends were considered wholly eligible because, as Johnson afterwards explained to Dr Percy, 'It was intended the Club should consist of such men, as that if only two of them chanced to meet, they should be able to entertain each other, without wanting the addition of more company to pass the evening agreeably.'[6] At first only seven passed this exacting test – Edmund Burke, by whom Johnson had been so impressed that he said of him, 'If a man were to go by chance at the same time with Burke under a shed to shun a shower, he would say – "This is an extraordinary man"', Oliver Goldsmith, Topham Beauclerk, Bennet Langton, Sir John Hawkins, and two others of whom we know less, Burke's father-in-law, Dr Nugent and a certain Anthony Chamier, a stockbroker who had 'quit business, and become, what indeed he seemed by nature intended for, a gentleman'.[7] They met at seven once a week in that friendly rendezvous, the Turk's Head in Gerrard Street, Soho, ordered a meal and generally lingered over their wine and talk until the small hours. By 1775 the membership had increased to thirty-five and some of the original members had drifted away, but in the beginning Johnson and Reynolds preferred the group to be intimate and exclusive, and Johnson was even momentarily annoyed when Garrick, hearing of the Club from Reynolds, said 'I like it much; I think I shall be of you.' '*He'll be of us?*' said Johnson, when the news reached him. 'How does he know we will *permit* him? The first Duke in England has no right to hold such language.'[8] This was a typical reaction on Johnson's part to Garrick's over-confidence, which perhaps would not have appeared such to anyone who had not shared their mutual history. When Garrick was eventually proposed Johnson warmly supported him, and he remained a valued member from then until his death.

Founding the Club was an astute move on Reynolds's part, for it gave Johnson the necessary scope for being what he now more or less admitted himself to be – a professional talker. Conversation was not only his greatest stimulus but his greatest pleasure, and now that he had reached his mid-fifties he was perfectly frank about regarding it as far more than a social activity or exchange of ideas: it was more like a chess championship or a wrestling match, to which, in his appetite for victory, he brought every skill and trick at his command, both legitimate and illegitimate. Talk had become a vocation even more than an amusement, and one cannot help lamenting Boswell's absence in those early days of the Club, when it contained no one capable of recording his frontal

OPPOSITE David Garrick in the finery of private life, by Jean-Baptiste van Loo, 1742

OVERLEAF Temple Bar, the archway dividing the Strand from Fleet Street: a painting by John Collett in 1760

attacks, his dazzling intellectual displays and his occasional recourse to rudeness and downright bullying. 'He fought on every occasion', said Reynolds, 'as if his whole reputation depended upon the victory of the minute, and he fought with all the weapons. If he was foiled in argument he had recourse to abuse and rudeness.'[9] 'The fact is,' as Augustine Birrell was to put it a century later, 'he had so accustomed himself to wordy warfare, that he lost all sense of moral responsibility, and cared as little for men's feelings as a Napoleon did for their lives.' This was a failing of which he was sometimes conscious, and which he usually regretted. 'He had one virtue', Reynolds remembered, 'which I hold one of the most difficult to practise. After the heat of the contest was over, if he had been informed that his antagonist resented his rudeness, he was the first to seek after a reconciliation; and of his virtues the most distinguished was his love of truth.' It was this basic quality of guide and mentor, even more than the stimulus of his ferocity and wit, which was most admired and valued by his contemporaries. 'He qualified my mind', said Reynolds, 'to think justly. No man had, like him, the faculty of teaching inferior minds the art of thinking.' Johnson himself was of course aware of this and regarded his talk – the serious and expository side of it – as creative in a lesser degree than his writing, but still comparable. In 1766, when his *Shakespeare* had been out for a twelvemonth and Boswell and Goldsmith were persistently teasing him to undertake something new, he replied, perhaps privately thanking God for the comfort of his pension, 'No, Sir, I am not obliged to do any more. . . . A man is to have part of his life to himself.' Almost at once an analogy occurred to him. 'A physician, who has practised long in a great city, may be excused if he retires to a small town, and takes less practice. Now, Sir, the good I can do by my conversation bears the same proportion to the good I can do by my writings, that the practice of a physician, retired to a small town, does to his practice in a great city.' 'But I wonder, Sir,' persisted Boswell, who rarely knew when to stop, 'you have not more pleasure in writing than in not writing.' To which Johnson, not choosing to pursue the matter further, replied, 'Sir, you *may* wonder.'[10]

Having a part of his life to himself now meant that he could leave London from time to time and pay leisurely visits to his friends. He had proposed himself to his step-daughter Lucy at Lichfield, but she had made it clear that at the moment he was not welcome. Her brother, Captain Jervis Porter, had died suddenly, and Johnson had written at once to offer sympathy, assuring her that if she now found herself embarrassed for money, 'I will endeavour to make what I have, or what I can get, sufficient for us both.'[11] But Lucy was not embarrassed; her brother had left her a fortune of ten thousand pounds, and she was unwilling to lose a moment before starting to build herself a grand new house in another part of Lichfield, and leaving the shop in Breadmarket Street for ever. A little disturbed by this sudden decision, Johnson offered to come and visit her in the summer, sending ten pounds for 'sheets and table-linen and such things', since he proposed to bring his servant Frank with him. But Lucy replied that there would not be room for him, even if Frank had a servant's bed at the Three Crowns, so the plan

OPPOSITE James Boswell aged about twenty-five: a portrait painted in Rome by George Willison during the early summer of 1765

165

was abandoned. The house still belonged to Johnson, and he was anxious that Kitty Chambers should continue to live in it and carry on her 'little trade' of toys and stationery and second-hand books which was all that remained of his father's ambitious business.

The house Lucy Porter built for herself after she had inherited her brother's fortune

He might have proposed himself to his friend John Taylor at Ashbourne, but Dr Taylor's wife had recently run away, leaving him in an unenviable situation as a target for curiosity and gossip, and the best that Johnson could do was to write to him frequently and affectionately, offering legal and personal advice. 'For the present I think it prudent to forbear all pursuit, and all open inquiry; to wear an appearance of complete indifference, and calmly wait the effects of time, of necessity, and of shame.'[12] The marriage had not been a happy one, and Dr Taylor was more disturbed by the possibility of financial claims than by any change in his domestic comfort; his spirits improved when Johnson was able to reassure him. 'To obtain a separate maintenance she must prove either cruelty to her person or infidelity to her bed, and I suppose neither charge can be supported. Nature', he added, 'has given women so much power that the law has very wisely given them little' – a piece of sophistry with which his friend would be thankful to agree.

If Taylor in the midst of his troubles was unwilling to be visited, there were others who were glad of Johnson's company, and with whom for a while he could drive depression away. With Bennet Langton in Lincolnshire he seems to have been in sufficiently good spirits, if one can judge by his behaviour on a steep hill behind the house, where, as Langton always remembered, he announced that he had not had a roll downhill for a long time, 'and taking out of his lesser pockets whatever might be in them – keys, pencil, purse or penknife, and laying himself parallel with the edge of the hill, he actually descended, turning himself over and over till he came to the bottom'.[13]

With Dr Percy, too, with whom he and blind Miss Williams spent part of the summer at Easton Maudit, he seems to have divided his time well enough, working on his

Shakespeare, reading ancient romances of chivalry in his friend's library and discussing the extraordinary discovery which was soon to make Percy's literary reputation. By chance, while staying with a friend in Shropshire, the rector had found an old folio manuscript 'lying dirty on the floor' in a cupboard where the servants were tearing it up to light the fire. Examining what remained, he found it to be a collection of old poems and ballads written in a seventeenth-century hand, and begged to be allowed to keep it. It proved to be a remarkable treasury of early poetry, which Percy, somewhat against the taste of his time, had always loved. Reinforced by contributions from scholarly friends, and with some help from Johnson in the writing of a grandiose dedication to the Duchess of Northumberland (to whom the rector, a Bridgnorth grocer's son, liked to believe himself related) it presently appeared as *Reliques of Ancient Poetry*, and made him famous.

In this same year 1765 Trinity College, Dublin, paid Johnson an unexpected compliment by creating him Doctor of Laws, thus making him, for the first time, 'Doctor' Johnson. He seems, however, not to have set great store by the Irish doctorate, and according to Murphy never used the honorary title until Oxford conferred it on him ten years later. His domestic life, too, was more comfortable than it had been for years. With his pension he was able to leave the chambers in Inner Temple Lane and rent a house in a cul-de-sac off Fleet Street called, appropriately enough, Johnson's Court. Here Miss Williams could be brought back safely under his own roof and Levett and Barber housed on an upper floor. A light and airy room was set aside as Johnson's study, and he even had some decent pieces of furniture and a silver standish which had been given him by an admirer. 'There Johnson sat every morning,' said Murphy, 'receiving visits, hearing the topics of the day, and indolently trifling away the time.' Levett obligingly 'attended at all hours, made tea all the morning, talked what he had to say, and did not expect an answer.' And if ever Johnson found himself without talk or company, 'chemistry afforded some amusement'.[14]

It was barely a month after the move into the new house that his eight-volume edition of Shakespeare was finally published, so that he was able to be idle with a good conscience and enjoy the praise with which – with a few virulent exceptions – the press and the town greeted its belated appearance. The splendid Preface, which Johnson out of his great love of Shakespeare wrote with more pleasure, perhaps, than any other part of the work, was immediately acclaimed, and remains an impressive *tour de force* today, when taste and critical method have wholly changed. It seems to the modern reader a waste of time on Johnson's part to go to great lengths to exonerate Shakespeare for his neglect of the classical unities; even more superfluous to complain that one looks in vain to Shakespeare for a moral message. But these were considerations of importance in Johnson's day, and the fact that these views were soon ridiculed by the new romantics was an accident of timing rather than judgment. Johnson's main purpose had been to restore the text of the plays as far as possible to what Shakespeare had written, and in this he achieved considerable success; though, again, he was unfortunate in that his edition was soon followed by others, notably Malone's, which performed the task more thoroughly, and raised the standards and methods of literary criticism to new levels. (Malone at least was fair enough to admit that Johnson's vigorous and comprehensive understanding threw more light on his author than all his predecessors had done.)[15] Macaulay's famous and derisory essay, of course, was the final blow – 'It would be difficult to name a more slovenly, a more worthless edition of any great classic' – and from then on, throughout the nineteenth century, Johnson's *Shakespeare* was dismissed by the romantics as a disaster of non-feeling, non-perception and non-scholarship. But in the twentieth century most serious critics, following Nichol Smith and Raleigh, have found in it much that is emotionally and aesthetically sensitive, as well as sometimes ludicrously astray, following the dictates of what Johnson's temperament as well as his period regarded as common sense.

Johnson's Court, off Fleet Street, where Johnson was again
able to house his extraordinary *ménage*

In October 1765, when the subscribers finally received their eight volumes, Johnson's reputation stood higher than ever, and with his numerous friends, the amusement of stimulating evenings at the Club and the improved comfort of his domestic life, one would imagine that he had at last achieved contentment. But it was not so. The in-scrutable malady which had pursued him all his life, the fears which were all the more difficult to confront because they were so illusive and irrational, had for some months been insidiously gaining ground, until now, when outwardly all seemed well, he found himself facing the horrors of a possible mental breakdown. With his morbid history he inevitably saw this, as he had done before, as the approach of insanity, remembering

Dr Swinfen's unforgivable diagnosis of more than thirty years ago, that 'he could think nothing better of his disorder than that it had a tendency to insanity, and without great care might possibly terminate in the deprivation of his rational faculties'. Murphy, learning this part of his early history from Johnson, was to put it even more strongly: Dr Swinfen's letter had stated quite bluntly that 'the symptoms indicated a future privation of reason'. Was it any wonder, then, that 'he was troubled with melancholy and dejection of spirit? An apprehension of the worst calamity that can befall human nature hung over him all the rest of his life.'[16]

In his present state of disquietude Johnson had done what he could, and it had been of no avail. He had tried to divert himself with company, had regretfully given up wine again, consoling himself with tea and lemonade, was struggling to keep his resolution of early rising (and for once in his life actually succeeding, for the space of six months, in leaving his bed at eight o'clock instead of two), had subjected himself to periodic fasts, which increased his insomnia, and continued to pray, to resolve and to accuse himself in his secret diary. Only one cryptic entry about this time seems to hint at the obsession which was later to become an uneasy secret – 'Went to tea. A sudden thought of restraints hindered me. I drank but one dish.'[17] 'Restraints' may have various meanings; it was a word common enough in the madhouses of the period, and we know that Johnson possessed both fetters and padlock. 'One must conclude', says Katharine Balderston, who first perceived the significance of certain references in Mrs Thrale's private memoranda, 'that Johnson actually kept these articles to enforce the strict confinement which he resorted to when his mind was seized by the delusion that he was insane.'

At some time during this unhappy period he refused for days together to leave the house, or even to see his friends. On one occasion, when Dr Adams arrived from Oxford and wished to call, he was told by Miss Williams that nobody had been admitted but Bennet Langton, and when Adams was finally allowed upstairs he found his old friend 'in a deplorable state, sighing, groaning, talking to himself, and restlessly walking from room to room'. 'He looked miserable,' Adams afterwards told Boswell; 'his lips moved, although he was not speaking.' One of the few remarks that he made to Adams left a most painful impression – 'I would suffer a limb to be amputated to recover my spirits.'[18]

This 'hypochondriack disorder', as Boswell called it, was not constant; it came and went, leaving him at times in an apparently normal state, but always unpredictable, always in danger of the old irrational and morbid nightmare. It was probably concern on the part of his friend Arthur Murphy – his 'dear Mur', as Johnson called him – which led to an unexpected transformation of Johnson's life. Murphy, as well as being a playwright and journalist, was also a popular man about town with many amusing and well-connected friends who would be normally quite outside Johnson's orbit. One of these was Henry Thrale, a rich brewer with a thriving business on the south side of the river in Southwark, where, being a man of the world as well as of commerce, he entertained his friends, especially those who could be relied on for good talk, and kept a splendidly lavish table. To Henry Thrale, therefore, who was fairly newly married and had a young and delightful wife to act as hostess, Murphy proposed that the celebrated

Mr Johnson should be asked to dinner – if only they could think of an excuse to account for this sudden invitation from a stranger.

An excuse was soon invented. 'It was on the second Thursday of the month of January 1765', wrote Mrs Thrale, 'that I first saw Mr Johnson in a room. Murphy, whose intimacy with Mr Thrale had been of many years' standing, was one day dining with us at our house in Southwark, and was zealous that we should be acquainted with Johnson, of whose moral and literary character he spoke in the most exalted terms; and so whetted our desire of seeing him soon, that we were only disputing *how* he should be invited, *when* he should be invited, and what should be the pretence. At last it was resolved that one Woodhouse, a shoemaker who had written some verses, and been asked to some tables, should likewise be asked to ours, and made a temptation to Mr Johnson to meet him. Accordingly he came, and Mr Murphy at four o'clock brought Mr Johnson to dinner.'[19]

The journey from Johnson's Court to Dead Man's Place, where Thrale had his town-house near the brewery, was not beyond walking distance for so stout a pedestrian as Johnson. Along Fleet Street and up Ludgate Hill, then down to Thames Street and over London Bridge was the route he and Murphy would take, either on foot or by hackney coach – probably the latter, since it was winter weather. The Borough was strikingly different from the City, not at all the sort of neighbourhood to which gentlemen were normally invited to dine. Thrale had his house there because of its proximity to the brewery, on which his wealth and consequence depended, and so lived surrounded by the sheds, yards, drying-grounds and alleys of a score of trades, and the innumerable taverns frequented by their journeymen and apprentices. This had been the area of the old Globe Theatre in Shakespeare's day, when players were classed as rogues and vagabonds and their performances not allowed on the City side of the river. The theatre had been burned down in 1621, and since then the rough and squalid quarter had been gradually colonized by Huguenot refugees from the Continent, bringing crafts and skills which gradually transformed it into a crowded and busy manufacturing area. Nobody knows how Dead Man's Place earned its forbidding name; there was a burial-ground nearby, but the name had existed long before the cemetery, and was perhaps an echo of some forgotten suicide or crime. The lanes and alleys all round it, as one can see from Rocque's contemporary map,[20] had taken theirs from the activities that went on in them – Fishmonger's Alley, Stonecutter's Yard, Carpenter's Yard, Harrow Dung-hill, Skin Market, Vinegar Yard, Packthread Ground, Foul Lane, Dirty Lane, Stoney Street, Whore's Nest, Clink Street – this last, of course, the street where the prison was. There were more slaughter-houses than one would have thought necessary. The gutters of Southwark, Johnson told Boswell, 'run with blood two or three times in the week'. It was not an area for elegant life, but it was one where money was made, and the brewers and vinegar-makers at least had handsome houses. The strong smells of brewing and tanning, the clatter of paper-mill and printing works, the tapping of broom- and hoop-makers, the cracking and splitting of firewood-choppers would be evident all through the narrow streets once London Bridge had been crossed. But when the hackney's fare had been paid and Mr Thrale's door opened, Murphy and Johnson stepped into a vastly comfortable world.

12

The Streatham Experience

HE Thrales lived mainly in Southwark because Henry Thrale, despite his elegant appearance and education, had down-to-earth ambitions as a businessman and intended to outbrew all rivals. His father, Ralph Thrale, had been a self-made man who had worked for most of his life in the Old Anchor Brewery, eventually buying it outright for thirty thousand pounds. His prosperity had not stopped there, for the brewery made his fortune and he had entered Parliament in 1741. He had also acquired (some say in return for an unlimited ten-year supply of ale and porter to the Duke of Bedford) a hundred acres of ground on Tooting Common, beside the village of Streatham, and there had built himself a solid country-house dignified by the name of Streatham Park.

Henry Thrale, his only son, had been given an expensive education, entering Oxford at the age of fifteen and then, not troubling himself with a degree, doing the Grand Tour at leisure in the company of a young nobleman, Ralph Thrale paying all their expenses. This was followed by a few rakish years about town, with Arthur Murphy one of his boon companions, and then, on the death of his father, Thrale in his middle twenties had inherited the brewery and a fortune, and had since dedicated himself to increasing his own consequence and making money.

For this dual purpose, and the equally important matter of getting heirs, it was necessary to be married, so after trying one or two disappointing heiresses who were unwilling to live in the Borough, he had settled on Hester Lynch Salusbury, a remarkable girl of twenty-one who had been promised a settlement of ten thousand pounds if she married suitably. There was no question of love on either side; the matter was settled between Henry Thrale and the girl's mother as a business transaction. The daughter's unwillingness was brushed aside, for Mrs Salusbury, who came of an ancient Welsh family but was now an impoverished widow, saw that the marriage would mean security both for herself and for her child. With a feckless and quick-tempered husband, she had for years, wrote Mrs Thrale, 'made her own candles, salted her own meat, ironed her own linen and her husband's and mine, and if he would have been but good-humoured, protested that she should have been happy'. He had, however, been a difficult character, and now that he was dead Mrs Salusbury found herself dependent on the financial promises of a brother-in-law. When her husband's debts had been

171

paid, there would be two hundred pounds a year for herself and a wedding portion of two thousand pounds for her daughter. If her daughter married an eligible man her uncle promised to increase this sum to ten thousand pounds, and also to settle something on Mrs Salusbury. This was an offer not to be refused, and since Thrale's wealth more than outweighed his commercial origins, the girl was soon persuaded to see reason. They had been married in St Anne's Church, Soho (Mrs Salusbury having a house in nearby Dean Street) in the autumn of 1763, and young Mrs Thrale had dutifully accepted her role as the wife of Southwark's most ambitious and gentlemanly brewer.

It was a dull life on the whole, for Thrale considered a wife's place to be in the drawing-room or the bedchamber, and he allowed her little freedom. She was discouraged from paying visits, was not allowed to ride, and permitted little authority even in her own household. The management of the kitchen, for instance, was Thrale's own province; he prided himself on being a gourmet, and planned the menus and ordered the meals himself, so that she never knew what was for dinner until the dishes came to the table. What was expected of her was to provide him with heirs, and to be agreeable when he entertained his friends, both of which she did to the best of her ability, exerting herself as hostess to his bachelor cronies through an exhausting sequence of pregnancies.

It was not exactly the married life she had envisaged, but the wealth and comfort round her made it more than tolerable, and she had an unusual capacity for keeping herself amused. For this she had largely her parents to thank, for realizing that their only child was exceptionally bright they had provided her with an excellent tutor. 'Although education', she wrote, 'was a word then unknown as applied to females, they had taught me to read, and speak, and think, and translate from the French, till I was half a prodigy.' At seventeen she had begun Latin, becoming so proficient that she was able to correspond in it with her tutor, the learned Dr Collier. She had also by this time developed a great facility in writing verses, in translating from several languages, tossing off epigrams and literary conceits, even making anonymous contributions to the magazines, all of which fed her self-esteem and conjured up visions of a literary future. 'I was now completely a spoiled child', she wrote many years later, 'and wrote odes for the peace and verses upon every, and upon no occasion. Imitations of English poets, too, which I fancied tolerable; but which on looking over my copies of late, appeared to me insupportable.'

She was tiny in stature, attractive in appearance though not beautiful, lively and charming in manner, accustomed to being petted and admired. While still in her teens she had met Hogarth, a London friend of her father's, and it was he who had first caught her imagination with his descriptions of Samuel Johnson, whose talk, he said, 'was to the talk of other men, like Titian's painting compared to Hudson's'. Hogarth also seems to have made several sketches of her for his dramatic genre painting, *The Lady's Last Stake*, though these have disappeared. It is probable, however, that the girl hesitating between giving up play and compromising her virtue is the only surviving likeness of the young Hester Lynch Salusbury before her marriage.

Eleven months after the wedding Mrs Thrale gave birth to her first child, a daughter, christened Hester Maria after her mother and grandmother. The baby soon had a succession of pet-names as well – Hetty, Niggy, Queen Hester – the last being before long shortened to Queeney, a name which remained with her for life. Within three months Mrs Thrale was pregnant again, dividing her time between the absorbing routines of the nursery, writing verses to amuse herself or her mother (since Thrale showed no interest in these sprightly performances) and taking pains to be as agreeable as possible to Murphy and other friends who frequently drove over to Southwark for a good dinner. Though no great talker himself, Thrale was a man who appreciated good conversation, especially if it led to vigorous arguments; he had, said Fanny Burney, 'a singular amusement in hearing, instigating and provoking a war of words, alternating triumph and overthrow, between clever and ambitious colloquial combatants'; and this naturally, after Murphy's impressive accounts, made him curious to meet Johnson. Murphy had been careful to give Mrs Thrale some 'general cautions not to be surprised at his figure, dress or behaviour', but it seems that, if he surprised them at all on this occasion, it was agreeably. He gave good advice to the shoemaker (of whose poems he privately held a poor opinion), urging him to give his days and nights to the study of Addison, and in general appeared so congenial that, as Mrs Thrale wrote in her journal, 'We liked each other so well that the next Thursday was appointed for the same company to meet – exclusive of the shoemaker.'[1] From then on, during the whole of that winter of 1765, Johnson drove out every Thursday to dine at Southwark.

ABOVE Hogarth's *The Lady's Last Stake*. Mrs Thrale claimed that, as a young girl, she sat to the artist for his preliminary sketches.

RIGHT Mrs Thrale in the early days of her marriage, from a portrait by Reynolds

The intimacy developed surprisingly fast, for by a happy chance both sides had something invaluable to offer. Thrale took a genuine pleasure in Johnson's conversation and was flattered to find himself host to a man so famous. If the 'Great Cham of litera-ture', as Smollett had christened him, was happy to come to his table, then other men of eminence would follow, and this was desirable for a man determined to be not only Southwark's famous brewer but also its Member of Parliament. For Mrs Thrale the attraction of Johnson was of a more personal nature. Her learning and intellectual vivacity were of no interest to her husband, whereas Johnson at once appreciated her quality, teased and coaxed her into lively arguments, even drew her into translating the 'Odes' of Boethius with him, each doing alternate stanzas. This was immensely stimulat-ing and flattering, and reopened a whole world which had been closed to her since her marriage. For Johnson too, and from the very beginning, the relationship was perfect. This charming and attractive little person, well trained in all the arts of flattery and complacency, was yet, surprisingly, not at all afraid to cross swords with him in argu-ment, with a mixture of respect and playfulness altogether disarming. She was of the type of woman to whom he was always most attracted – feminine, intelligent, well bred and well informed, with a lively sense of independence which was yet properly under control in her relations with men. Johnson had no use for what he called 'honeysuckle wives', invariably sweet and clinging; such women bored him, however much he approved their proper subjugation. (He always on principle took the husband's side in any marital dispute.) He liked attractive women to have spirit and some learning, since it made them more amusing. 'It is a paltry trick indeed', he said on one occasion, 'to deny women the cultivation of their mental powers, and I think it is partly a proof we are afraid of them, if we endeavour to keep them unarmed.'[2] At the same time he was very easily antagonized by any behaviour which he regarded as presumptuous or unfeminine. He was firmly, Mrs Thrale noted in her journal, 'of opinion that the delicacy of the sex should always be inviolably preserved, in eating, in exercise, in dress, in everything.' She herself perfectly fulfilled all these requirements, and seemed besides to take an almost filial pleasure in keeping Johnson amused and making him comfortable.

His affection for her husband is more difficult to interpret, since Thrale himself has left nothing comparable to his wife's letters and diaries to illuminate his character. He strikes one as a fairly dull dog – cool, unemotional and selfish; but this may be unfair, and his wife, who never loved him, was scrupulous to admit that his 'sobriety, and the decency of his conversation, being wholly free from all oaths, ribaldry and profaneness, make him a man exceedingly comfortable to live with, while the easiness of his temper and slowness to take offence add greatly to his value as a domestic man';[3] and Arthur Murphy accounted reasonably enough for his popularity with men: 'His education at Oxford gave him the habits of a gentleman; his amiable temper recommended his conversation, and the goodness of his heart made him a sincere friend.'[4]

The sincerity of their friendship was before long put to the test, for in spite of his appearance of normality in company, Johnson in the following year was rapidly approaching a time when the dreaded symptoms of fear and horror, with the old illusion (if such it was) of threatening insanity, would make it undesirable and even dangerous for him to be alone. He had by this time confided his dread of madness to the Thrales, who at first tended to discount it; until one day, calling on him unexpectedly in town, they overheard such wild utterances of misery that Thrale immediately decided to offer help. A clergyman was on the point of leaving as they came in, and Johnson, according to Murphy, was 'on his knees . . . beseeching God to continue to him the use of his understanding'. 'I felt excessively affected with grief,' Mrs Thrale wrote afterwards, 'and well remember my husband involuntarily lifted up one hand to shut his mouth, from provocation at hearing a man so wildly proclaim what he could at last persuade no one to believe; and what, if true, would have been so very unfit to reveal.'[5] Thrale judged it best to leave his wife alone with Johnson in order to coax him to 'quit his close habitation in the court and come with us to Streatham', where he could try the effects of country air and a more soothing way of life. Evidently she prevailed without much difficulty, for Johnson was installed at Streatham by midsummer and lived practically as a member of the family for the next three months.

Streatham Park as Johnson knew it

Nothing could have presented a greater contrast with his ordinary life; it was like landing on another planet, and as he recovered his balance in these charming surroundings Johnson began to experience a placid happiness. Quite apart from the comfort of a luxurious existence, in which his needs were met by servants and his idle hours amused by Mrs Thrale, it was for Johnson a new and altogether enchanting experience to find himself involved in the everyday affairs of a young family. 'Queeney' was now a precocious child of two years old, so intelligent and pretty that her mother had had her painted by Zoffany, sitting on a cushion beside her cradle and playing with her grandmother's spaniel. The previous year had seen the birth of a second daughter, but this one had died 'of the watery gripes', and Mrs Thrale was now pregnant for the third time, hoping eagerly for a son. At the time of the birth and death of the second baby Thrale had been in the thick of a parliamentary election and had been returned without opposition as member for the Borough of Southwark. There had been no time for mourning; she and Johnson had both put their energies into the campaign and shared in the satisfaction of Thrale's success.

Another enterprise in which they collaborated with amusement was the compiling of a little book of Anna Williams's poems – a project for which Johnson had written proposals as long as fifteen years ago, and then apparently forgotten. Miss Williams's poems were too few even for a small volume, so the two of them put their heads together and each wrote a contribution, Mrs Thrale's being a light-hearted ballad, *The Three Warnings*, about Death coming to old Farmer Dobson, and Johnson's a simple allegory, *The Fountains*, with which he teased and pleased Mrs Thrale by saying that the heroine was a sketch of her own character. In spite of their help, however, Miss Williams must have been disappointed by the poor success of her long-cherished anthology, which 'turned out a thin flat quarto, which it appears sold miserably: I never,' wrote Mrs Thrale, 'saw it on any table but my own'.

All these small interests and amusements had been a distraction and a help when the 'vile melancholy' threatened, but it was not until his three months' domestication with the Thrales that Johnson really began to mend. Streatham lay still in unspoiled country, untouched as yet by the smoke and noise of the Borough. (So empty, indeed, was the lonely stretch of common which had to be crossed by anyone coming from London that highwaymen found it a profitable area, and Thrale himself on one occasion had been robbed of thirteen guineas, his watch, and silver shoe-buckles.) The house was surrounded by a large and pleasant garden where Johnson could walk if he felt inclined, or visit the walled enclosure where salads and vegetables were grown for the kitchen and mellow brick walls and glasshouses ripened superb peaches. He had his own room now permanently provided and could lie as late as he liked, secure in the knowledge that Mrs Thrale would good-humouredly preside over his tea and toast and that the dinner at three or four o'clock would be delicious. Even his appearance had notably improved, for Thrale, who was particular in such matters, saw to it that clean linen and well-brushed garments were laid out for him, his shoes cleaned and clasped with silver buckles, even his wig changed for a better one when necessary. Johnson's own was apt to be singed by the candle from late-night reading, so when there was company Thrale's valet was instructed to intercept him on his way to the dining-room and replace the frizzled object with a fresh one.

The only flaw in this halcyon period was that Mrs Salusbury, who from the beginning had spent long periods at Streatham with her daughter, found Johnson's presence and manner irritating, and was not altogether successful in concealing her feelings. He for his part responded with open dislike and a certain amount of teasing, aimed at her 'superfluous attention' to foreign politics as reported in the newspapers and her 'willingness to talk on subjects he could not endure'.[6] Mrs Thrale was devoted to her mother, who seems on the whole to have been a highly sensible and agreeable woman, so their dissensions were particularly distressing in the midst of nursery cares and the sicknesses of pregnancy, when she was also responsible for coddling Johnson back into a state of health – a task which, she admitted, 'though distressing enough sometimes, would have been less so had not my mother and he disliked one another extremely, and teased me often with perverse opposition, petty contentions, and mutual complaints'. Fortun-

OPPOSITE Mrs Salusbury in her widow's weeds, by Zoffany

ately for everyone's happiness this hostility wore out in time, and they became friends at last; though not until Johnson had been more or less a member of the Thrale household for six years. In Zoffany's majestic portrait of Mrs Salusbury in her widow's dress (a nun-like but handsome habit concealing the evidences of age and showing only the face and hands) she appears as a woman intelligent, probably reserved, perhaps even a trifle censorious. Certainly Mrs Thrale had loved her all her life, and as she regarded Johnson now with considerable affection their persistent bickering plagued her. It would not, of course, occur when Thrale was present; he was entirely master in his own house and had even been known to silence Johnson when he had talked too long on one subject; his wife could only hope by patience and tact to make them friends – 'excellent as *they both* were, far beyond the excellence of any other man and woman I ever yet saw'. [7]

It was, of course, absurd of Johnson to allow himself to be so irritated by Mrs Salusbury, but then, as Mrs Thrale soon discovered, with all his intellectual force and rationalism, in some ways Johnson was the most inconsistent being alive. He could be astonishingly rude in the heat of argument – with a 'roughness in his manner which subdued the saucy and terrified the meek' – and at the same time cherish the illusion that he was 'well-bred to a degree of needless scrupulosity'. 'No man', he insisted – not observing, Mrs Thrale was amused to note, the 'amazement of his hearers' – 'no man is so cautious not to interrupt another; no man thinks it so necessary to appear attentive when others are speaking; no man so steadily refuses preference to himself, or so willingly bestows it on another, as I do; nobody holds so strongly as I do the necessity of ceremony, and the ill effects which follow the breach of it: yet people think me rude . . .'. [8] Indeed, they often did, and he as often was; though one suspects that rude answers are more often remembered than civil ones, especially the rough retort which is spiced with wit. There was at times a concealed comic element in Johnson's bludgeoning which those who did not know him failed to detect. His intimate friends were well aware of it, but others could be misled. 'It is much to be wished', wrote Miss Reynolds, Sir Joshua's sister, 'that the many jocular and ironical speeches which have been recorded of him had been marked as such, for the information of those who were unacquainted with him.' Mrs Thrale knew this very well, and was more than once amused to record an apparent incivility which had either concealed an element of jest, or been turned at the last minute to comic advantage. 'Dr Johnson delighted in his own partiality for Oxford; and one day, at my house, entertained five members of the other university with various instances of the superiority of Oxford, enumerating the gigantic names of many men whom it had produced, with apparent triumph. At last I said to him, "Why, there happens to be no less than five Cambridge men in the room now." "I did not", said he, "think of that till you told me; but the wolf don't count the sheep."'

The contrast between his opinions and his behaviour Mrs Thrale found often puzzling, until she learned to recognize the conflict that must always exist in an obstinately rational man who is also highly emotional. He would be impatient with expressions of grief over the loss of relations or friends – 'We must either outlive our friends, you know, or our friends must outlive us; and I see no man that would hesitate about the choice'

178

– yet when he himself lost a friend by death his suffering was obvious. 'The truth is, nobody suffered more from pungent sorrow at a friend's death than Johnson, though he would suffer no one else to complain of their losses in the same way.' He disapproved of cosseting the sick, and 'when one asked him gently, how he did? – "Ready to become a scoundrel, Madam," would commonly be the answer: "with a little more spoiling you will make me a complete rascal . . .".' Yet during his convalescence he would make her sit up at night by exploiting his 'pathetic manner, which no one ever possessed in so eminent a degree,' so that she was afraid to leave him. 'I lie down,' he told her piteously, 'that my acquaintance may sleep; but I lie down to endure oppressive misery, and soon rise again to pass the night in anxiety and pain.' She suffered discomfort and exhaustion on many occasions, being required even to pray by his sickbed, which 'required strength of body as well as of mind, so vehement were his manners, and his tones of voice so pathetic', yet was fair enough to admit that 'he made his company exceedingly entertaining when he had once forced one, by his vehement lamentations and piercing reproofs, not to quit the room, but to sit quietly and make tea for him, as I often did in London till four o'clock in the morning'.

There was no end to the contradictions to be discovered in this extraordinary man. One of the most surprising was that with all his morbid melancholy and self-pity he could be the most amusing companion imaginable. Murphy had always insisted that he was 'incomparable at buffoonery', and Mrs Thrale herself was soon of opinion that 'if he had had good eyes, and a form less inflexible, he would have made an admirable mimic'. He had, in fact, much of the talent that he affected to despise in actors, and could himself so easily terrify or burlesque in conversation that he belittled the player's art, even once describing Garrick as 'a player – a showman – a fellow who exhibits himself for a shilling'. 'No man loved laughing better,' said Mrs Thrale, and when the amusing fit was on him 'his laugh was irresistible'. This infectious if erratic gaiety, together with the power and variety of his conversation soon made a notable difference in the company to be found at the Thrales' two homes, particularly at Streatham, where as time went on the more ambitious entertaining was done. After his three months' convalescence in their care Johnson found himself unable to be happy away from them, and fell into the comfortable habit (with Henry Thrale's full approval) of spending Monday night to Saturday morning with them, returning to Johnson's Court only for the weekend, to give Miss Williams and Levett and Barber the benefit of his company and to make sure that they had good dinners at least on the Saturday, Sunday and Monday. Miss Williams's life must have been tedious enough during the week, with Levett out on his mysterious rounds and only the Negro boy for company; but at least she could go to bed at a reasonable hour, and Johnson more than once in compensation took her with him on country holidays.

Henry Thrale now had the satisfaction of playing host to men eminent in the literary and artistic world who would never have come his way if it had not been for the magnetic presence of Johnson. Sir Joshua Reynolds, by far the most celebrated painter of his day, newly knighted in 1769 and President of the first Royal Academy, was a frequent guest; so was David Garrick, whose fame and riches had done nothing to spoil his charm; Edmund Burke, too, whom Johnson so much admired and who was now a formidable figure of the political opposition; Dr Burney the eminent musician, whose daughter Fanny would eventually meet and wholly captivate Johnson; and that eccentrically absurd Irishman, Dr Goldsmith, who some people claimed had no right to the title of 'Doctor' and who often seemed more like a half-wit than a man of genius. (Walpole was said to have described him as an 'inspired idiot'.) To all of them Thrale was an admirable host, intelligent, courteous, easy-going, yet quite capable of keeping his guests in order if the situation required it. A man who could civilly silence Johnson on occasion was more than equal to the social ineptitudes of Goldsmith, who longed to be liked and to shine in company yet whose tactlessness often landed him in trouble. He was 'certainly a man extremely odd', Mrs Thrale observed in her journal. 'The first time he dined with us, he gravely asked Mr Thrale how much a year he got by his business?' Thrale, surprised and annoyed by the question but outwardly unruffled, had answered, 'We don't talk of those things much in company, Doctor; but I hope to have the honour of knowing you so well that I shall wonder less at the question.'[9]

Henry Thrale, a man who could silence
Johnson on occasion: the portrait painted by Reynolds
for the library at Streatham

Good talk, even with Johnson as the star turn, was not the only attraction of an evening at Thrale's, for he kept a splendid, even ostentatious table, and the wine, though he himself was a moderate drinker, would be as plentiful and as choice as one could wish. An Irish clergyman, one Dr Campbell, who had a taste for good living and metropolitan pleasures, dined one day in 1775 at Thrale's, where he found ten or a dozen gentlemen and only one other lady beside Mrs Thrale. 'The dinner was excellent, first course soups at head and foot removed by fish and a saddle of mutton – second course a fowl they called Galena at head, and a capon (larger than some of our Irish turkeys) at foot; third course four different sorts of ices, viz., pineapple, grape, raspberry and a fourth; in each remove I think there were fourteen dishes. The two first courses were served in massy plate.'[10] (This same cleric, by no means too prim to relish some of the repartee to be heard in male company, noted in his diary one of Murphy's less presentable anecdotes of Johnson: 'Murphy gave it – on Garrick's authority – that when it was asked what was the greatest pleasure, Johnson answered f***ing, and the second was drinking. And therefore he wondered why there were not more drunkards, for all could drink though all could not f***.')[11]

It was, apart from his intellectual powers and agility of imagination, his gift for the homely simile or metaphor which made so many of Johnson's remarks both pungent and memorable. In a discussion about descriptions of night, he was prepared to give the poet Young his due, even in comparison with Dryden and Shakespeare – yet 'We must not', he told Mrs Thrale, 'compare the noise made by your tea-kettle there with the roaring of the ocean.' This was the sort of remark that everyone remembered, like his saying, when someone was rashly praising Corneille above Shakespeare, 'Corneille is to Shakespeare as a clipped hedge is to a forest' – a simile so precise that it stays with one for ever – on a par, at least, with his description of a politician with 'a mind as narrow as the neck of a vinegar cruet'. Even to sombre or painful subjects he brought this every-day familiar touch, illustrating an often profound thought with an image simple enough for a child to remember. To Mrs Thrale's cheerful proposition that occasional quarrels between lovers did more good than harm, he replied, '*All* quarrels ought to be avoided studiously, particularly conjugal ones', and added, with evident feeling, 'The cup of life is surely bitter enough, without squeezing in the hateful rind of resentment.' How could she ever forget that image, even without noting it down, as she did, in her private journal?

His deep emotional conviction of the bitterness or 'vacuity' of life was never wholly forgotten, even among the pleasures of Streatham; it was, in fact, the omnipresence of misery which made pleasure so important. When one of Thrale's friends spoke casually against 'giving halfpence to common beggars' because 'they only lay it out in gin and tobacco', Johnson at once demanded, 'Why should they be denied such sweeteners of their existence? . . . Life is a pill which none of us can swallow without gilding; yet for the poor we delight in stripping it still barer, and are not ashamed to show even visible displeasure, if ever the bitter taste is taken from their mouths'[12] – a homely image which, one imagines, silenced the company, since everyone would be familiar with the unpleasant pill or bolus made palatable in a coating of gold-leaf by the apothecary. Sigmund Freud, with whom one cannot imagine Johnson much agreeing, was to make precisely the same point, though without the poignant image: 'Life as we find it is too hard for us; it entails too much pain, too many disappointments, impossible tasks. We cannot do without palliative remedies. . . . There are perhaps three of these means: powerful diversions of interest, which lead us to care little about our misery; substitutive gratifications, which lessen it; and intoxicating substances, which make us insensitive to it. Something of this kind is indispensable.'[13]

All of these palliative remedies Johnson found to perfection with the Thrales. Powerful diversions of interest there were in plenty, for a well-ordered family life with a growing nursery of children was a new and absorbing experience, and he 'loved', he told Mrs Thrale, 'to see a knot of little misses dearly'. As the years passed, and first Queeney and then the others became conversible, he played games with them, composed funny poems, pretended to be a giant who lived in a castle, was 'good-humouredly willing to join in childish amusements, and hated to be left out of any innocent merriment

181

that was going forward.'[14] He was as happy when Thrale was away at the brewery and there was no male company, as when coaches came rolling up the gravel and there was formidable conversation after dinner. He began to speak of Southwark and Streatham as 'home', to take it for granted that he had his own room in either house, to address Thrale as 'Master' and his wife as 'Mistress', to comment favourably or otherwise on the dishes at dinner, even to join in Thrale's passion for hunting, following the hounds 'with a good firmness' on an old hunter and distinguishing himself so well that the Tory member for Petersfield, 'one-speech Hamilton', called out, 'Why, Johnson rides as well, for aught I see, as the most illiterate fellow in England.'[15]

Johnson's emotional involvement with the Thrales, beginning in mutually advantageous friendship, but as the years went by developing into something dangerously deep, was remarked by his friends at first with some annoyance, since he was now rarely to be found at home and no longer appeared so regularly at the Club. It remained for Boswell, however, on one of his rare visits to London in 1768, full of his own Edinburgh affairs and intoxicated with self-importance over the publication of his *Corsica*, to detect at once the extent of the change in Johnson's life, and to focus his jealous attention on Mrs Thrale. He had decided, now that Paoli had been dealt with, that Johnson was to be his next and greatest subject; and in all the confidence of success and with techniques improved by experience was determined to anatomize Johnson with a minuteness and fidelity never before attempted. And what did he find? That Johnson was now a lion among opulent strangers; that he was petted and displayed by a brewer's wife who had social and literary ambitions – or so the gossip went; that the great man had advised the lady to keep a journal, and to write down everything that struck her imagination, or that she found interesting. Thoroughly alarmed, and unsettled even further by hearing that Johnson was annoyed by his having published an extract from one of his letters, Boswell made nervous inquiries and found that he was neither in London nor at the Thrales', but visiting his friend Robert Chambers, now Principal of New Inn Hall, Oxford, and Vinerian Professor of Law. There was no time to be lost if he was to capture the territory so promisingly explored more than four years ago, and in a matter of hours Boswell was in the 'fly' on his way to Oxford.[16]

The summer-house at Streatham: a fanciful early 19th-century reconstruction. The actual summer-house is still preserved at Kenwood.

13

'Nothing of the bear but his skin'

UN to earth at last in the comfortable quarters of his young friend Robert Chambers – 'The house is a good one, and genteely furnished' – Johnson proved to be in a better humour than Boswell had feared, and they were soon back in the give-and-take of their old relationship. Johnson had, it is true, been annoyed by the ostentatious use of what he had privately written, but the momentary irritation had passed, and when Boswell, already anxious to establish his claim to further material, 'thought it right' to ask if there were any objection to his publishing his friend's letters after his death, he received a good-humoured reply: 'Nay, Sir, when I am dead, you may do as you will.'

He was not, however, to get off scot-free, for Johnson was bored by Boswell's self-publicizing antics over his Corsican adventures, and told him, 'I wish you would empty your head of Corsica, which I think has filled it rather too long.' This, of course, was impossible: Boswell saw himself now as the celebrated author of two books on the subject – a history of the island and an account of his own tour – and was going to extravagant lengths to draw attention to himself as a pundit on Corsican affairs and the friend of Paoli. He was even sending to the newspapers anonymous announcements of the movements of 'Corsica Boswell', and was soon to attend Garrick's Shakespeare Jubilee in Stratford-upon-Avon dressed in his costume of a Corsican chieftain with *Viva la Liberta* conspicuously embroidered in gold round the crown of his hat. All this Johnson saw as the conceited capering that it was, and might well have applied to Boswell the jest he had fastened on Richardson, as a man who 'could not be contented to sail quietly down the stream of reputation, without longing to taste the froth from every stroke of the oar.'[1]

There were some sessions of talk over cups of tea and one or two suppers in Chambers's rooms with 'madeira and warm port negus', but nothing particularly memorable was said, apart from an astonishing contribution to natural history: 'He said swallows certainly sleep all the winter; many of them conglobulate themselves by flying round and round, and then all in a heap throw themselves under water, and lie in the bed of a river.' This, Boswell observed, 'appeared strange to me. I know not if Mr Johnson was well founded in it.' (Obviously he was not, and was simply repeating a theory fairly common at the time, when the habits of migratory birds were little understood.)

Johnson in fact was closely engaged in helping Chambers compose his Vinerian Lectures on law, a subject far more attractive to him than Boswell's provocative chatter. 'The law', he had told Mrs Thrale severely, when she 'declared against it' as tedious, 'is the last result of human wisdom acting upon human experience for the benefit of the public.'[2] His helping Chambers, like so many of his anonymous activities, was a secret. The lectures evidently were a success, for a few years later Chambers, still only in his middle thirties, married a beautiful girl of fifteen and went as a Supreme Court Judge to Bengal, where before long he achieved a knighthood and the office of Chief Justice.

Boswell managed before he left, however, to draw Johnson out on a subject highly congenial to himself – adultery. One of his great plans at the moment was for an advantageous marriage, and this and related subjects were much on his mind, so that he was relieved to hear Johnson arguing like a lawyer on points of inheritance and property, considering adultery far more criminal in a woman than in a man, 'because it broke the peace of families and introduced confusion of progeny.'[3] Proud rather than otherwise of his own lecherous habits, Boswell was delighted to hear that, provided a man did not insult his wife, he did her no injury 'if, for instance, from mere wantonness of appetite, he steals privately to her chambermaid. Sir,' Johnson told him, 'a wife ought not greatly to resent this. . . . A wife should study to reclaim her husband by more attention to please him.' This was splendid news for the potential bridegroom, and Boswell was enchanted to find the great moralist 'grown liberal' on a point so much to his liking. 'But,' said Mr Chambers, 'suppose a husband goes a-whoring, and then poxes his wife.' 'Why, Sir, if he poxes her, it is a bodily injury, and she may resent it as she pleases.' Boswell was struck by an uneasy thought. Was it not hard, he asked, 'that one deviation from chastity should so absolutely ruin a woman?' Johnson: 'Why, no, Sir; the great principle which every woman is taught is to keep her legs together. When she has given up that principle, she has given up every notion of female honour and virtue.'[4] This down-to-earth reply was edited into a more decorous statement when Boswell decided to include it in his biography; it could not stand as it was, but the idea was too pleasing to be left out. He relieved his feelings the following day, when he returned to London, with a spree recorded cryptically in his journal: 'Got red-haired hussy; went to Bob Derry's, had brandy and water. . . . Then once. Then home with her. . . . Horrid room; no fire, no curtains, dirty sheets, etc. All night . . .'.[5]

One curious detail had caught his eye before he parted from Johnson: for the first time, so far as he could remember, his friend was wearing a watch, a new and handsome one in a tortoiseshell case; the first, according to Hawkins, that he had ever possessed. There was a Greek inscription engraved on the dial-plate, 'The night cometh, when no man can work' – a reminder of death and admonition against wasting time which in Johnson's case was peculiarly apt. Even disagreeably so, it seems, for when next they met Boswell saw that the dial-plate had been changed and that there was now no inscription, a simplification which Johnson accounted for by saying that 'it might do very well upon a clock which a man keeps in his closet', but for a watch to be carried on the person it might be thought ostentatious. This was reasonable enough, but no doubt there was a more sombre motive. Johnson's extreme dread of death was interesting to Boswell, who deliberately introduced the subject at every opportunity. 'Is not the fear of death natural to man?' he asked one day, coming fresh from watching the executions at Tyburn. 'So much so, Sir,' replied Johnson, 'that the whole of life is but keeping away the thoughts of it.' A little while later Boswell, watching him narrowly, reintroduced the subject and provoked a reaction more violent than he had expected. 'To my question, whether we might not calm our minds for the approach of death, he answered, in a passion, "No, Sir, let it alone. It matters not how a man dies, but how he lives. The act of dying is not of importance, it lasts so short a time." He added, with an earnest look, "A man knows it must be so, and submits. It will do him no good to whine." I attempted to continue the conversation. He was so provoked, that he said, "Give us no more of this;" and was thrown into such a state of tumult that he expressed himself in a way that alarmed and distressed me; showed an impatience to have me leave him, and when I was going away, said, "Don't let us meet tomorrow."' For once, Boswell had been dismissed with his tail between his legs, and was alarmed to realize the risk he had taken. 'I went home exceedingly uneasy. All the harsh observations which I had ever heard made upon his character crowded into my mind; and I seemed to myself like the man who had put his head into the lion's mouth a great many times with perfect safety, but at last had it bit off.'[6]

Among the many subjects which Johnson preferred to talk about there was one 'which he loved to relate with all its circumstances, when requested by his friends'. This was no less than his having a private conversation with the King, an honour which he had neither sought nor expected, and which was, therefore, particularly flattering to his reputation. 'I find', he told a gathering at Reynolds's who were eager for details, 'it does a man good to be talked to by his Sovereign.'[7] The meeting had taken place in Buckingham House, which George III had bought some years before and settled on Queen Charlotte, this predecessor of Buckingham Palace being then known as 'the Queen's house'. The King's librarian, Mr Frederick Barnard (who happened also to be the King's natural brother, hence his appointment) had enlisted Johnson's help in the formation of the library, and Johnson occasionally visited it in order to look over the books and give advice. Hearing of this the young King, anxious to show a proper respect for literature, had expressed a desire to meet him, and was accordingly conducted by Mr Barnard with a lighted candle to where Johnson was sitting with a book by the library fire, 'in a profound study'.

The conversation, once Johnson had 'started up', followed a well-meaning if somewhat pedestrian course, the King asking Johnson if he were writing anything, and being told that he was not; that he thought he had already done his part as a writer. 'I should have thought so too,' said the King, 'if you had not written so well.' This piece of politeness was really the climax of the interview, though other matters were touched on, the King suggesting that the literary biography of the country should be written, and that Johnson was the man to undertake it. On this second compliment the conversation came to an end, leaving Johnson glowing with satisfaction and the King, perhaps, relieved that the thing was done. According to Northcote, Reynolds's friend and biographer, he had been 'more afraid of this interview than Dr Johnson was, and went to it as a schoolboy to his task'.

Now that he was blessedly free from the necessity of working, Johnson was no longer tied to London. Loving the city and its company as he did – that 'fountain of intelligence and pleasure' – he yet found a passion for travel beginning to assert itself; a long journey or a short one, it was the distraction of movement that he loved, and was discovering to be one of the most sovereign remedies for his melancholy. Some time after his three months' sojourn with the Thrales he had made one of his periodical visits to Lichfield, not intending to stay long, but had found his mother's old servant, Catherine Chambers, mysteriously ill, and in doing what he could to relieve her, besides deciding the future of the house once she would be gone, had been unable to return to London for nearly six months. 'Kitty', as he had always called her, was now nearly sixty, and had grown dropsical and infirm; she had been bed-ridden already for eight months when Johnson found her. Lucy Porter was living in her new house in another part of Lichfield and was presumably doing her best for their old servant, but it was clear that Kitty was sinking, and Johnson wrote urgently to his own physician, Dr Lawrence, for advice, admitting that he could not be exact about her symptoms, since 'neither she nor her attendants are very good relators of a case'. Kitty lingered on from June to October, slowly dying. Johnson himself, as always when he was miserable (Lucy was brusque and he was longing to return to the Thrales) was again unwell, 'miserably disordered', yet felt himself held at Lichfield by 'the shackles of destiny'. On a Sunday in October 1767 he wrote in the notebook in which he recorded his prayers: 'Yesterday . . . at about ten in the morning I took leave for ever of my dear old friend Catherine Chambers, who came to live with my mother about 1724, and has been but little parted from us since. . . . I desired all to withdraw, then told her that we were to part for ever; that as Christians we should part with prayer, and that I would, if she was willing, say a short prayer beside her. She expressed great desire to hear me, and held up her poor hands, as she lay in bed, with great fervour, while I prayed, kneeling by her. . . . I then kissed her. She told me that to part was the greatest pain that she had ever felt, and that she hoped we should meet again in a better place. I expressed with swelled eyes and great emotion of tenderness the same hopes. We kissed and parted, I humbly hope, to meet again, and to part no more.'

This done, he was at last free to bespeak 'a place in the first vehicle that shall have a vacancy', and return to London. He was longing, he wrote to Mrs Thrale, to be in Streatham again, 'in that place which your kindness and Mr Thrale's allows me to call my *home*'. While he was away Mrs Thrale had given birth to a son, and since the longed-for heir seemed likely to live, the family was absorbed in a special domestic happiness. In Lichfield, on the other hand, there had been 'not one day of pleasure'. Lucy, with whom he had always hoped to have an affectionate relationship, had become a little stiff and reserved in middle age, leading a spinsterish life with her dogs and cats and not responding to the occasional endearments – 'My dear dear love' . . . 'My dear darling' – in Johnson's letters. She had received him civilly enough ('Miss Lucy is more kind and civil than I expected . . . though a little discoloured by hoary virginity') but it was useless to look for any evidence of affection. 'Lucy', he told Mrs Thrale, 'is a philosopher, and considers me as one of the external and accidental things that are to be taken and left without emotion.' Prosperity had not made her more obliging; she still remained 'a very peremptory maiden'. This lack of warmth made him long all the more to return to Streatham and its delights, and above all to the company of his 'Dearest Lady'.

His own household, when he returned to it, seemed drearier than ever by comparison. Miss Williams and Levett went on with their own obscure concerns, holding a minimum of communication with one another; presumably there was a female servant somewhere in the nether regions, since coals must be carried, dishes washed and rooms sometimes cleaned, as well as an occasional dinner fetched from the local tavern; but with Johnson so often from home there was little or nothing for Frank the Negro to do. He was occasionally taken to help wait at table when Johnson dined with Reynolds or other friends, and once or twice had accompanied his master on country visits; but before his long absence in Lichfield Johnson had decided that he would be improved by a little further education. Frank was now at least twenty-two, a difficult age for a schoolboy, but there was apparently a humble grammar school at Bishop's Stortford that was willing to have him, and he was placed in the charge of the late headmaster's widow.[8] Here he was to remain for the next four years, receiving letters from Johnson from time to time, urging him to 'be a good boy' and to attend diligently to his reading. Frank no doubt profited from this experiment, for when he returned in 1772 he was at least well spoken and literate, an improvement which (according to Anna Williams, who thought it a waste of money) had cost Johnson some three hundred pounds. Poor Miss Williams had little beyond household and small financial matters to occupy her, and was apt to

ABOVE Lucy Porter, Johnson's step-daughter, in middle age, 'a very peremptory maiden'.
RIGHT Francis Barber, Johnson's Negro servant: a portrait believed to be by Reynolds

be irritable over trifles. She was 'very attentive', said Hawkins, 'to the conduct of this his favourite', and 'when she took occasion to complain to his master of his misbehaviour, would do it in such terms as these: "This is your scholar! your philosopher! upon whom you have spent so many hundred pounds."' No doubt it contributed something to the harmony of the household to have Frank out of the way for four years, improving his grammar and spelling at Bishop's Stortford.

During these years Johnson's life proceeded, paradoxically, on three levels; it was almost as though he were living three separate lives. His friends, and the ever-widening intellectual circle which his fame had brought him, saw him to perfection as the Johnson whom Boswell immortalized – the Great Cham of literature, impressive dictator of famous Club and late-night gatherings in taverns, the most potent and formidable talker of his time. This massive image is nowhere better preserved than in a quick retort of Boswell's: 'When I called upon Dr Johnson next morning, I found him highly satisfied with his colloquial prowess the preceding evening. "Well," said he, "we had good talk." "Yes, Sir; you tossed and gored several persons."' Johnson's entertainment value, no less than the force of his thinking, was vastly appreciated by his eminent contemporaries, in spite (or because) of the always implicit element of danger. An opponent might be tossed and gored one evening, to be treated with disarming partiality the next. As Goldsmith (who was skinned alive on more than one occasion) said, 'Johnson, to be sure, has a roughness in his manner; but no man alive has a more tender heart. *He has nothing of the bear but his skin.*'

At the same time, there was a very different Johnson to be found in Southwark and Streatham, a Johnson of whom Boswell, and even his more intimate friends, knew little. At Thrale's dinner-table he was in his accustomed glory, but behind the scenes, in the day-to-day affairs of domestic life, he was a confidant and friend whom Boswell would scarcely have recognized. As his affection for Mrs Thrale deepened, so did her dependence on his company, comfort and advice; with Thrale more often out of the house than in it, and in any case indifferent to most domestic or maternal perplexities, Johnson had gradually become indispensable – so closely concerned in all their family affairs that Mrs Thrale could write to him, half playfully but also with truth, 'Can we do anything without you?'

Yet even this impression of comparative happiness – and there *was* a great deal of tranquil happiness in the early years – is far from being the whole picture. On a deep and hidden level, for the most part contended with in silence but eventually, to her great dismay, imparted to Mrs Thrale, Johnson wrestled with his old demon, leaving a trail of anguish through his prayers and meditations which, taken alone as evidence of his state of mind, would leave an impression of almost unalloyed misery. As early as the autumn of 1768 Mrs Thrale was startled to turn up by chance the dark underside of an apparently pleasant day's outing into the country on Johnson's birthday. 'We had taken Mr Johnson a little tour into Kent,' she wrote in one of her scraps of journal – being already as keen a recorder as Boswell – '. . . and soon after our return he went to town

OPPOSITE Mrs Thrale aged thirty, a few years after she first became acquainted with Johnson

188

for a day or two, during which time I went into his apartment to see that all was left as it should be, and found in an open drawer not even shut together these remarkable lines, of which I could not forbear taking a copy . . .'. The birthday, however cheerful it had seemed, had been recorded by Johnson in a very different manner. 'I have now begun the sixtieth year of my life. How the last year has past I am unwilling to terrify myself with thinking. This day has been past in great perturbation . . . and my distress has had very little intermission. . . . This day it came into my mind to write the history of my melancholy. On this I purpose to deliberate. I know not whether it may not too much disturb me. . . .'[9] How could it be that a fine day spent driving in a coach with his beloved 'Master' and 'Mistress' – one of his favourite pleasures – could have been passed in such sombre reflections? She already knew something of the pitfalls of Johnson's temperament, and had been happy to see how much the normal family life of Streatham had done for his health and spirits. Had he not written to her that very spring, 'I count the friendship of your house among the felicities of life'? Over the next few years, with pity and reluctance, she would learn a great deal more than she wished to know.

In 1768, after much preparatory work and propaganda by Joshua Reynolds, the Royal Academy was founded in London, the first institution of its kind where painters could officially exhibit their works and students receive instruction. Reynolds was appointed by the King as first President and in his turn bestowed a number of honorary (and almost wholly meaningless) dignities on several of his friends. Johnson was appointed Professor of Ancient Literature and Goldsmith Professor in Ancient History, while both Boswell and Baretti were made Secretaries for Foreign Correspondence – Baretti for his distinction in modern languages and Boswell, presumably, on the strength of the success of his *Corsica*. There were no duties to perform and no rewards apart from the titles themselves. 'There is no sallary annex'd,' Goldsmith wrote plaintively to his brother, 'and I took it rather as a compliment to the institution than any benefit to myself. Honours to one in my situation are something like ruffles to a man who wants a shirt.'

Baretti was perhaps the only one who benefited by this distribution of 'ruffles', for within a few months of his appointment he found himself in Newgate, charged with murder, and the evidence offered by his Academy colleagues argued strongly in his favour. The incident which had led to his arrest was so typical of the earlier hazards of the streets at night that it could have served as the model for a couplet in Johnson's *London*. He had been pestered in a persistent manner by a prostitute, and when he threw her off had been attacked by her attendant bullies, one of whom, in the struggle which followed, he had fatally wounded with his pocket-knife. Johnson and Burke both visited him in prison, chary of holding out too much hope, since he had certainly carried a knife and killed his man. ('I wear it', Baretti had pleaded, 'to carve fruit and sweetmeats, and not to kill my fellow-creatures.') At the trial, however, the evidence in

OPPOSITE Joseph Baretti, who tutored Queeney Thrale in languages, accompanied Johnson and the Thrales to France, and quarrelled with nearly everybody

191

favour of his good character, his sobriety, learning, and even physical timidity won the day, and Baretti was acquitted. Garrick, Johnson, Burke, Beauclerk, Goldsmith and Reynolds each contributed a favourable opinion; Garrick's testimony, in particular, was a turning-point. Why, asked the prosecution, if this foreigner, this Italian, was such a peaceable character, was he carrying a knife? Because, said Garrick, that was the custom abroad; it was well known that in foreign inns only forks were provided. 'When *you* travel abroad,' counsel persisted suspiciously, 'do you carry such knives as this?' 'Yes,' answered Garrick firmly, 'or we should have no victuals.' So Baretti was acquitted, and received back with relief and rejoicing by his friends – by all, that is, except Boswell, who had always detested him, and told Murphy in private that he hoped he would be hanged.

Baretti had been unfortunate, for London in the late seventeen-sixties was a safer and cleaner place than the city Johnson had first known more than thirty years ago. Credit for much of this improvement was due to Henry Fielding as Bow Street magistrate: his inauguration of the first small metropolitan police force had done much to reduce the appalling crime wave of the late seventeen-forties. Pickpockets, thieves and highwaymen still plied their trade, but they were far from being the universal menace they had once been, when 'Cruel with guilt, and daring with despair', the midnight murderer in any back street and alley was a danger to be reckoned with. A great deal, too, had been done by the Act of 1751, which by increasing the tax had reduced the dangerous consumption of raw spirits among the poor. Hogarth's *Gin Lane*, engraved in 1750, had been no exaggeration; gin of crude quality was so cheap as to be practically free, and in slum districts was sold in every kind of shop, back-yard and cellar, reducing whole local populations to a sort of gin-inflamed insanity in which any crime was possible. Drunkenness in the streets, like prostitution, was still a disturbing problem, but the kind of street affray which had nearly cost Baretti his life was becoming rarer.

Another improvement, and one which made private visiting in London more agreeable, was the recent abolition of what Boswell described as 'the unhospitable, troublesome and ungracious custom of giving vails to servants'. This practice had been a nuisance to all – except the servants; particularly so to people of modest means, since a man leaving his host's house after dinner would find all the servants assembled in the hall with outstretched hands. Johnson might often, in the past, have had to refuse invitations which for this reason he could not afford to accept, but now the abolition of compulsory tipping had removed a disagreeable embarrassment. Wages – a footman's wage, exclusive of vails, was about eight pounds a year – were supposed to be increased to compensate, but this was not always done and there had been some ugly riots.[10] Johnson, since the talk that day had been about Scotland, chose to be on the servants' side and easily spoiled Boswell's boast that it was the Scots who had first done away with the pernicious system – 'Sir, you abolished vails, because you were too poor to be able to give them.' On another occasion, when servants were again the subject of

Boswell's talk, Johnson for once was at a loss for a reply. 'I put a question to him upon a fact of common life, which he could not answer, nor have I found anyone else who could. What is the reason that women servants, though obliged to be at the expense of purchasing their own clothes, have much lower wages than men servants, to whom a great proportion of that article is furnished, and in fact our female house servants work much harder than the male?' It would take a long time, a couple of centuries at least, before anyone would seriously study that conundrum.

Boswell had by now made up his mind that he must be Johnson's biographer, and had cautiously broached the subject. The detailed information he wanted would 'come out by degrees', Johnson told him, without deliberate sessions of question and answer. Meanwhile it was more congenial to give his young friend occasional lessons in pronunciation, since the broad Scotch accent with which he had first come to London was embarrassing him. Johnson on the whole was reassuring – 'Sir, your pronunciation is not offensive.' He himself, after thirty years of London, still had traces of his old Lichfield accent. 'When people watch me narrowly, and I do not watch myself, they will find me out to be of a particular county.' These occasional lapses, Boswell noted, were '*there*, pronounced like *fear*, instead of like *fair*; *once* pronounced *woonse* instead of *wunse*. . . . Garrick sometimes used to take him off, squeezing a lemon into a punchbowl, with uncouth gesticulations, looking round the company, and calling out, "Who's for *poonsh*?"'[11]

These comic imitations of Garrick's, always a popular item in his private repertoire, were sometimes repaid by Johnson in his own coin. Garrick, for instance, had converted Shakespeare's *Winter's Tale* into an entertainment called *Florizel and Perdita*, and when Mrs Thrale, praising his talent for light poetry, misquoted a line as, 'I'd smile with the simple and feed with the poor', Johnson was quick to retaliate. 'Nay, my dear lady, this will never do. Poor David! Smile with the simple! What folly is that? And who would feed with the poor that can help it? No, no; let me smile with the wise, and feed with the rich.' Boswell lost no time in repeating this sally to Garrick, and 'wondered to find his sensibility as a writer not a little irritated by it'.[12]

Romantic and sentimental attitudes towards the simple life had always provoked Johnson's contempt and inspired some of his most devastating rejoinders, yet on occasion he would still speak of visiting the Hebrides as though he meant it, and would even propose more primitive adventures. When Boswell one day expressed a fancy for buying St Kilda, the most remote island of them all, he was astonished by Johnson's response: 'Pray do, Sir. We will go and pass a winter amid the blasts there. We shall have fine fish, and we will take some dried tongues with us, and some books. We will have a strong built vessel, and some Orkney men to navigate her. We must build a tolerable house: but we may carry with us a wooden house ready made, and requiring nothing but to be put up. Consider, Sir, by buying St Kilda, you may keep the people from falling into worse hands. . . . I'll be your Lord Chancellor, or what you please.'[13]

Such speeches were taken as pleasantries, but Boswell was serious about the proposed tour to the Hebrides; it was the only scheme by which he could have Johnson to himself for a prolonged period, out of the reach of Mrs Thrale. His own visits to London, now that he had married his cousin Margaret Montgomerie and was beginning to practise as an advocate, were necessarily rare, and Johnson in any case was usually inaccessible at Streatham, where Boswell had been invited only once, in the month before his marriage. Besides, the thought of taking that great urban figure, that giant of literary London into the unknown and primitive world of the Western Isles was so bizarre as to be irresistible. What might not come of such an extraordinary juxtaposition, which only Boswell would know, and only Boswell write? The waste of opportunity, with Johnson perpetually out of reach, was a constant worry. 'What a pity it is,' he wrote to Reynolds, 'that he loathes so much to write, and since that is the case, what a pity it is that there is not constantly with him such a recorder of his conversation as I am. I hope next month to be again in London and resume that office.'[14]

That office, though Boswell did not know it, had already been quietly assumed by Mrs Thrale, who was keeping an album called *The Children's Book* and a number of other journals filled with miscellaneous anecdotes and observations. Johnson was already one of her chief subjects, whose behaviour and conversation she recorded in a haphazard way without any conscious system. 'These anecdotes', she wrote, 'are put down in a wild way just as I received or could catch 'em from Mr Johnson's conversation; but I mean one day or another to digest and place them in some order.' It was not until 1776, to mark one of their wedding anniversaries, that Thrale presented her with six handsome quarto volumes of blank paper, bound in calf with scarlet labels and the title, *Thraliana*, lettered in gold. This, coming from Henry Thrale, was an unusual encouragement of his wife's passion for recording, with which he appears never to have shown much sympathy. Johnson, on the other hand, had approved from the beginning of their acquaintance, and had, as she wrote on the first page of her first new volume, 'advised me to get a little book, and write in it all the little anecdotes which might come to my knowledge, all the observations I might make or hear, all the verses never likely to be published, and in fine everything which struck me at the time.'[15]

From this extraordinarily variable medley of memoranda, and from the letters which she and Johnson exchanged whenever they were apart, we catch glimpses of a man who seems to have nothing to do with the old background of club and tavern, and who appears wholly absorbed in the joys and sorrows, the excitements and anxieties, even the childish jokes and festivities of family life. In the early months of 1768 he had plunged once more into Thrale's political activities, writing letters and announcements to canvass the Borough for the coming election, which promised to be an unusually stormy one because of the riots aroused by the Government's proceedings against Wilkes. John Wilkes, atheist and radical, was an object of extreme abhorrence to Johnson, as to the Tory government and to the King, whom he was accused of libelling in his subversive news-sheet, *The North Briton*. To the mob, however, which had no conception of him as a brilliant political adventurer, he was a hero and a tribune of the people; now that he was in England again, standing once more for Middlesex after four years' exile, there were riotous demonstrations in the City, where coaches were held up and public speakers shouted down with cries of 'Wilkes and Liberty!' Southwark, however, was still a safe seat for Thrale, and he was duly elected. His wife supported the campaign with all the energy she could muster in these last weeks of her fourth pregnancy, enter-taining influential constituents to dinner – so many of them unknown to her by sight that she had to keep lists of names on the back of her menu card – and encouraging Johnson in his efforts. By the time the issue was decided Johnson had retreated to the quiet of Oxford and she was able to lie in at Streatham in comparative peace. The child was another girl, christened Anna Maria after her great-aunt, the first Lady Salusbury. 'I design to love little Miss Nanny very well,' Johnson wrote to Mrs Thrale, 'but you must let us have a Bessy some other time.' He had hoped, always fondly remembering Tetty, that she would be named Elizabeth, but for this he had to wait another year, when he stood godfather to the fourth daughter.

The Thrale nursery now seemed in a flourishing condition. One baby had been lost, but three survived – a very satisfactory record for the time. Queeney, the eldest, was healthy and unusually intelligent, so that her mother was already eagerly at work to turn her into a prodigy. She was 'four years and nine months old,' Mrs Thrale recorded, 'when I lay in of Lucy; and then I first began to teach her grammar, showing her the difference between a substantive and an adjective as I lay in bed: she has made since then a progress so considerable, that she this day . . . parsed the first couplet of Pope's Iliad, beginning of her own accord at the vocative case. . . .' The difficulty with this intelligent and self-possessed child was that she could already seem somewhat forbidding. She was firmly Johnson's favourite and would remain so, but her mother found her dis-turbingly lacking in affection. She was 'exquisitely pretty . . . her complexion delicate and her carriage uncommonly genteel,' Mrs Thrale wrote in the winter of 1768, yet 'her temper is not so good; reserved to all, insolent where she is free, and sullen to those who teach or dress or do anything towards her.' This was the child to whom Johnson would soon be writing playful and tender letters beginning 'Dear Sweeting', or 'My sweet, dear, pretty little Miss', and from whom he would receive replies both well mannered and well spelt. He had a sure and imaginative touch with children and found it both easy and delightful to be on affectionate terms – not so difficult, perhaps, when he had only to play the part of indulgent grandfather, which suited him marvellously well.

Mrs Thrale, indeed, in spite of the privileges and comforts of her life had to face tragic misfortunes where her children were concerned, to a degree that seems abnormal even in an eighteenth-century family. In sixteen years she gave birth to twelve children, of whom only four survived; her own good health and physical resilience, the well-run nursery and the attendance of careful physicians were no match for the mysterious mishaps and infections which carried off one child after another as indifferently as if she had been living in the rookeries that Levett attended in the back alleys of Fleet Ditch. Almost every winter she found herself contending with the fatigues and dis-comforts of pregnancy, almost every spring she gave birth to a child more likely to die than to survive. She herself, it seems, was a born survivor, one of those rare women whose energy and optimism recover after every setback, leaving their allies and enemies exhausted or stranded by the way.

Early in 1772 Mrs Thrale's mental and physical resources were put stringently to the test when she discovered – to her own as well as everyone else's amazement – that

Henry Thrale was on the brink of bankruptcy and the famous brew-house heading for disaster. How Thrale could have been so reckless no one could understand, but the fact was that, shrewd money-maker though he was, he had fallen completely under the spell of an inventor called Humphrey Jackson, who believed he had discovered a method of brewing without either malt or hops, by a purely chemical system which, undertaken on a vast enough scale, would bring unheard-of profits. Thrale had said nothing of this to his wife and she had asked no questions, having been brought up by both mother and husband to believe it was improper for her to meddle in business matters. Johnson thought otherwise, and had strongly advised her to interest herself in the brewery as a means of being more agreeable to her husband: 'He cannot talk to you about his business, which you do not understand; nor about his pleasures, which you do not partake. . . .' Sensible advice it seemed at the time, but Mrs Salusbury poured scorn on Johnson's suggestion. Had her daughter nothing better to do, she inquired, than to become 'my Lady Mashtub'? 'So,' scribbled Mrs Thrale in her new leather-bound volume, 'I went on in the old way, brought a baby once a year, lost some of them and grew so anxious about the rest, that I now fairly cared for nothing else, but them and her; and not a little for Johnson, who I felt to be my true friend, though I could not break, through my chains to take his advice as it would have helped to kill my poor Mother, whose health now began to decline, and who was jealous enough of Mr Johnson's influence as it was. . . .'[16]

Thrale at last became so 'pensive and gloomy' that questions had to be asked, and the disastrous truth was gradually confessed. Not only had he ruined a whole year's brewing by adopting Jackson's methods without trial, but he had also thrown away vast sums on another scheme to 'conjure some curious stuff, which should preserve ships' bottoms from the worm. . . . Twenty enormous vats!' wrote Mrs Thrale distractedly, 'holding 1,000 hogsheads each – costly contents! Ten more holding a *thousand barrels* each were constructed to stew in this pernicious mess, and afterwards erected on I forget how much ground, bought for the ruinous purpose.' To make matters worse, one of the City's major banks had collapsed, setting off a financial panic. Thrale had no more available capital and no alternative, it seemed, to bankruptcy – a prospect which paralysed him with shock and made him incapable of action.

At this point, since her husband now 'begged for counsel and comfort', Mrs Thrale conferred with her mother and Johnson and all three set their wits to retrieving the situation. Mrs Salusbury contributed her life's savings, Johnson and Mrs Thrale examined the accounts of the brewery, got rid of Jackson (whom the men in the brewery referred to as 'that *Fiend*'), raised money by various means, made necessary practical changes in process and management, and at last found the danger reduced to a tolerable debt, with bankruptcy averted. 'Money was raised,' said Mrs Thrale, 'the beer was mended, our whole conduct in the management of our trade was changed, and we grew prosperous and loved each other.'[17]

The disaster had, after all, been narrowly avoided. Thrale began to breathe again, and Johnson and Mrs Salusbury became friends. 'My mother's amiable behaviour on the occasion endeared her to Mr Johnson, and his active friendship reconciled her to him: Mr Thrale saw his wife capable to be trusted, and I saw that he was not insensible to the tenderness which it was my duty to show him; so all went better after the year 1772 than before.'[18] It was not only her generous behaviour in parting with her savings that had made Johnson see Mrs Salusbury in a more kindly light. For some time it had been known that the pain of which she sometimes complained was due to cancer – 'admitting of no cure,' her daughter miserably wrote, 'nor even of any hope' – and this, with her patient fortitude, was more than enough to rouse his deepest compassion. He no longer teased her about the newspapers, but sat and talked as though they were old friends; while she for her part, touched by this new gentleness, gave him, before he went off to Lichfield in October, a chair-seat worked by Mrs Thrale in the days, said the note accompanying it, 'when she was a good little girl and minded her book and needle'.

Mrs Thrale's cheerful statement that 'all went better' when the worst of the crisis was over was euphemistic, being written several years later, when the memory of her worst experiences had faded. At the end of the summer, worn out with work and anxiety, she had given birth prematurely to yet another girl, who 'looked black and could not breathe freely', and who lived only a few hours. She herself, as usual, recovered quickly, but the blithe statement that 'we grew prosperous and loved each other' was only partly truthful and partly ironic. For Thrale never quite recovered from the shock of his near-failure, as though the whole episode had been an insult to his pride, and his rescue by wife and mother-in-law something he found difficult to forgive. The polite, withdrawn, rather dull man whom we meet in the pages of Boswell and Fanny Burney came into being at the time of the brewery catastrophe.

For Johnson on the other hand, as for his 'dear Mistress', the experience had been curiously rewarding. They had both become personally involved in the management of the brewery and were to remain so – a situation to which some strain from Johnson's shop-keeping ancestry responded. Calculations of profit and loss, the practical processes of brewing, prices of malt and hops and the orders and complaints of customers, all appealed to a robust and practical element in his nature. 'They have in this country a very prosperous hay harvest,' he wrote to Mrs Thrale from Lichfield as soon as he arrived there, 'but malt is five and sixpence a strike, or two pounds four shillings a quarter. Wheat is nine and sixpence a bushel.' And again, a few days later, 'The price of malt has risen again. It is now two pounds eight shillings the quarter. Ale is sold in the public houses at sixpence a quart, a price which I never heard of before. . . .'[19] It was almost as though Johnson, rather than Thrale, were the 'eminent brewer'.

14

'Mr Boswell will be at last your best physician'

 HE winter of 1772 was a difficult and depressing one for the Thrales. The threatened catastrophe, it is true, had been averted, and neither had time or inclination to mourn overmuch for the loss of a sickly infant; but the reform of the brewery was complicated and exhausting, Thrale so bad-tempered and morose that his workmen preferred to deal with his wife or Johnson, while Mrs Salusbury's painful approach to death made even cheerful Streatham a place of mourning. 'Nobody can guess', wrote Mrs Thrale in her *Children's Book*, 'what a winter this has been to me, and big with child too again, God help me!'

LEFT Hester Maria ('Queeney') Thrale, aged about fifteen, by Reynolds, and RIGHT a caricature of Henry Thrale in 1772

With Mrs Thrale distracted between nursing her mother in the country and attending to the affairs of the brewery in Southwark, Johnson spent more time than usual at home, presenting himself only on Tuesdays at Southwark for dinner and discussion. He even absented himself altogether for seven weeks during the winter, visiting Lichfield and Ashbourne but keeping in close touch with Mrs Thrale through frequent and confidential letters. 'Calamity Thrale', it seems ('It will be Calamity Thrale in good earnest by and by'), was being as unhelpful as ever, harsh to the brewery staff and flying into unaccountable rages – 'Nor can all the influence I have over him,' wrote Mrs Thrale, 'make him speak a kind word to a customer.' She relied on Johnson's advice at every turn, and if it had not been for her mother's state would have been glad to have him back with them at Streatham. 'All the good we enjoy,' she told him, 'all the flattery we receive, all the pleasure we bestow, comes ultimately, if not immediately, from you.'[1]

For Johnson, too, the temporary loss of Streatham was a deprivation, for he had found it a quiet and comfortable place to work in and his leisure hours, even when there was only nursery company, were always pleasant. He had become fast friends with Queeney and had begun a correspondence with her, adjusting himself with ease to the level of an eight-year-old: 'I am glad to hear of the prosperity of my hen. Miss Porter has buried her fine black cat. So things come and go. . . .'[2] At Streatham, too, he had been able to indulge his passion for chemistry, and had persuaded Thrale to allow a little brick furnace to be built in the kitchen-garden, where he smelted ore and extracted essences before an admiring audience of children and servants; until, that is, Thrale himself joined the group one day and was so horrified by the possibility of an explosion that he put an end to the experiments.

Since Johnson had been able to work at Streatham he had produced two political pamphlets and was doing a little desultory revision of his Dictionary for a new fourth edition. The pamphlets – *The False Alarm*, a fierce legalistic defence of Parliament's action against Wilkes, and *Thoughts on the Late Transactions Respecting Falkland's Islands*, a balanced examination of the arguments for Spanish or British possession – caused no great stir, though the former attracted considerable abuse for its extreme diehard politics. His name, as a result, was put before Lord North as a possible candidate for Parliament, a suggestion that came to nothing. The thought of Johnson as a Member of Parliament has comic possibilities; but it is probable that the pamphlets were written only as part of his political support for Thrale.

Back in Johnson's Court with his sombre household, or idling away the time in Lichfield and Ashbourne, his old enemy, neurasthenia, began stealthily to gain ground, so that by the end of May 1773, weak from a persistent bronchial cough and in misery with an eye infection which made reading impossible, he was begging to be fetched 'home'. 'My eye is yet so dark that I could not read your note. I have had a poor darkling week. . . . I wish you could fetch me on Wednesday. I long to be in my own room.'[3] There was no resisting this piteous appeal, though there was every reason against his returning to Streatham. Mrs Salusbury was sinking fast, and the horrors of a cancer death, in those days of meagre knowledge and no anaesthetics, left her daughter little inclined for another burden. There was, besides, an unpleasant atmosphere in the house, due to the revelations of scurrilous news-sheets. Thrale, true to his character as a well-to-do gentleman, had always had his molls and mistresses in the area – a fact which Mrs Thrale philosophically accepted, together with those periods when, clapped or poxed, he would spend a fretful interval under the regimen of his physicians. This time, however, his scrapes had got into the newspapers and the scandal-sheets were retailing the escapades of a Borough brewer 'more famed for his amours than for his beer'. This vein (after several issues) being exhausted, they had gone on to an examination of Thrale's home life, and were piously delighted to report 'how an eminent Brewer was very jealous of a certain Author in Folio, and perceived a strong resemblance to him in his eldest son'. Nobody who knew them took this scurrilous gossip seriously, but it was unpleasant, and to have to receive the ailing Johnson back into the household at this particular moment must, for Mrs Thrale, have been an unwelcome duty. Yet how could she refuse? Though hardly yet (to borrow one of Mrs Thrale's expressions) 'fit for a dark room and straw', he was still clearly in need of the care which only she could give. 'I hope I shall not add much to your trouble,' he had written; 'I long to be under your care.' He had added to this brief letter an apparently trivial query which may or may not have had significance for them both – 'Have you got your key?'[4]

This is the first hint at an uncomfortable secret which the two of them had evidently been sharing for some time, and which Katherine Balderston first tracked down in 1942, in her meticulously scholarly edition of *Thraliana*. It is easy to make too much of this curious detail, so carefully concealed by both Johnson and Mrs Thrale as to suggest melodramatic possibilities almost certainly remote from the truth. It had to do, of course, with Johnson's fear of madness, and it seems clear, from the evidence of two letters published only in 1932, that to allay the obsessive feelings of guilt which so persistently tormented him Johnson had evolved a fantasy of imprisonment – a sort of corrective game, though serious enough, in which he was the captive penitent and Mrs Thrale the gaoler. This make-believe severity of treatment – solitude, padlocked door, restrictions on food and drink – absolved him emotionally from the sense of sin which tormented him after indulgence (or so we must suppose) in voluptuous day-dreaming. ('His passions', said Reynolds, 'were like those of other men; the difference only lay in his keeping a stricter watch over himself.') The suppression, in the interests of Christian morality, of Johnson's own strongly sexual nature had left subconscious scars, fears that he secretly dealt with through this weird make-believe of penance and absolution. (The fantasy had been growing on him at least two years before, when he had written in his diary, 'De pedicis et manicis insana cogitatio' – insane thoughts of handcuffs and fetters.)

These two letters appear to have been written during the difficult and anxious last weeks before Mrs Salusbury's death, when Johnson too was being nursed at Streatham, according to his own peculiar prescription. The first is from him to Mrs Thrale, written in French – perhaps to defeat possible curiosity on the part of the servant who carried it from his room to hers. Its tone is one of piteous self-abasement; imploring her to decide whether or not he is to remain a prisoner; what is to be allowed him, and what forbidden; even what he may eat and drink. He accuses her of neglecting duties and forgetting promises, condemning him perpetually to beseech her in a manner 'que la resouvenance me fait horreur.'[5] (His choice of words suggests subservence, or at least that he wishes to be afraid of her, for his own sake, 'A madman', he once observed to Boswell, 'loves to be with people whom he fears; not as a dog fears the lash, but of whom he stands in awe. . . . Madmen are all sensual in the lower stages of the distemper. They are eager for gratifications to soothe their minds, and divert their attention from the misery which they suffer: but when they grow very ill, pleasure is too weak for them, and they seek for pain.')

Mrs Thrale's answer is equally extraordinary, though couched in terms of tenderness and respect. 'What care can I promise my dear Mr Johnson that I have not already taken? . . . If it be possible, shake off these uneasy weights, heavier to the mind by far than fetters to the body. Let not your fancy dwell thus upon confinement and severity. . . . I foresaw some ill consequences of your being here while my Mother was dying thus. . . .' (Confinement to his room, it appears, was not continuous, but was a part of the ritual to which he attached obsessive importance. Mrs Thrale's tone, as usual, is cheerful and sensible.) 'If we go on together your confinement shall be as strict as possible except when company comes in, which I shall more willingly endure on your account.' The erotic undertones in the situation seem entirely to have escaped her; or, if she felt a vague uneasiness, she was careful to go on as though she had noticed nothing. 'Dissipation,' she told him, 'is to you a glorious medicine, and I believe Mr Boswell will be at last your best physician. . . . Farewell,' she concluded, 'and be good; and do not quarrel with your governess for not using the rod enough.'[6]

It was a troublesome and embarrassing situation, though subtly flattering to her vanity, since he had placed himself so totally in her power. The reason for the locked door and spells of seclusion must, for Johnson's sake, be kept secret, and she referred to it, even in her diary, only obliquely. 'Poor Johnson!' she wrote in *Thraliana* after his death, 'I see they will leave *nothing untold* that I laboured so long to keep secret; and I was so very delicate in trying to conceal his fancied insanity, that I retained no proofs of it – or hardly any';[7] and later, when the 'fancied insanity' was found to have been confided to others, 'How many times has this great, this formidable Doctor Johnson kissed my hand, ay and my foot too, upon his knees! . . . but the fetters and padlocks will tell posterity the truth.' After her own death, a padlock was one of the minor items in the sale of her effects, with a note written in her hand: 'Johnson's padlock; committed to my care in the year 1768.' The fetters, if ever they existed, have never been found.

Mrs Salusbury's sufferings came to an end in June and Johnson abandoned the rituals of melancholy to comfort Mrs Thrale in a loss which, despite her temperamental resilience, was deeply felt. Her relationship with her mother had so far been the most important and formative of her life, her filial feelings and her own maternal ones the strongest emotions she had so far experienced. She still had much of the emotional character of a responsive child, and it was this, as well as Johnson's paternalism, which had so easily settled their relationship in an affectionate pattern. In her present loss Johnson was able to comfort her better than anyone, through the pity and tenderness for her mother which had conquered the old dislike. He had sat with Mrs Thrale at her bedside and had been present at the end. 'Yesterday,' he wrote in his diary, 'as I touched her hand and kissed it, she pressed my hand between her two hands, which she probably intended as the parting caress. . . . This morning, being called about nine to feel her pulse, I said at parting, God bless you, for Jesus Christ's sake. She smiled, as pleased. She had her senses perhaps to the dying moment.'

Her death, in a very real sense, was a relief, but it left her daughter emotionally prostrated. Johnson, too, though recovering from his recent bout of neurasthenia, was in a self-critical and discouraged state of mind. Four days later he turned again to his diary. 'My memory has been for a long time very much confused. Names, and persons, and events, slide away strangely from me. . . .' He had even forgotten the resolutions with which he had so often flattered himself with hopes of amendment. 'Whether I have not lived resolving, till the possibility of performance is past, I know not. God help me, I will yet try.'

The time had come when, if he were to do it at all, he must make good his promise to go with Boswell to the Hebrides. Henry Thrale, now that the affairs of the brewery were looking up, was restoring his image by transforming the Streatham house from a solid but unspectacular abode into an impressive country mansion, and in the process making it temporarily uninhabitable. A handsome library wing had been added and many of the rooms were being entirely remodelled, including Johnson's, which was at present, Mrs Thrale told him, 'pulled to pieces'. To make matters worse, 'My children have got the measles, and nothing goes quite right with me.'[8] If he had not already had the infection, she told him, he had better keep away.

Boswell had been urging the tour into Scotland for some time, even enlisting the aid of his more eminent Scottish acquaintances, who wrote flattering letters to Johnson, pressing him to come. Now at last the matter had been settled by chance. Johnson's Oxford friend, Robert Chambers, was about to take up his appointment in Bengal, and in August would be travelling to Newcastle to take leave of his family. Since the Scottish Court of Session rose on the twelfth of August, Johnson decided to travel with Chambers that far, and then to join Boswell in Edinburgh. 'Mr Boswell, an active lively fellow,' he wrote to Taylor, 'is to conduct me round the country. What I shall see, I know not, but hope to have entertainment for my curiosity, and I shall be sure at least of air and motion.'

Johnson's motive was, as usual, diversion; he had also hopes of improving his health by exercise and fresh air. 'I fancy', he had written to Taylor, who was as corpulent as himself, 'that neither of us uses exercise enough.' Boswell's intentions, on the other hand, were more devious. He had for a long time been vexed by Johnson's intimacy with the Thrales, and his suspicion that Mrs Thrale was collecting material was a nagging worry. The tour to the Hebrides would put the great man in his pocket for a considerable period – only nine days short of three months, as it turned out – during which he could record his conversation and rapidly enlarge his stock of biographical matter. He had had little chance to proceed with his grand design, for now that he was a practising advocate, a married man and a father, he had neither time nor money for more than brief and occasional visits to London. He had managed a few days at Easter, on Good Friday breakfasting with Johnson on hot cross buns (the buns being provided for himself and Levett, while Johnson took only tea without milk), and afterwards going to church with him at St Clement Danes. He had been asked to dinner, too, on Easter Day, rather to his surprise, for he had 'never supposed he had a dinner at home'. This, of course being a Sunday, Johnson had explained: 'I generally have a meat pie on Sunday: it is baked at a public oven, which is very properly allowed, because one man can attend it; and thus the advantage is obtained of not keeping servants from church to dress dinners.' Boswell had accepted the invitation in a flurry of curiosity. 'I supposed we should hardly see knives and forks, and only have the pie which he mentioned. But to my surprise I found everything in very good order. . . . We had a very good soup, a boiled leg of lamb and spinach, a veal pie, an excellent rice pudding, pickled walnuts and onions, porter and port wine. I dined as well as ever I wished to do.'[9]

Now the plans were settled at last, and Boswell even had the satisfaction of having been elected a member of the exclusive Club. Though he had 'assiduously and earnestly recommended' himself, 'as in a canvass for an election into Parliament', not all the members were anxious to have him, but Johnson had carried the day. 'They knew,' he said, 'that if they refused you, they'd probably never have got in another. I'd have kept them all out.' So Boswell returned to Edinburgh highly satisfied – this was in May – to think out the details of the journey and wait for August. His parting from Johnson had been as extraordinary as anything he had so far recorded of the great man's oddities of behaviour. There had been a slight temporary cooling of affection between Johnson and Bennet Langton, due to Langton's taking offence at a 'drubbing' in argument, and Johnson in return had chosen to be extravagantly amused over Langton's solemnity in the matter of making his will. He and Boswell had made such a joke of this, strolling along the Strand on the night they parted, that – eagerly preserved in Boswell's journal – it would become one of those absurd incidents that are never forgotten. Boswell had deliberately 'cherished' Johnson's merriment, 'calling out "Langton the testator, Langton Longshanks." This tickled his fancy so much that he roared out, "I wonder to whom he'll leave his legs?" And then burst into such a fit of laughter that he seemed almost in a convulsion; then in order to support himself he laid hold of one of the posts which were then at the side of the pavement and bellowed forth such peals that in the dark silence of the night his voice resounded from Temple Bar to Fleet Ditch.'[10]

It was precisely this kind of eccentric behaviour, quite as much as his vaunted wisdom and memorable conversation, that appealed to Boswell's fancy, so that it was at least a part of his design in coaxing Johnson into the wilds of Scotland to place him in situations dramatically remote from the normal pattern of his life. Goldsmith, jealous as always, had told Boswell that 'he would be a dead weight for me to carry, and that I should never be able to lug him along through the Highlands and Hebrides': but Boswell knew better. His instinct – that of a journalist of genius – told him that some of his best material would come from luring Johnson into the sort of primitive company and surroundings that he normally abhorred. The dream of the simple life, sentimentally praised by Rousseau and the new romantics, was a notion he always took pleasure in deflating. There had been, for instance, a recent occasion when a 'learned gentleman' had talked at length on the happiness of primitive life, supporting his views with those of an English officer who had lived for a time in the wilds of America, in Indian territory, and whom he had quoted as saying, 'Here I am, free and unrestrained, amid the rude magnificence of nature, with this Indian woman by my side, and this gun, with which I can procure food when I want it; what more can be desired for human happiness?' 'If a bull could speak,' said Johnson, 'he might as well exclaim – "Here am I with this cow and this grass; what being can enjoy greater felicity?"'[11] – another example of his gift for collapsing philosophical pretensions with a homely prick from the kitchen or even the midden.

The thought of Johnson among barren mountains or 'contending with seas' in an open boat appealed to Boswell's sense of incongruity. He had often racked his brains for outlandish situations, and then demanded to know what Johnson would do in them. 'If, Sir,' he had once asked him, 'you were shut up in a castle, and a new-born child with you, what would you do?' 'Why, Sir,' said Johnson, 'I should not much like my company.' But would he, Boswell persisted, take the trouble of rearing it? Johnson was evidently bored by so futile a subject, but the questions continued. 'Why, yes, Sir,' Johnson admitted, 'I would; but I must have all conveniences. If I had no garden, I

ABOVE From a sketch by Sir Thomas Lawrence: James Boswell in middle age. LEFT Johnson sketched in the clothes he wore on the Highland tour, carrying his 'large English oak stick'

would make a shed on the roof, and take it there for fresh air. I should feed it, and wash it much, and with warm water to please it, not with cold water to give it pain.' But even this was not enough. Was not hot water, Boswell asked, relaxing? And what about education? Would he not teach the child? 'No, I should not be apt to teach it.' But, since he admitted to pleasure in teaching men, 'Would not you have a pleasure in teaching it?' 'No, Sir, I should *not* have a pleasure in teaching it.'[12] After this, to avoid an explosion, the conversation had been allowed to turn to more rational matters, such as the rise and fall of population in Russia. The future biographer, however, still dreamed in private of situations equally bizarre, and believed that in the Western Isles (which he had never seen) they would inevitably find them.

Boswell was not mistaken. The hundred days which he and Johnson spent together in Scotland, often in wild surroundings and in continuously bad weather, provided him with a variety of adventures, absurd incidents and memorable confrontations such as he had hardly dreamed of. He felt, he told Lady Macleod at Dunvegan, like 'a dog who has got hold of a large piece of meat, and runs away with it to a corner, where he may devour it in peace, without any fear of others taking it away from him.[13] And for Johnson himself, though he felt 'but poorly' at the start, caught cold in the Isles, suffered hard going and squalid conditions and learned the horrors of seasickness, it was a period of unusual experience and interest, on which he would look back with satisfaction. 'I cannot but laugh', he said to Boswell when they had reached Skye, 'to think of myself roving among the Hebrides at sixty. I wonder where I shall rove at four-score?'[14]

Johnson arrived in Edinburgh prepared for a rough and possibly perilous journey. 'He wore a full suit of plain brown clothes with twisted-hair buttons of the same colour, a large bushy greyish wig, a plain shirt, black worsted stockings, and silver buckles,' and when travelling 'wore boots and a very wide brown cloth greatcoat with pockets which might have almost held the two volumes of his folio dictionary'. To complete the picture, he 'carried in his hand a large English oak stick'. (This stick, lost in the course of the journey by the Highlander acting as baggage-man, was marked off with nails as a measure, showing a foot and a yard.) He had equipped himself besides with a pair of pistols, with gunpowder and bullets, but being assured by Boswell that they were unlikely to meet robbers, handed these over to Mrs Boswell to keep for him in a drawer. He left also in her care 'a pretty full and curious diary of his life', which he had once allowed Boswell to dip into, and which he was eventually to destroy before his death. If only, Boswell lamented, his wife had had the wit to copy the whole thing out while they were away! But Mrs Boswell by no means shared her husband's obsessive interest in Johnson, and even, it seems, took a certain dislike to their famous guest which she was not altogether successful in concealing. 'I know', Johnson wrote when the tour was over, 'Mrs Boswell wished me well to go.' The truth was, Boswell admitted, 'his irregular hours and uncouth habits, such as turning the candles with their heads downwards, when they did not burn bright enough, and letting the wax drop upon the carpet,

OPPOSITE A kindly portrait by Reynolds of his friend Johnson, who at this time (1775) was ailing both physically and mentally

206

could not but be disagreeable to a lady. Besides,' he shrewdly added, '. . . she thought he had too much influence over her husband. She once in a little warmth made . . . this remark upon the subject: "I have seen many a bear led by a man, but I never before saw a man led by a bear." '[15] Johnson's opinion of Mrs Boswell, on the other hand, was calmly tolerant. She had 'the mien and manners of a gentlewoman', he wrote to Mrs Thrale, but otherwise nothing much to recommend her. 'She is in a proper degree inferior to her husband; she cannot rival him, nor can he ever be ashamed of her.' This was true enough, and no doubt he considered it a handsome compliment.

Nor was he over-impressed by Edinburgh, even after a conducted tour of the city. 'Most of their buildings are very mean, and the whole town bears some resemblance to the old part of Birmingham.' Boswell occupied an apartment in St James's Court, one of those high cliff-like tenements of the Old Town, lying in the shadow of the Castle Rock in a maze of steep and narrow streets – 'very handsome and spacious rooms level with the ground on one side of the house,' Johnson reported, 'and on the other four stories high.' But in spite of recent by-laws against slops being thrown out of windows, these precipitous 'wynds' with their open sewers smelt much as they had always done, and when Boswell walked arm-in-arm with his guest through the dusk he 'could not prevent his being assailed by the evening effluvia of Edinburgh'.[16] Despite this unfortunate detail, however, Boswell was soon indulging in 'old Scottish sentiments', regretting the loss of Scotland's independence through the Act of Union, thereby provoking Johnson to an equally romantic indignation. 'Sir, never talk of your independency, who could let your Queen remain twenty years in captivity, and then be put to death without even a pretence of justice, without your attempting to rescue her; and such a Queen, too! – as every man of any gallantry of spirit would have sacrificed his life for.'[17]

Such a display of feeling was just the sort of material Boswell was hoping for, and nothing was allowed to escape his diligent note-taking, though a good many remarks and incidents would be suppressed when eventually, a year after Johnson's death, he published his *Tour to the Hebrides*. The labour of detailed recording was very great, occupying many hours of the day and night, so that Johnson at one point expressed surprise that they were 'so little together'. It could not be helped – 'My journal is really a task of much time and labour' – and it was an essential part of Boswell's genius, as important as his prodigious memory and the brilliant intimacy of his writing, that he could compel himself to sit up these long hours with his notebooks when he might have been taking his ease in Johnson's company, or even sleeping. Johnson, too, was spending his available leisure with pen and paper, keeping a 'book of remarks' and writing long serial letters to Mrs Thrale which he suggested she might keep, since they would be useful if ever he decided to write about his journey. He did not, apparently, make up his mind to do this until they were already in a wild part of the Highlands, forced to dismount so that their horses might feed and rest. Here were the rugged solitudes he had come to see; he sat on the bank of a stream and gazed about him. 'The phantoms which haunt a desert are want, and misery, and danger. . . . Man is made unwillingly acquainted

OPPOSITE Flora Macdonald, who herself related to Johnson the dramatic story of
Prince Charles's escape after the '45 Rebellion

Edinburgh, which Johnson for some reason decided 'bears some resemblance to the old town of Birmingham'

with his own weakness, and meditation shows him only how little he can sustain, and how little he can perform.' Such a vision was more realistic than Boswell's, and less romantic. 'Whether I spent the hour well I know not,' he wrote later, preparing his own account, 'for here I first conceived the thought of this narration.'[18]

The first part of the journey was civilized enough, travelling by coach up the east coast to St Andrews and Aberdeen, attended by Boswell's Bohemian manservant – 'a fine stately fellow above six feet high, who had been over a great part of Europe, and spoke many languages'. There was good academic company at St Andrews and Aberdeen (at the latter Johnson was given the freedom of the city and wore his diploma in his hat) and if Dundee had 'nothing remarkable' to offer, it was at least the prelude to a fascinating visit to Lord Monboddo, which Boswell could not resist suggesting, although (or, more probably, because) he knew that Monboddo and Johnson, who had never met, cordially disliked one another. Monboddo was an eminent lawyer and judge, five years younger than Johnson and already celebrated for what was then regarded as intellectual eccentricities. He had thought and written much on the origins of language and the evolution of man – he is best described as a pre-Darwinian evolutionist – and his reasonably sensible conclusions on both subjects had earned him a great deal of ridicule. The notions that had made him something of a laughing-stock had to do with his theory of the descent of man. The great apes, he maintained, in the remote past had shared with *Homo sapiens* the same distant ancestor – a proposition shocking to anyone who believed, as most people did, in Adam and Eve and the Book of Genesis. Human speech, he argued, must have developed originally from the grunts of animals, and it was, therefore, not impossible that an orang-utan might be taught the rudiments of speech. All this seemed ridiculous enough in the seventeen-seventies, but the theory that finally turned Monboddo into a joke was his supposition that somewhere in the world, among pygmies or bushmen or other legendary human variants, a tribe might be found which still had traces of a tail, thus proving his point that man and ape in the past had been related.[19]

All this, of course, Johnson thought highly ridiculous and laughable, especially in an eminent judge and classical scholar. 'There would be little in a fool doing it; we should only laugh; but when a wise man does it we are sorry. Other people have strange notions, but they conceal them. If they have tails, they hide them; but Monboddo is as jealous of his tail as a squirrel.' Monboddo, on the other hand, considered Johnson overrated as a writer and his formidable reputation undeserved. The idea of a confrontation between two such powerful and antipathetic minds was irresistible. Since Boswell knew Lord Monboddo well, both as a lawyer and as a friend of his father, Joseph was sent ahead with a letter as they approached his territory, with the happy result that they were invited to dinner.

Lord Monboddo: an anonymous sketch

They first saw the domain of Monboddo through pouring rain on a bleak moor – 'a wretched place, wild and naked, with a poor old house' – and found their host awaiting them at the gate, an astonishing little figure less than five feet high, clad in a farmer's suit with his wig protected from the downpour by a little round hat. (The courts being in recess, he was busy getting in his harvest.) 'In such houses,' said he in welcome, pointing to a crumbling turret, 'our ancestors lived, who were better men than we.' 'No, no, my lord,' said Johnson, 'we are as strong as they and a great deal wiser' – a reply which made Boswell tremble lest there would be 'a violent altercation . . . before we got into the house'. But there was nothing of the kind, for Monboddo had the manners of a gentleman, and Johnson, who had been warned, was on his best behaviour. They discussed Homer and emigration and ancient history, and Johnson amiably examined Monboddo's young son in Latin and found him proficient. Dangerous subjects were avoided, and Monboddo, who himself believed in early rising, cold baths, naked exercise, unheated houses and a diet of raw vegetables, handsomely set his principles aside in the matter of dinner, which included soup, ham, peas, lamb and moor-fowl. Johnson ate with his usual appetite, only observing afterwards to Boswell, 'I have done greater feats with my knife than this.' The only moment of danger came during a dispute as to 'whether the savage or the London shopkeeper had the best existence' – Monboddo, as usual, arguing for the simple life, and Johnson naturally supporting the London tradesman. But both behaved with decorum, Johnson in fairness admitting privately to his companion, 'I don't know but I might have taken the side of the savage equally, had anybody else taken the side of the shopkeeper.' ('He could, when he chose it,' Boswell noted, 'be the greatest Sophist that ever wielded a weapon.')

So the evening appeared to have gone off remarkably well, and Johnson from that time maintained a half-friendly, half-comical interest in Monboddo, whose theories he could not approve, but whose character he respected. He had no means of knowing that his host's politeness had concealed an almost hysterical dislike, and that in some respects this remarkable judge's prejudices were as violent as his own. Five years after Johnson's death Monboddo dropped the mask and wrote as he felt: 'Dr Johnson was the most invidious and malignant man I have ever known, who praised no author or book that other people praised, and in private conversation was ready to cavil at and contradict everything that was said. . . .' Even his Dictionary was no more than a laborious performance. 'There are many works useful and even necessary, which require no genius at all; and dictionary-making is one of these.' How outrageous it would have seemed to Monboddo that his own name should be remembered only because Dr Johnson thought him comical! For time has proved, as a great neurologist[20] in our own time has pointed out, that 'Monboddo was right, or at least as nearly right as anyone then could be, about human evolution. But he is forgotten, or worse still, is remembered only because Johnson laughed at him.'

Once they had crossed from east to west and reached Inverness, the real adventure began. There were few roads in the Highlands and none in the Isles, so from this point they were obliged to go on horseback, into a country, as Johnson triumphantly wrote, 'upon which perhaps no wheel has ever rolled'. The weather, as usual in these parts in autumn, was uniformly bad, rain and wind making the going difficult, mist obscuring the hills, and no doubt (since such things are a part of Highland life) in the few fine intervals midges rising in clouds from the sodden heather. They had four horses, three to ride and one for the baggage, with always a pair of Highlanders on foot to lead them, since in most places there were no regular tracks and only a local man would know the way over steep rocks and treacherous bog. Inns were rare and primitive, often no more than a huddle of huts where the fire smoked, food was short and the beds might be

A weaver's cottage on the island of Islay, Inner Hebrides, about 1800

verminous. If there were no inn, and no gentleman's house within reach (Boswell was well armed with introductions) the only shelter would be a crofter's dwelling of turf and stones, where there might be nothing to eat and nothing to sleep on but hay or heather. If the traveller 'finds only a cottage,' Johnson noted, 'he can expect little more than shelter, for the cottagers have little more for themselves; but if his good fortune brings him to the residence of a gentleman, he will be glad of a storm to prolong his stay'.

The poverty of the Highlands was everywhere painfully apparent, and its cause immediately attracted Johnson's interest as a rare phenomenon – a country forcibly and unwillingly dragged out of medieval feudalism into a low form of modern social economy. Before the Union of 1707 Highland chiefs and lairds had ruled over their territories and waged war on one another exactly as they had done in the Middle Ages. The clans were family tribes, of which every member bore the chief's name, paid for his patch of land with part of its produce, and in return was protected from the marauding of quarrelsome neighbours. The chief's word was law; he could hang a man or starve him in a dungeon; 'the laird at pleasure can feed or starve, can give bread, or withold it';[21] his power, in his own primitive and barren territory, was absolute. This had now, since little more than half a century, been changed. The law was supposed to operate as in England – which was impossible, since there were too few magistrates; tenants now had to pay rent for their miserable holdings, which was difficult in the Isles where money was practically non-existent; the lairds and chiefs had no more authority, and since the defeat of '45 had not even been allowed to carry arms or wear Highland dress – a rule which they either ignored, or evaded by becoming absentee landlords, leaving their lands to be managed by 'tacksmen' while they themselves lived in genteel economy in Edinburgh. The resulting poverty of the tenant farmers had driven them into a rage for

213

Johnson and Boswell entertained in the Highlands: a fanciful anonymous sketch

emigration, especially in absentee areas. Where the laird, himself often poor, remained at home and struggled to meet his obligations, the people stayed too; but some regions were being rapidly depopulated. 'He that cannot live as he desires at home,' Johnson wrote, 'listens to the tale of fortunate islands, and happy regions, where every man may have land of his own, and eat the product of his labour without a superior.' The American colonies might benefit, but what in the end would happen to the Hebrides? 'For nobody born in any other parts of the world will choose this country for his residence, and an island once depopulated will remain a desert.'[22]

Boswell and Johnson were both intent on gathering information, but for very different purposes. Boswell's subject, of course, was Johnson himself – how he would react, what he would say, how he would impress, amaze or alarm the natives. He was fully conscious of himself as the inspired interpreter of a unique subject, and his journal of their jaunt, when finally trimmed into publishable form, was to become, as all the world knows, one of the most entertaining books ever written. The book which Johnson was methodically compiling was very different. The history, the manner of life and foreseeable future of a unique people were his concern, and his *Journey to the Western Islands of Scotland* is in its own way almost equally enthralling. Inevitably eclipsed, after his own death, by the sheer entertainment value of Boswell's hilarious volume, it has been undeservedly neglected, and even gave some offence at the time, as we shall see. But it still remains a perceptive and sympathetic piece of observation, and anyone wishing to know about the human conditions through which Boswell skilfully conducted his celebrity will do well to read the two accounts together.

The savagery still smouldering under the surface of Highland life, in spite of civilized manners ('I never was in any house of the Islands where I did not find books in more languages than one') struck Johnson with a kind of horror. When they had been ferried across to Skye and were being entertained by Sir Alexander Maclean at Armadale, he was pleasantly struck by the ancient custom of the pipes being played during dinner. (Ignorant of and indifferent to music as he was, Johnson appeared fond of the bagpipe, and Boswell observed that he stood for some time 'with his ear close to the great drone.') But when the significance of the tune was explained to him, it was an echo of savagery. Long ago, he was told, the Macdonalds of Glengary had been at enmity with their neighbours at Culloden, and coming upon their village on a Sunday to find 'their enemies at worship, they shut them up in the church, which they set on fire'. The music at dinner, it appeared, was 'the tune that the piper played while they were burning'.[23]

Ruined churches everywhere, and what seemed to him the debasement of religious life under the rule of Calvinism, saddened and shocked him; but the details of ordinary life were his chief interest. The universal passion for whisky, for instance, which even a poor old woman in a turf hut would offer the travellers with 'true pastoral hospitality'. 'A man of the Hebrides,' he noted, '. . . as soon as he appears in the morning, swallows a glass of whisky; yet they are not a drunken race . . . but no man is so abstemious as to refuse the morning dram.' His curiosity on this point overcame his scruples when he and Boswell arrived at Inverary drenched with rain. 'After supper Mr Johnson, whom I had not seen taste any fermented liquor during all our expedition, had a gill of whisky brought to him. "Come," said he, "let me know what it is that makes a Scotsman happy,"' afterwards pronouncing it 'preferable to any English malt brandy'.

On more than one occasion, when they were not taking precautions against vermin in a primitive inn, or (as on Iona) sleeping on hay in a barn, they stayed with the local laird in his castle, which always proved to be less grand than one would imagine. A castle in the Isles was usually, Johnson found, 'a single tower of three or four stories. . . . I know not whether there be ever more than one fireplace. . . . In every castle is a well and a dungeon. . . . They are built for safety, with little regard to convenience, and with none to elegance or pleasure. It was sufficient for a laird of the Hebrides if he had a strong house, in which he could hide his wife and children from the next clan.'

The ventilation everywhere was bad, sash-windows being the favourites, with no means yet arrived at for keeping them open. 'He that would have his window open must hold it with his hand, unless . . . there be a nail which he may stick into a hole, to keep it from falling. When the room was full, as it usually was, 'a stranger may be sometimes forgiven, if he allows himself to wish for fresher air'. Even in a gentleman's house, 'well-built and elegantly furnished', there were sometimes inconvenient surprises. At such a house in Skye, after a good supper, 'I undressed myself, and felt my feet in the mire. The bed stood upon bare earth, which a long course of rain had softened to a puddle.'[24] And who that had never been in Skye before would expect to have his rest disturbed by weasels? 'There are in Skye neither rats nor mice, but the weasel is so frequent, that he is heard in houses rattling behind chests or beds, as rats in England.'[25]

The food, in which Johnson was eagerly interested, was extremely variable. In inns it was sometimes so nasty as to be uneatable, and he would go to bed hungry. In private houses the meat compared poorly with that of England – too fresh, being mostly killed after the guests' arrival – and the poultry were inclined to be skinny, though 'good enough'. Barley-bread and oatcakes were the usual fare, 'to which unaccustomed palates are not easily reconciled', and there was a sad absence of custards and tarts. The table-linen was usually elegant, but the knives, he noticed, were neither bright nor sharp, perhaps because it was only a few years since 'the men who had knives, cut the flesh into small pieces for the women, who with their fingers conveyed it to their mouths' – as Johnson himself did when eating fish, being short-sighted and afraid of bones. For the Scottish breakfast, however, he had nothing but praise. Soon after the morning dram 'may be expected the breakfast, a meal in which the Scots . . . must be confessed to excel us. The tea and coffee are accompanied not only with butter, but with honey, conserves and marmalade. If an epicure could remove by a wish, in quest of sensual gratifications, wherever he had supped he would breakfast in Scotland.'[26] He did, however, take exception to haddocks first thing in the morning, and seems not to have encountered porridge.

For Boswell, without any doubt, the highlight of the whole journey was the night they spent in the house of Allan Macdonald, Laird of Kingsburgh in Skye, for 'Kingsburgh's' wife was none other than the celebrated Flora Macdonald, who in the '45 had helped Prince Charles Edward to escape, disguised in women's clothes, from the Isle of Lewis. Here Johnson slept in the bed the Prince had slept in, and Flora Macdonald herself related the dramatic story of the escape. There was a good fire, an excellent supper and plenty to drink; this was one of several exciting occasions when Boswell drank too much, being already intoxicated by his own success in managing Johnson, keeping him in a good temper and stimulating him to talk. He was more than prepared to tolerate the occasional snubs and buffets that came his way – 'the risk', as he put it, 'of mortification from repulses'. The success of the journey was due, he was justified in believing, to 'the happy art which I have of contriving that he shall be easy wherever he goes. . . . I have also an admirable talent of leading the conversation . . . starting topics, and making the company pursue them. Mr Johnson appeared to me like a great mill, into which a subject is thrown to be ground.'[27]

Kingsburgh himself, a fine and handsome man who took no notice of the ban on Highland dress, was the kind of figure to whom Boswell's romantic imagination responded. 'He had his tartan plaid thrown about him, a large blue bonnet with a knot of black ribbon like a cockade, a brown short coat of a kind of duffle, a tartan vest with gold buttons and gold buttonholes, a bluish filibeg [Highland kilt] and tartan hose. He had jet-black hair. tied behind with screwed ringlets on each side, and was a large stately man, with a steady sensible countenance.' But alas, this noble and amiable person was a poor hand at managing his affairs, and with his famous wife was already planning to emigrate to America. The rage for emigration was spreading like a contagion. 'Last year,' Boswell was told, 'when the ship sailed from Portree for America, the people on shore were almost distracted when they saw their relations go off; they lay on the ground and tumbled, and tore the grass with their teeth. This year there was not a tear shed. The people on shore seemed to think that they would soon follow. This is a mortal sign.'

There was even a dance called 'America', in which Boswell joined one night after dinner at Armadale: 'A brisk reel is played. The first couple begin, and each sets to one – then each to another . . . and so it goes on till all are set a-going, setting and wheeling round each other. . . . It shows how emigration catches till all are set afloat.' This cheerful habit of calling on the fiddler or piper and dancing a reel or two after dinner was not one that Boswell enjoyed, but he knew that it promoted 'social happiness' – what else were the younger members of a family to do? – and on several occasions obligingly joined in and 'beat the ground with prodigious force'. Johnson meanwhile looked on benignly, or investigated his host's library, since with all that noise going on conversation was impossible. He was, in fact – though he concealed it surprisingly well – never entirely easy in any of the isles. There was little intellectual company, and once he had asked all the questions that interested him – whether on Skye, Raasay, Coll, Mull or Iona – he was apt to take refuge in books or brooding silence. On the island of Coll, where they had been driven by a storm and the violence of the weather delayed them for several days, he became gloomy and irritable. 'I want to be on the mainland,' he told Boswell, 'and go on with existence. This is a waste of life.' (One of his grievances was that in the isles he could neither receive letters from Mrs Thrale, nor send them to her.) But for Boswell even the rough weather had its compensations, for at least he saw Johnson as sick as himself – 'He got up, and looked out of the cabin hatchway, and was as pale as death. He then went to bed again, and was quiet all the time' – and on another appalling crossing observed Johnson in his bunk, 'having got free of sickness . . . lying in philosophic tranquillity, with a greyhound of Coll's at his back, keeping him warm.'

217

There were some diverting moments, certainly, in Johnson's discomforts, as when Miss Macleod at Dunvegan, finding that Johnson had caught cold and was not in the habit of wearing a nightcap, made him a large flannel one, and persuaded him to drink some brandy before going to bed.

His docility in female company was always a source of astonishment to Boswell. There was the doctor's young wife, for instance, at Coirechtachan, a 'neat, pretty little girl' of sixteen, who delighted everyone by sitting on Johnson's knee, 'and upon being bid by some of the company, put her hands round his neck and kissed him. "Do it again," said he, "and let us see who will tire first."' Laughing with the rest, Boswell could hardly believe it. 'To me it was a very high scene. To see the grave philosopher – the Rambler – toying with a little Highland wench!' It seems not to have struck him that the incident was even more delightful to Johnson than to the onlookers.

By the first week of November, back on the mainland, Boswell was congratulating himself on the great success of their 'jaunt'. Johnson had been better tempered and easier to manage than he had anticipated. 'During the whole of our tour he showed uncommon spirit, could not bear to be treated like an old or infirm man, and was very unwilling to accept of any assistance; insomuch that, at our landing at Icolmkill, when Sir Allan Maclean and I submitted to be carried on men's shoulders from the boat to the shore, as it could not be brought quite close to land, he sprang into the sea and waded vigorously out.' His manners, too, had been unusually pleasing: when Boswell remarked on his courtesy at Inverary, where he met the somewhat alarming Duchess of Argyll, Johnson had replied – whether complacently or mischievously we shall never know – 'Sir, I look upon myself as a very polite man.'

But now, approaching Auchinleck, there were hazards ahead, for Boswell's father had invited them to stay, and to refuse would certainly give great offence. So Johnson was warned, and told what subjects to avoid, especially politics and religion. Lord Auchinleck was slightly the older of the two, and in his own way equally formidable. 'His age, his office and his character had long given him an acknowledged claim to great attention, in whatever company he was; and he could ill brook any diminution of it' – which Boswell might equally well have said of Johnson. A fierce Whig and a no less rigid Presbyterian, he had read none of Johnson's works and had a strong prejudice against him by hearsay, referring to him contemptuously as 'a Jacobite fellow'.

The first day went reasonably well, in spite of the rain, but on the following day, which was equally wet, some local gentlemen called, evidently so much in awe of both Johnson and his host that there was 'little conversation'. One of them eventually plucked up courage to ask Johnson how he liked the Highlands. 'The question seemed to irritate him, for he answered, "How, Sir, can you ask me what obliges me to speak unfavourably of a country where I have been hospitably entertained? Who *can* like the Highlands? I like the inhabitants very well."' The gentleman, we are not surprised to learn, 'asked no more questions'.

But worse was to come. Next day, dining with the local minister, who was rash enough to make some offensive references to the Church of England, Johnson exploded – 'Sir, you know no more of our Church than a Hottentot' – and in a matter of hours was engaged in a furious battle with Boswell's father. This clash between his two great deities, both of whom inspired him with love and terror, so frightened Boswell that he was scarcely able to remember how it began, and – more extraordinary still – could not bring himself to record their contradictions and insults. It had started with Lord Auchinleck's collection of medals, which contained a coin of Oliver Cromwell's, which in turn led disastrously to Charles I and the even more explosive subject of Whigs versus Tories. 'They became exceedingly warm and violent, and I was very much distressed by being present at such an altercation between two men, both of whom I reverenced; yet I durst not interfere.'

This surely was the dialogue of all dialogues to preserve in the pages of his journal. But Boswell's terror was too great, and he took refuge in decorum: 'It would certainly be very unbecoming in me to exhibit my honoured father and my respected friend as intellectual gladiators, for the entertainment of the public; and therefore I suppress what would, I dare say, make an interesting scene.' An interesting scene indeed, which inspired Lord Auchinleck to bestow on his opponent the apt nickname of 'Ursa Major'! But Boswell for once is silent, denying himself a sensational climax to their incomparable journey, described at last in a grand phrase, as 'the transit of Johnson over the Caledonian Hemisphere'.

Lord Auchinleck, Boswell's father, in 1754, about twenty years before he met and quarrelled with Johnson: a portait by Allan Ramsay

15

'Life has not many things better than this...'

UCH an adventure was bound to have repercussions. Soon it was widely known that Johnson was preparing to publish an account of his travels, and everyone who had come in contact with him was eager to know what he would say of the Highlands in general and themselves in particular. Inevitably his candour gave offence, for as Dickens was to discover some seventy years later, a country which hospitably receives a famous writer expects in return to be extravagantly praised. So Johnson's plain speaking in describing what he saw, particularly the barrenness of the country and the absence of trees, was an outrage, and his views on the authenticity of Macpherson's *Ossian* – a great point of literary pride in Scotland – made him a monster. Briefly, what James Macpherson had done was to collect a number of Gaelic ballads and poems, handed down by oral tradition all over the Western Highlands, and 'translate' them into a romantic saga which he claimed to have derived from ancient manuscripts. Where there were gaps Macpherson filled them in, presenting the whole as a continuous epic written in the Gaelic tongue by Ossian, a semi-mythical bard. Johnson was sure that the whole production was a fraud, and said so. If it were not, why were the original manuscripts never produced? Since Macpherson with rude violence demanded a public apology, while still bringing no evidence to support his claim, Johnson dismissed him with contempt. 'Everything is against him. No visible manuscript: no inscription in the language: no correspondence among friends: no transaction of business, of which a single scrap remains in the ancient families. . . . If he had not talked unskilfully of *manuscripts*, he might have fought with oral tradition much longer.' The climax came with threats of physical assault, which Johnson took with sufficient seriousness to replace the great oak stick which had been lost in Scotland, and to write a letter which effectually silenced his adversary:

> I received your foolish and impudent note. Whatever insult is offered me I will do my best to repel, and what I cannot do for myself the law will do for me. I will not desist from detecting what I think a cheat, from any fear of the menaces of a ruffian.[1]

Had his opponent gone to the lengths he threatened, there was no doubt, said Boswell, 'that, old as he was, he would have made his corporal prowess be felt as much as his intellectual'. In private Johnson was willing to admit that Macpherson had 'found

James Macpherson, whose pretended translation of Ossian
was denounced by Johnson as a fraud

names, and stories, and phrases, nay passages in old songs, and with them has blended his own compositions', which is the view generally accepted today. Johnson's outspoken condemnation of the semi-fraud made him exceedingly unpopular in Scotland, though there were serious men even there who privately agreed with him.

His candid observations on Highland life, too, inevitably gave offence to some of the families who felt that their hospitality had been abused, but this was only to be expected and made no difference to the real friends he had made in Skye and elsewhere, to whom he sent barrels of porter from Thrale's brewery and copies of his own works. He was, after all, celebrated as the champion of plain speaking, and when his friend Dr Barnard, soon to be Bishop of Killaloe, suggested that if Johnson went to Ireland he might treat the Irish more roughly even than the Scots, he replied in the politest manner, 'Sir, you have no reason to be afraid of me. The Irish are not in a conspiracy to cheat the world by false representation of the merits of their countrymen. No, Sir; the Irish are a *fair people* – they never speak well of one another.'

Perhaps the greatest effect of the Scottish tour was that it turned Johnson into an almost obsessive traveller. The figure of popular legend, of a man permanently anchored in London, endlessly laying down the law in clubs and taverns, could hardly be further from the truth. In the last ten years of his life he was almost more often on the road than at home – three months of 1774 spent wandering in Wales, a month in France the following year, frequent journeys up and down between London and the midlands, between London and Brighton, to Bath, to Bristol and of course, as often as possible, to Oxford. The great plan of a tour to Italy with the Thrales was destroyed, as we shall see, by a family disaster, but the journey through Wales and the exploration of Paris and other French cities strengthened his newly discovered appetite for travel, of which he could never have enough. 'If I had money enough,' he wrote to Mrs Thrale, 'what would I do? Perhaps . . . I might go to Cairo, and down the Red Sea to Bengal, and take a ramble in India?' He was henceforth addicted to this favourite remedy for the 'vacuity of life':

A view of the Steyne at Brighton in 1778. Thrale had bought a house there in 1767, and Johnson accompanied the family on several lengthy visits, which he found dull: 'I do not much like the place.'

movement from one place to another created an illusion of achievement, and every day brought fresh subjects of curiosity.

Wales, however, proved to be something of a disappointment, though agreeable enough as a means of passing the time. The original plan had been for Italy, but since Mrs Thrale on the death of her uncle had inherited the run-down estate of Bach-y-Graig, Thrale had decided to visit Flintshire first – 'to take possession', as Johnson explained in a letter, 'of at least five hundred a year, fallen to his lady'. They travelled in Thrale's own comfortable coach with four fast horses, dining and sleeping at inns good or bad, according to luck – 'Never was so noisy nor I think so disgustful a lodging,' wrote Mrs Thrale at Edensor; 'I durst hardly venture to bed at all, there were so many rude, drunken people about' – or in the houses of convenient friends. It was not all pleasure, for Queeney had caught cold and coughed incessantly, while Thrale and Johnson were often silent and not always in the best of humours. ''Tis so melancholy a thing,' Mrs Thrale scribbled in her journal, 'to have nobody to speak to about one's clothes, or one's child, or one's health, or what comes uppermost. Nobody but *Gentlemen*, before whom one must suppress everything except the mere formalities of conversation and by whom everything is to be commended or censured.'[2]

She was soon to discover, from bouts of sickness on the journey, that she was again pregnant, an unwelcome discovery which briefly depressed her spirits; but not for long, for when the men were silent or critical she felt herself 'obliged to be civil for four'. Johnson at least had the pleasure of showing Lichfield to his friends and his friends to Lichfield, staying at the Swan, visiting Lucy Porter, Peter Garrick and the budding poetess Anna Seward before moving on to Ashbourne, where Dr Taylor entertained them handsomely to three weeks of sightseeing tours and good dinners. Johnson, too, was keeping a journal of the tour, a sober and brief affair, since Wales made little appeal to his imagination and he probably shared Thrale's disappointment in the derelict condition of Bach-y-Graig and its woods. After 'three months from home among dunces of all ranks and sorts', as Mrs Thrale privately put it, the party was electrified on the journey home by the news that Parliament was dissolved, and that they must hurry back to Southwark to start canvassing.

This was stimulating news for Thrale, and perhaps also for Johnson, who enjoyed his part in an election bustle; but Mrs Thrale's journal strikes a note of dismay as she learns that their destination is not to be beloved Streatham, but the gloomy Borough. 'So all my hopes of pleasure blow away. I thought to have lived at Streatham in quiet and comfort, have kissed my children and cuffed them by turns, and had a place always for them to play in, and here I must be shut up in that odious dungeon, where nobody will come near me, the children are to be sick for want of air, and I am never to see a face but Mr Johnson's. Oh what a life that is! and how truly do I abhor it!'[3]

Was she already feeling that Johnson's company, where there was no escape, could be an intolerable burden?

The tour to France in the following year was a much more lively enterprise. Thrale had been successfully returned to Parliament, vigorously supported by Mrs Thrale's canvassing throughout the Borough, and by Johnson's rapidly written political pamphlet, *The Patriot*, aimed at the pretensions of 'the mob'. (It is worth remembering, as Donald Greene has pointed out, that 'most of Johnson's contemporaries would have

The last two pages of Mrs Thrale's *Welsh Journal*

There was an old Mr. Lowndes dined with us, and got very drunk talking Politics with Will Burke & my Master after Dinner. Lord Verney & Edmund came home at Night very much flustered with Liquor, & I thought how I had spent three Months from home among Dunces of all Ranks and Sorts, but had never seen a Mandrunk till I came among the Wits— this was Accidental indeed, but what of that? it was so.

30. Sept: when I rose Mr. Thrale inform'd me that the Parliament was suddenly dissolved & that all the World was to bustle that we were to go to Southwark not to Streatham a canvass away. I heard the first part of this report with Pleasure, the latter with Pain; nothing but a real Misfortune could I think affect me

so much as the thoughts of going to Town thus to settle for the Winter before I have had any Enjoyment of Streatham at all, & so all my hopes of Pleasure blow away. I thought to have lived at Streatham in Quiet & comfort have kissed my Children & cuffed them by turns, & had a Place for them always to play in; & here I must be shut up in that odious Duageon, where nobody will come near me, the Children are to be sick for want of Air, & I am never to see a face but Mr. Johnson's— Oh what a Life that is? and how truly do I abhor it.

at Noon however I saw my Girls, & thought Susan vastly improved. at Evening I saw my Boys & liked them very well too, How much is there always to thank God for! but Dare not enjoy poor Streatham lest I should be forced to quit it.

agreed with him that there are limits of ignorance below which the privilege of partici-pating in the government of a country should not be extended'.)[4] Working together to promote Thrale's interest, they found the excitement of the crowds contagious. 'A rough fellow one day,' Mrs Thrale recorded,'. . . a hatter by trade, seeing Mr Johnson's beaver in a state of decay, seized it suddenly with one hand, and clapping him on the back with the other, "Ah, Mr Johnson," says he, "this is no time to be thinking about *hats*." "No, no, Sir," replies our Doctor in a cheerful tone, "hats are of no use now, as you say, except to throw up in the air and huzza with" – accompanying his words with the true election *halloo*.'[5]

Mrs Thrale by the late summer of 1775 was in good health, and for once not pregnant. In April she had given birth to a fragile girl who would not live long, and in July had lost her younger boy, Ralph, who had suffered brain damage from meningitis; but Queeney, Harry and the two smaller girls were in excellent health, and though Thrale was not yet willing to go as far as Italy, all were agreed that a month in Paris would be an interesting experience. The two little daughters were settled with a governess in Kensington and Harry, the most attractive of all the children and his father's favourite, was attending day-school. 'A better or finer, a wiser or kinder boy than Harry', his mother wrote, 'cannot be found: he goes to Jenning's free school here in Southwark, and is half adored by master and scholars, by parents and servants . . . he is so rational, so attentive, so good; nobody can help being pleased with him.'

It was a propitious moment for a holiday, and in September the Thrales set out for Dover with Queeney and Johnson, taking Baretti as courier and interpreter, a man-servant called Samuel Greaves, and Mrs Thrale's personal maid, Molly. Baretti, that talented, impecunious and difficult man, had for the past two years been tutoring Queeney in Spanish and Italian and had become more or less an inmate of the household, living at Streatham, Johnson told Boswell, 'as at an inn'. 'I suppose he meant,' the latter noted, 'gave value for what he got, and did not mind whether the landlady liked him or no.' Already there was a certain antagonism between the two, but for the month in France Baretti's usefulness outweighed his disadvantages.

The party followed the usual course of well-to-do English tourists – visits to churches, art galleries, the theatre, the opera, the Palais Royal, Versailles, Fontainebleau (where with other visitors they were able to stare at the royal family at dinner) and the normal round of sightseeing and shopping. Both Mrs Thrale and Johnson kept a diary of the tour, but the two accounts are very different. Refusing to speak French – he wrote it fairly well but was unwilling to risk conversation – Johnson found few Frenchmen with whom he could converse in Latin, and seems in any case to have been disinclined to do more than make brief notes of places visited and things observed. Mrs Thrale, on the other hand, rattled away in schoolgirl French and wrote detailed accounts of her usually lively impressions. Both of them show a certain insular prejudice against the foreigner, and no doubt in pre-Revolutionary France there were many things that shocked them. 'The great in France', said Johnson with truth, 'live very magnificently, but the rest very miserably. There is no happy middle state as in England' – and then added, with true British contempt, 'The shops of Paris are mean; the meat in the markets is such as would be sent to a gaol in England. . . . The French are an indelicate people. . . . France is worse than Scotland in everything but climate.' There were details of French manners, certainly, which displeased all the party – ladies of quality blowing down the spouts of tea-pots when they would not pour, a footman putting sugar into Johnson's coffee with his fingers, young ladies hawking and spitting, a court lady's close-stool open beside her bed as the visitors were shown through, not to mention the crude behaviour of the lower orders in Paris, where 'the women sit down in the streets as composedly as if they were in a convenient-house with the doors shut'.[6]

The splendid libraries and monasteries he visited were undoubtedly the greatest pleasures of Johnson's tour. Religious houses in those days were a regular part of any traveller's itinerary, and since monks could be relied upon to speak Latin he was able to indulge the sympathetic curiosity he had always felt towards the monastic life. 'If I were to visit Italy,' he had once written to Baretti, 'my curiosity would be more attracted by convents than by palaces,' and here, to his satisfaction, he was respectfully received by several orders, in Paris spending a whole day with the English Benedictines – 'meagre day; soup meagre; herrings, eels, both with sauce; fried fish; lentils. . . . I parted very tenderly from the Prior'. (This same Prior, Father Cowley, assured him that in future a cell would always be kept ready for his use – a civility which has led some people to suppose that Johnson had secret leanings towards conversion. It is true that he was emotionally attracted to 'a Church where there are so many helps to get to heaven', but he also saw too much that he could not swallow. 'I would be a Papist if I could. I have fear enough; but an obstinate rationality prevents me.')[7]

Mrs Thrale, too, through the good offices of a convent-bred friend of hers, derived as much pleasure and interest from her visits to convents as from anything in the tour. What could be more enthralling, after all, than to see how these religious ladies of good family lived in their grated cells? The Poor Clares of Rouen shocked her, certainly – in dirty habits, rheumatic and foul-smelling, they were committed to a life of privation and misery that she could hardly believe commendable to God. But the Benedictines and the English 'Blue' and 'Austin' nuns lived very comfortably – 'Their beds are soft, their linen fine, their table plentiful and their house convenient'; they had even a library and billiard-room, with card-tables, backgammon and chess. The Benedictine ladies in particular had silver cups and forks at table and 'their house full of lap-dogs, cats and parrots.' Where was the reputed hardship of monastic life, she wondered, when 'a well-endowed convent is of all others the most perfect refuge from poverty'?[8]

How Henry Thrale amused himself during this 'month of extreme expense, some pleasure, and some profit' is less clear. He paid for everything, apart from personal shopping (Johnson himself bought a French wig, a new hat and a pair of white stockings), was entertained and gave some dinners in return, listening with amiability to a great deal of multilingual conversation. At least he enjoyed himself sufficiently to decide on a further foreign adventure in the same company, and with Baretti planned an ambitious tour of Italy for the following spring.

The Abbess of one of the French convents had been anxious to have explained to her 'the nature and cause of the rebellion in America', which the Thrales as well as Johnson, being Tories, naturally regarded as disgraceful treachery. Fighting had been going on sporadically since January 1775, and Lord North's Government had officially declared war a month before the Thrales left for France. Johnson had been pressed into service for propaganda purposes, and had rapidly produced a pamphlet, *Taxation No Tyranny*, which soon became notorious for the severity of its opinions. Even the Government felt obliged to tone down some of his remarks, but on the whole one would admit today that Johnson's arguments, though harshly stated, were logical from the Tory point of view – namely, that a colony which depends for defence on the mother country should contribute to that defence by paying taxes; that a Crown colony has no right to secede without the Crown's consent; and that any such defiance should be dealt with by force of arms. 'The situation of 1775', as an eminent American authority has pointed out, 'was duplicated within the United States itself in 1861, when Lincoln made the decision that Johnson advocated. . . . If it was right for the Southern states to be denied the power of secession in 1860, it was equally right for the thirteen colonies to be denied the power of secession in 1776.'[9] But Johnson's arguments, however sound theoretically, were expressed in so satirical a manner that his prejudice against the Americans became obvious, and did more harm than good to the party he was enlisted to support. Even Boswell was embarrassed by his tone and wished he had never written on the subject. Boswell, however, did not share Johnson's horror of slavery, which prejudiced him emotionally against the Americans, and which he had many times very forcibly expressed; he was shocked, therefore, by his rudeness in describing the Resolutions of the American Congress as 'too wild for folly and too foolish for madness', and then demanding, 'How is it that we hear the loudest yelps for liberty among the drivers of negroes?'

In March 1776, when Boswell managed to escape from his Edinburgh duties for a few weeks, he was surprised to find that Johnson had moved house, and was now to be found at No. 8 Bolt Court, another alley off 'his favourite Fleet Street'. This was to be his final home for the years that remained to him, and here it was that there gradually assembled that eccentric and quarrelsome household that we know best from his own ruefully comical descriptions. Miss Williams of course was in charge, treated always by Johnson with respectful indulgence despite the 'peevishness' which others remarked and which had clearly grown more acrimonious with age. Levett, too, was an old man now, still conducting the remains of his humble practice from the garret. Frank the Negro appears to have married by this time, since there are references in letters to his English 'Betsey', but his wife and children seem to have lived elsewhere until a year before Johnson's death, when they were absorbed into Bolt Court with the rest. From at least 1778 there were several newcomers who contributed vigorously to the quarrelling and complaints which went on both above and below stairs: these were Mrs Desmoulins (Tetty's old friend) and her daughter, to whom Johnson allowed half a guinea a week – 'above a twelfth part of his pension,' as Boswell calculated – and a room which they shared with an unaccountable young female called Poll Carmichael. Who this young person was nobody knows. It has been suggested that she was possibly the prostitute whom Johnson found ill and exhausted in the street one night and carried home, having her 'taken care of with all tenderness for a long time, at considerable expense, till she was restored to health', but this is a random guess, and Johnson himself admitted that he could not 'rightly remember' how she came among them. He had 'some hopes' of her at first, he told Mrs Thrale, but soon discovered her to be 'a stupid slut', as well as a great quarreller and maker of trouble. The final member of this incongruous household, which Johnson sometimes in jest referred to as his 'seraglio', was a servant, Mrs White, of whom nothing is known except that he left her a hundred pounds in his will.

Since such a coalition was hardly likely to produce harmony, Johnson's charity at home can be said to have wrecked his domestic peace. 'He really', wrote Mrs Thrale, 'was oftentimes afraid of going home, because he was so sure to be met at the door with numberless complaints; and he used to lament . . . that they made his life miserable from the impossibility he found of making theirs happy, when every favour he bestowed on one was wormwood to the rest.' He treated the theme as comedy in his letters: 'Williams hates everybody; Levett hates Desmoulins, and does not love Williams; Desmoulins hates them both; Poll loves none of them' – and later, 'Discord and discontent reign in my humble habitation as in the palaces of monarchs. . . . There is as much malignity amongst us as can well subsist, without any thoughts of daggers and poisons': but his heart sank each time he returned to Bolt Court, where the atmosphere of sulks and vendettas made him more eager than ever for the peace and comfort of Streatham or Ashbourne, or better still, the enchantment of a spring journey to Italy in the company of Henry Thrale and his 'dearest of all Ladies'.

There was time before leaving, however, for a quick round of his old friends at Oxford, Birmingham, Lichfield and Ashbourne, and with Boswell at hand for company such a 'jaunt' was not to be resisted. Travelling part of the way by the rapid post-chaise which Johnson loved – 'Life has not many things better than this' – they put up at Oxford and Birmingham, finally reaching Lichfield after a journey so crammed with friendly encounters and good conversation that Boswell must have sat up the better part of each night to record it. At Lichfield they settled at the Three Crowns, next door to Johnson's own house, which Boswell visited 'with reverence', and were in the midst of visiting and dining and enjoying themselves when, at breakfast with Lucy Porter on the third morning, a letter arrived from the Southwark brewery clerk with the news that Harry Thrale had suddenly died, and that the bereaved parents were anxious to have Johnson back in London.

Why this boy's death should have so affected Johnson, Boswell was at a loss to understand. True, Harry was the Thrales' only surviving son and the third child they had lost within a year, but was it reasonable to describe his death as 'one of the most dreadful things that has happened in my time', or to exclaim with anguish, 'This is a total extinction to their family, as much as if they were sold into captivity'? But Johnson had genuinely loved Harry, 'as I never expect to love any other little boy'; had responded with delight to his intelligence and charm, and among other playful arrangements had loved to give him a penny each time he came to his room to call him in the morning. Even on his own account, he assured Boswell, he 'would have gone to the extremity of the earth to have preserved this boy'. But Johnson also knew what this sudden death, in the midst of life and health and apparently from a ruptured appendix, would mean to his 'Master' and 'Mistress'; how easily it could reduce to ruin their whole fabric of family life. It is perhaps not too fanciful to say that Johnson's own life was never quite the same after Harry's death, for the effect of this loss on the apparently unemotional Henry Thrale was a perceptible and disastrous damage to personality, subtly affecting the lives of all of them in turn. His hope, his belief in the future died in that moment; he became neurotically withdrawn and restless, no longer capable of application, devoting himself at last to an obstinate gluttony as the only comfort and consolation left him in this world. So came about the self-induced thrombosis which heralded his death, leaving Mrs Thrale free to do as she pleased with the rest of her life, and Johnson, to his dismay, deprived of the emotional support on which he had depended too much.

This unimaginable sequence, however, was to develop slowly over the next few years. When Johnson and Boswell returned to London – in no great hurry, after several days spent with Dr Taylor at Ashbourne – it was to find that Mrs Thrale, unable to bear the emotions of Harry's funeral, had fled with Queeney to Bath, and that Thrale was brooding in solitude at Southwark. There was little that Johnson could do to help, beyond writing frequent letters and undertaking to visit the 'two babies', Susy and Sophy, at Kensington. Their mother had heard with great alarm that they had caught chicken-pox, but he found them, he told her, 'indeed a little spotted with their disorder, but as brisk and gay as youth and health can make them. I took a paper of sweetmeats, and spread them on the table. They took great delight to show their governess the various animals that were made of sugar, and when they had eaten as much as was fit, the rest were laid up for tomorrow.'[10] Johnson's sure touch with children, always easy and affectionate, was only one of many emotional ties which bound him to the Thrale household.

From the time of Harry's death, however, the family life at Streatham began to change, and Johnson's impregnable position, very gradually, to weaken. Of this at first he had no idea, and in some respects the social life that he increasingly shared was gayer and more various than before. Henry Thrale had been too stunned to undertake the Italian tour, but his restlessness demanded change and movement – extensive trips to London, holidays in Brighton and Bath, bigger and grander dinner-parties with impressive company, eventually a house of his own at Brighton and a succession of elegant rented ones in town. From all this social activity, and in spite of two more childbirths in successive years (two more unwanted girls, of whom one survived), Mrs Thrale, resilient as ever, derived brilliant benefit as her circle of acquaintance widened. Even the exclusive Bluestockings, those formidable intellectual ladies of whom Mrs Elizabeth Montagu was the queen, admitted her more or less into their circle – a promotion which gratified her even more than her social success. This, too, however, she now enjoyed to a degree unknown before – was presented at Court, spent a good deal on clothes and jewelry, was frequently mentioned in the newspapers and to some extent achieved her ambition to be regarded as a social and literary lioness. None of this, of course, could she have achieved simply as the wife of Henry Thrale: but as the hostess in whose drawing-room the now legendary Dr Johnson could be seen

OPPOSITE Johnson: the Reynolds portrait commissioned by Henry Thrale for his new library at Streatham

228

and heard, with Burke, Garrick, Reynolds, Dr Burney and others, she had achieved a status that was the crown of her career. To mark the advancing eminence of the Thrale family, Reynolds was commissioned to paint thirteen portraits of themselves and their friends for the handsome newly built library at Streatham. Mrs Thrale with Queeney, now a self-possessed thirteen-year-old, was hung over the fireplace, Henry Thrale above the doorway, Johnson, Garrick, Goldsmith, Burke, Dr Burney, Reynolds himself and other notables disposed about the room over the bookcases. Baretti was originally one of these, but his quarrelsome nature and increasing jealousy of Mrs Thrale where Queeney was concerned, soon disqualified him for the role of esteemed friend. He 'went away from Thrale's', Johnson told Boswell, 'in some whimsical fit of disgust, or ill-nature, without taking any leave,' and it is probable that after this piece of rudeness his portrait was regarded less favourably than the rest.

It is entirely typical of Johnson that in this last period of his life, when his health was beginning to fail and the drama was approaching which would destroy his happiness, we receive impressions on every hand of a Johnson so much at ease, so lively in wit and delighting in old and new friendships, that if it were not for his letters and diaries we might suppose him in old age to have achieved contentment. But he was no more consistent now than he had ever been: no period of his life shows a more extraordinary pattern of contradictions.

These were the years when, working partly in the comfortable library at Streatham, he was producing what he at first modestly described to Boswell as 'little lives, and little prefaces, to a little edition of the English poets', but which developed, as he became more deeply involved, into his major critical work. The 'little lives' blossomed into judicious and highly readable biographies, stirring up both admiration and hostile criticism. At the end of four years' sporadic labour he wrote that he had 'finished the Lives of the Poets, which I wrote in my usual way, dilatorily and hastily, unwilling to work, and working with vigour and haste'. It had been, however, one of his more pleasurable undertakings, with Mrs Thrale often working as amanunensis and copyist and reading aloud from Johnson's proof-sheets at the Streatham breakfast-table in what was 'certainly', as Fanny Burney remembered, 'the most sprightly and agreeable meeting of the day'.

Fanny Burney herself contributed not a little to Johnson's sociable gaiety during these last years of Streatham, for she undoubtedly possessed at least some of the qualities that he found most enchanting in a woman; since she was also young enough to have been his granddaughter they fell easily into a playful and affectionate relation. It had been, of course, the greatest possible sensation at Streatham when it was discovered that Dr Burney's unobtrusive daughter was the anonymous author of *Evelina*, the most sensationally best-selling novel of the day, and from that moment Johnson teased, admired and petted her in the loving and provocative manner in which he was adept. She was for ever running from the room to hide her blushes, or to record the tone of his talk in diary or letter: 'Johnson has more fun, and comical humour, and love of nonsense about him, than almost anybody I ever saw. . . .' 'In the evening he was as lively and as full of wit and sport as I have ever seen him. . . .' 'Dr Johnson was in the utmost good humour. . . .' 'At tea we all met again, and Dr Johnson was gaily sociable.' 'Dr Johnson, as usual, came last into the library; he was in high spirits and full of mirth and sport.' 'Dr Johnson was charming, both in spirits and humour. I really think he grows gayer and gayer daily, and more *ductile* and pleasant. . . .' The Burneys, father and daughter, were a valuable addition to the regular Streatham circle, for while Fanny could amuse Johnson during the afternoon Dr Burney was happy to sit up with him at night, thus relieving Mrs Thrale of an exhausting duty when, during her last pregnancies, staying up to make tea for him sometimes long past midnight caused her legs to 'swell like columns'.

Yet, to compare the observations of Boswell, Mrs Thrale and Fanny Burney with the surviving fragments of Johnson's own meditations is to turn from daylight to darkness. (All three of them, aware by this time that the great man could hardly live for ever, were recording everything about him which struck them as memorable, and Fanny Burney even found amusement in observing Boswell observing: 'The attention which it excited in Mr Boswell amounted almost to pain. His eyes goggled with eagerness; he leant his ear almost to the shoulder of the Doctor, and his mouth dropped open to catch every syllable that might be uttered; nay, he seemed not only to dread losing a word, but to be anxious not to miss a breathing, as if hoping from it, latently or mystically, some information.')

Johnson's own brief comments on himself about this time are almost invariably gloomy. 'When I survey my past life, I discover nothing but a barren waste of time with some disorders of body, and disturbances of the mind very near to madness; which I hope He that made me will suffer to extenuate many faults, and excuse many deficiences. Yet much remains to be repented and reformed.' And again, before Easter 1779, 'I am now to review the last year, and find little but dismal vacuity, neither business nor pleasure; much intended and little done. My health is much broken; my nights afford me little rest. I have tried opium, but its help is counterbalanced with great disturbance; it prevents the spasms, but it hinders sleep. O God, have mercy on me.' Despondently reviewing his seventieth year, he makes a note that he is maintaining Mrs Desmoulins and her daughter – 'other good of myself I know not where to find, except a little charity.'[11]

The 'little charity' is an extraordinary understatement even by Johnson's exacting standards. He was still at this time supporting Levett and blind Miss Williams as well as the tiresome Poll Carmichael; sending regular money to Tom Johnson, an impoverished cousin, and paying for the keep of a lunatic female of his mother's family. His letters and diaries abound with notes of sums given, contrived or begged from friends, and Frances Reynolds among others remembered his often emptying his pockets for the needy: 'As he returned to his lodgings about one or two o'clock in the morning, he often saw poor children asleep on thresholds and stalls, and . . . used to put pennies into their hands to buy them a breakfast.'[12] Johnson's day-to-day charity, which he dismissed so lightly, went always to those who needed it, whether or not they were deserving. 'It is sufficient that our brother is in want,' he had once written in a sermon; 'by which way he brought his want upon him, let us not too curiously inquire. We likewise are sinners.'[13]

A sinner for whom he had neither liking nor admiration, but for whom he went to great lengths in an attempt to save him from the gallows, was the Reverend William Dodd, the handsome and fashionable London parson who in 1777 found himself in Newgate on a charge of forging a broker's bond for £4,200 – a crime which he immediately (upon arrest) repented and confessed, returning the money and evidently hoping that his singular lapse in behaviour would be overlooked. He had some years before been tutor to the young Lord Chesterfield, godson and heir of Johnson's one-time 'patron', and finding himself in debt after a few seasons of luxurious living, had forged his wealthy pupil's signature. Unfortunately for Dr Dodd, and in spite of his confession and restitution, forgery, together with some two hundred other offences under the 'Bloody Code', was still a hanging matter. Lord Chesterfield made no move for his defence, and the Lord Chief Justice, Lord Mansfield – who according to Horace Walpole 'never felt pity, and never relented unless terrified' – was adamant; so that 'the unfortunate Dr Dodd', as he came to be called, was sentenced to be hanged.

Public reaction to the trial was emotional and extraordinary, producing a record number of petitions to Parliament and the King – the biggest supported by twenty-three thousand signatures on a scroll of parchment thirty-seven and a half yards long – and Johnson, at Dodd's own request, was implored to help. This he immediately did, working at speed and in considerable distress of mind to compose, first, Dodd's speech before the Recorder at the Old Bailey at the passing of sentence, then letters of appeal from Dodd to the King and from Mrs Dodd to the Queen, the draft of the great petition which consumed so much parchment, and finally, a farewell address to the condemned

ABOVE Fanny Burney, later Madame d'Arblay: a portrait by her cousin, Edward Burney. LEFT The ill-fated Dr Dodd, whom Johnson attempted to befriend

man's fellow convicts in Newgate, the true authorship of all of these, of course, being kept secret.

The Convict's Address to his Unhappy Brethren, published at the time of the hanging, was the occasion of one of Johnson's most famous observations, intended (though this is not usually remembered) to deflect suspicion as to who might have written it. When a Mr Seward expressed a doubt that it was not Dodd's own, 'because it had a great deal more force of mind in it than anything known to be his', Johnson carefully replied, 'Why should you think so? Depend upon it, Sir, when a man knows that he is to be hanged in a fortnight, it concentrates his mind wonderfully.'

This for nearly two hundred years has been quoted as a grim jest, but Johnson's feelings in the affair had nothing to do with wit. Apart from his horror at the atrocious punishment, and disgust at 'the days when the prisons of this city are emptied into the grave', it particularly distressed him that the shame of a public execution should fall on a clergyman of the Church of England. Would it not be more in the interests of religion, he asked in one of his appeals, 'to bury such an offender in the obscurity of perpetual exile, than to expose him in a cart, and on the gallows, to all who for any reason are enemies to the clergy?' Deportation was punishment enough, but less dreadful for a clergyman than hanging.

When all appeals had failed, as he had feared they would, Johnson addressed himself to the almost impossible task of writing a final letter to Dodd, to be read on the morning of his execution. He had that day received the condemned man's grateful farewell, written at midnight – 'Accept, though *great* and *good* heart, my earnest and fervent thanks and prayers for all thy benevolent and kind efforts on my behalf. Oh! Dr Johnson! . . . You was my Comforter, my Advocate, and my Friend![14] – and now must summon whatever words might conceivably help to support him in his final ordeal.

Dodd apparently fell into a deep sleep after writing to Johnson, but waking a little after four in the morning 'did not immediately recollect what he was to suffer, and the moment that he did . . . expressed the utmost horror and agony of mind'.[15] A few hours later, in showery weather and before the greatest crowds ever assembled since the execution of Jonathan Wild, Dr Dodd endured with calm and dignity the slow cart journey from Newgate to Tyburn, and died without a struggle. Is it too much to suppose that in Johnson's words, as much as in his own prayers, he had found strength and comfort?

Dear Sir,

That which is appointed to all men is now coming upon you. . . . Be comforted: your crime, morally or religiously considered, has no very deep dye of turpitude. It corrupted no man's principles; it attacked no man's life. It involved only a temporary and reparable injury. Of this, and of all other sins, you are earnestly to repent; and may God, who knoweth our frailty and desireth not our death, accept your repentance. . . .

In requital of those well-intended offices which you are pleased so emphatically to acknowledge, let me beg that you make in your devotions one petition for my eternal welfare.

I am, dear Sir, Your affectionate servant,
Sam: Johnson[16]

16

'The night cometh...'

HE last years of Johnson's life are so overshadowed by the drama which violently and finally estranged him from Mrs Thrale that it is impossible to see them clearly except from the intimate vantage-point of Streatham. Boswell's account of these four years occupies almost a quarter of his whole biography, this being the period when he was able to spend more time with Johnson than was usually possible, and when his hero's genius for talk and zest for company were as great as ever, if not greater. But Boswell was never, in the early stages, aware of the sleeping volcano which was to erupt in scandal, and in any case was always jealous of Mrs Thrale and anxious to belittle her personal importance to Johnson. So, although the final volume of the *Life* is by far the most detailed part of his great work and the most enjoyable, we need other evidence as well if we hope to come any closer to the truth. Mrs Thrale's own private memoranda and her published *Anecdotes* are, of course, invaluable, though they must always – particularly the *Anecdotes* – be read with caution, as an injured and indignant woman's self-justification. Fanny Burney, too, makes her over-emotional and scandalized contribution, and Johnson's own diaries and letters shed a lurid and melancholy light. But to understand the whole story as it unfolds one needs more than evidence: knowledge of the human heart, with all its irrational violence, is also necessary.

If Henry Thrale had outlived Johnson, as in the normal course he would expect to do, things would have been very different; Johnson would have been nursed and cared for to the end. But Thrale in middle age – he was only fifty-two when he died – seemed set on a course of self-destruction from which wife, physicians and friends were powerless to deflect him. He suffered his first stroke in his sister's house at the reading of a will, when he learned that his brother-in-law had died insolvent and that the large sums he had invested with him had vanished. He presently recovered, but remained lethargic; only constant movement from place to place, frequent and opulent entertaining and a slavish passion for the celebrated Sophy Streatfeild, kept him awake. (Miss Streatfeild, we remember, prettiest and most languishing of the 'Blues', was famous for being able to weep tears on request, even in the middle of dinner.) Another stroke cost him his seat in Parliament, since news of his condition had got abroad and he was in no state to be shown to the electors. Yet nothing would induce him to stop overeating. 'After the

James Boswell in 1786, while he was working on his *Life of Johnson*

denunciation of your physicians this morning,' Johnson warned him, 'such eating is little better than suicide.' But such advice, like the pleading of his wife and the shocked protests of Fanny Burney and Mrs Montagu, only encouraged him to beckon the footman for another dish. Even the ominous warning of his physician, that 'either there must be *legal* restraint or certain death',[1] was brushed aside. And so the end came.

On April 3rd 1781, after eating so much of eight courses at dinner that 'the very servants were frighted', Thrale retired to bed early, apparently none the worse. But when Queeney presently went into his room she found him lying on the floor, and to the girl's startled question he replied, 'I choose it; I lie so o' purpose', and would not move. His doctors were instantly summoned and Johnson sent for, but 'one violent fit of the apoplexy followed another', and nothing could be done. One of his physicians, wrote Mrs Thrale, 'seeing death certain, quitted the house without even prescribing. . . . Johnson who was sent for at 11 o'clock never left him, for while breath remained *he* still hoped.' But by six o'clock on the morning of the 4th Thrale was dead, and the friendship which Johnson had always acknowledged with gratitude was over. 'I felt almost the last flutter of his pulse, and looked for the last time upon the face that for fifteen years had never been turned upon me but with respect or benignity. Farewell. May God that delighteth in mercy, have had mercy upon thee.'[2]

To Mrs Thrale, who once more could not face a funeral and had fled with Queeney to Brighton, Johnson wrote almost daily, offering what comfort he could and making no secret of his own loss. 'No death since that of my wife has ever oppressed me like this. . . . I am afraid of thinking what I have lost. I never had such a friend before.' The consolations he offered from a distance were partly practical and partly, as one would expect, religious: since he had no inkling of what the sequel to her widowhood would be, it could never strike him that the future he earnestly hoped for was somewhat barren. God, he assured her, had given her 'happiness in marriage to a degree of which without personal knowledge, I should have thought the description fabulous'. (Had he really had no suspicion of the lack of love between them?) God could now, if she addressed herself to Him, give her 'another mode of happiness as a mother, and at last the happiness of losing all temporal cares in the thoughts of an eternity in heaven'.[3] Even in these early days of her affliction it is unlikely that Mrs Thrale regarded this pious prospect with enthusiasm.

For in the death of Thrale there was an element which his widow, at least in the privacy of her own thoughts, was quick to acknowledge – the possibility of freedom. There could be an end to her connection with the brewery trade and all its plebeian associations, which she had come to hate. During Thrale's decline she had had to take an ever-increasing part in the firm's management, and she was sick to death of it. Her husband had treated her generously enough in his will; two thousand pounds a year or thirty thousand pounds outright if the brewery were sold, the daughters besides being handsomely provided for; and now she was eager to be rid of her 'golden millstone'. 'Perhaps I may rid my hands of it,' she confided to her diary, '. . . I am half inclined to hope for happiness once more'; and within two months was able to write ecstatically, 'Well! Here have I with the grace of God, and the assistance of good friends, completed – I really think very happily – the greatest event of my life. I have sold my brew-house to Barclay the rich Quaker for £135,000. . . . I have by this bargain purchased peace and stable fortune, restoration to my original rank in life, and a situation undisturbed by commercial jargon, unpolluted by commercial frauds, undisgraced by commercial connections.' At last she was back on the social level of her Welsh ancestors.[4]

But there was another influence which had been unconsciously at work for some time past, and which now began to insinuate itself into her thoughts and feelings in a disturbing manner. Some two years before, at a musical evening given by Dr Burney, she had met the Italian singer Gabriel Piozzi, and had been so misguided in her attempts to liven up what proved to be a very dull party – imitating the singer's gestures behind his back and making faces – that Dr Burney in a whisper had reproved her. She had quite forgotten the incident when two years later she encountered Piozzi at the door of a bookseller's shop in Brighton, and he, apparently not much caring to be accosted, did not recognize her. In such unpromising beginnings can the seeds of irresistible passions germinate. Piozzi had by this time become sufficiently celebrated for Mrs Thrale to covet him as a singing-master for Queeney; she was also moved by his appearance, for she saw, or fancied she saw, a touching resemblance to her father. So Piozzi became one of Streatham's most regular and agreeable frequenters, and Mrs Thrale began to pay attention to music, through the music-master, with an interest she had never discovered before. This innocent beginning had a disquieting undertone, discernible even in the early entries in *Thraliana*: 'Piozzi is become a prodigious favourite with me; he is so intelligent a creature, so discerning, one can't help wishing for his good opinion. His singing surpasses everybody's for taste, tenderness and true elegance: his hand on the forte-piano too is so soft, so sweet, so delicate, every tone goes to one's heart, I think; and fills the mind with emotions one would not be without, though inconvenient enough sometimes. . . .'

On the day before Thrale died Mrs Byron, grandmother of the poet, watching the singing-master at the harpsichord, had whispered, 'You know, I suppose, that that man is in love with you?' – and was lightly snubbed for her impertinence. Now, little more than a year after Thrale's death, his widow had to admit to herself that it was *she* who was in love, and never having known the touch of passion before, it was only with the greatest difficulty that she kept her secret.

Secret it had to be for the present, since she guessed well enough at the outcry if she should choose to marry Piozzi. She had already refused three proposals from self-interested gentlemen, and had had to bear a good deal of suggestive gossip in the newspapers as to whether or not she intended to marry Johnson. Such a grotesque possibility had never entered her head, but it was freely discussed all over London and Boswell had distinguished himself by writing an indecent *Ode* only the day after Thrale's funeral. This he had recited at various (we must assume all-male) gatherings, and if any of it reached Mrs Thrale's ears, as it probably did, it is not surprising that she began to loathe him. A few lines from this *Ode by Dr Samuel Johnson to Mrs Thrale* are a fair sample of the whole:

> My dearest lady! view your slave,
>   Behold him as your very SCRUB,
> Eager to write as author grave,
>   Or govern well the brewing tub . . .
>
> Ascetick now thy lover lives,
>   Nor dares to touch, nor dares to kiss,
> Yet prurient fancy sometimes gives
>   A pre-libation of our bliss.
>
> Convulsed in love's tumultuous throws,
>   We feel the aphrodisian spasm;
> Tir'd nature must at last repose,
>   Then Wit and Wisdom fill the chasm.[5]

That Johnson ever heard of the outrageous squib one cannot imagine; otherwise he would surely have tossed Boswell into the nearest gutter, as he had once thrown an insolent fellow and his chair from the side of the stage into the pit. There is no evidence that he had ever dreamed of marrying Mrs Thrale. He was infirm and ailing and past seventy, while she was a vivacious and attractive forty. What he hoped for, and apparently counted on, was a continuation of the comforting intimacy they had so long enjoyed, and it seemed that this was what she wished for too. When he was ill early in 1782 she wrote in her diary, 'If I lose *him* I am more than undone: Friend, Father, Guardian, Confidant! God give me health and patience – what shall I do?' He had certainly been her greatest support and stand-by after Thrale's death, acting as one of his executors, helping her to sort out the brewery problems and arrange the sale, bustling about in all the commercial concerns that he so curiously enjoyed. He had been reluctant to see the brewery sold, and had tried to persuade her to continue, but on that point at least she knew where happiness lay. Only months before Thrale's death, when the mob in the Gordon Riots had invaded the brewery and were preparing to set fire to it, she had come very near to losing all she possessed, and wanted no more of it. (The brewery had been saved by the presence of mind of John Perkins the manager, who regaled the crowd with beer and food while a messenger ran for the troops.) Johnson, who during the riots had seen Newgate, the Fleet Prison and the King's Bench burning and the night sky red with fires, understood at last her desire to be rid of responsibility; but he must also have known that the sale of the brewery would make him less essential than before.

By chance, it seems, rather than by design, Mrs Thrale was now often out of reach. She had decided to let Streatham, ostensibly for reasons of economy, but also, no doubt, because a freer life in Mayfair, Brighton and Bath was more to her taste. Johnson was too unwell to travel much, and began to be uneasily aware that she was drifting away.

Newgate Gaol in 1790. Ten years earlier, Johnson had watched it burning in the Gordon Riots: 'one might see the conflagration fill the sky from many parts.'

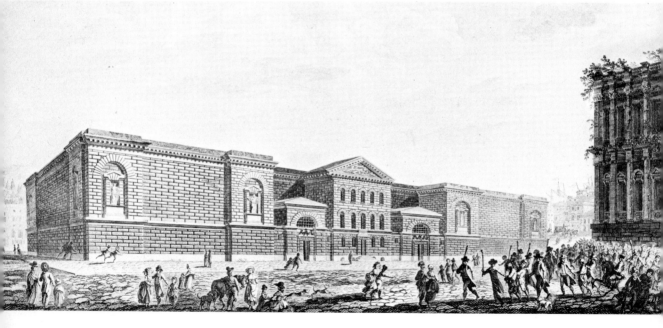

238

'Do not neglect me, nor relinquish me,' he wrote plaintively. 'Nobody will ever love you better or honour you more. . . .' Clearly he had as yet no suspicion of her feeling for Piozzi. Only a month before, hearing that their Italian friend was returning from a visit to Milan, he had assured her, 'When *he* comes and *I* come, you will have two about you that love you' – little suspecting how near he was to the truth.

By the autumn of 1782 her feelings – and also, it seems, Piozzi's – were an open secret to everyone but Johnson. Fanny Burney had long suspected it, and was now told; even Queeney could no longer be kept in ignorance if her mother seriously intended marriage. She did intend it, or at least passionately desired it; yet more than a year of argument and anguish had still to be endured before she finally resolved to defy the world and even – though she put this off as long as she dared – to make a clean breast of it to Johnson.

Her long delay, her agonized vacillation between love and prudence seem extraordinary to us today, and need some explaining. What was the matter with Piozzi, that the idea of her marrying him should strike her friends and advisers with such dismay? In the first place he was a middle-class foreigner, which made him socially undesirable. (Thrale's origins had been a good deal humbler than Piozzi's, but then he had inherited wealth, which made all the difference.) In the second place he was a Roman Catholic, in an England in which anti-Catholic prejudice was still extreme, and of which the Gordon Riots had been an ugly symptom. Worse still he was not well off, being one of a large family and having only the money he earned by singing and teaching. Most ignominious of all – and this is the point we find hardest to get in focus – he was a *performer*, a 'fellow who exhibits himself for a shilling', as Johnson had contemptuously said of Garrick – and therefore immeasurably beneath a wealthy brewer's widow. The snobbery of the age in this respect was a fact of life and Mrs Thrale was aware of it; but she must have wondered why Garrick and Burney should be allowed such social success if nobody was prepared to permit it to Piozzi. Part of the trouble, no doubt, was that he was a quiet, soft-mannered, reserved man whose English was far from perfect and who was, therefore, not likely to shine in a social assembly. Besides, since for so many reasons he was a poor match, it was clear that at the age of forty Mrs Thrale was awake for the first time to sexual passion, a discovery that her contemporaries met either with obscene jokes or shocked embarrassment. But when everything is considered – even Queeney's objection that such a stepfather would prejudice her chances of a prestigious marriage – there still lingers the feeling that everyone concerned (except, perhaps, Piozzi, who remained philosophically calm) was hysterical, venomous and unreasonable, and that Mrs Thrale's long months of misery were unnecessary.

As those months dragged by Johnson was surely aware that something was being concealed from him, and that Mrs Thrale's attention was elsewhere. He was almost perpetually ailing now, and like many sick men imagined that his symptoms and sufferings, his bronchial asthma and gout, his swellings and his dropsy, would be the things she would most wish to read about in his letters. (He once bewailed to Dr Brocklesby 'that sickness had made him a peevish, selfish, ungrateful, snarling dog'.[6] But Mrs Thrale, though she continued to express affectionate concern, could no longer spare much thought from her own troubles. She had even, in private, been exasperated when Johnson apparently approved of a passing scheme for her taking her daughters to Italy. 'I begin to see', she wrote angrily in *Thraliana*, '. . . that Johnson's connection with me is merely an interested one – he *loved* Mr Thrale I believe, but only wished to find in me a careful nurse and humble friend for his sick and his lounging hours: yet I really thought he could not have existed without *my conversation*, forsooth. He cares more for my roast beef and plumb pudden which he now devours too dirtily for endurance: and since he is glad to get rid of me, I'm sure I have good cause to desire the getting rid of *him*.'[7]

A bad-tempered outburst, to be sure, but at least it was written for herself alone: despite the increasing anguish of her own unconfessed perplexities she continued to harbour Johnson from time to time, and faithfully to answer his plaintive letters. After finally leaving Streatham she took him with her for several weeks to Brighton, where as Fanny Burney noted, he was so gloomy and bad-tempered that he was soon pointedly excluded from invitations. 'I was really quite grieved to see how unamiable he appeared, and how greatly he made himself dreaded by all. . . . He is almost certainly omitted, either from too much respect or too much fear.'[8] And in London, where Mrs Thrale had taken a house in Argyll Street, he had his own room as before whenever he chose to use it. There were still occasions when she could coax him into a happy humour, when he would be gay and amusing in the old way, and for the moment forget his gloomy forebodings and the gossip about Piozzi in the newspapers. But in April 1783 he took leave of her, though he did not know it, for the last time. Matters had come to a crisis in the family, with the daughters and their advisers, as well as Fanny Burney, imploring Mrs Thrale to give up seeing Piozzi before her reputation was irretrievably lost. She was in a state bordering on collapse, worn down by the endless pressures and indecisions. 'Sometimes I prevailed entirely,' wrote Fanny afterwards, 'then she repented her compliance, then her senses seemed to fail her; then she raved – then she was seized with a sort of stupor – then she used to fall suddenly asleep, and talk aloud . . . frightful period!' At last, after a night of tears and prayer, she decided to sacrifice everything for her daughters; sent for Piozzi, who was convinced of the hopelessness of the situation only after an abrasive interview with Queeney, and wept through an agonized farewell as he left for Italy. She now determined on retirement in Bath, where she would see no one, and it was at this point, too distracted to care whether finally or not, that she parted from Johnson. 'I took leave of Mrs Thrale,' he wrote in his diary. 'I was much moved. I had some expostulations with her. She said that she was likewise affected. I commended the Thrales with great good will to God; may my petitions have been heard!'[9]

Six weeks later, about three in the morning, Johnson woke to find that he had suffered a stroke and lost the power of speech. He at once made a prayer in Latin to test his mental powers, and when these proved to be unaffected, wrote a note to his servant Frank and waited for daylight. Frank 'came in talking, and could not immediately comprehend why he should read what I put into his hands', but the emergency was somehow explained, and Dr Brocklesby, his friend and best physician, sent for. Another medical friend, Dr Heberden, was also summoned, and after the usual dosing and blistering in two or three days his speech began to return. His first concern was to write a long and melancholy account to Mrs Thrale: 'I am sitting down in no cheerful solitude to write a narrative which would once have affected you with tenderness and sorrow, but which you will perhaps pass over now with the careless glance of frigid indifference.' His physicians, he told her at the end, gave him great hopes, 'but you may imagine my situation. . . . I hope you will sympathize with me . . . I have loved you with virtuous affection, I have honoured you with sincere esteem. Let not all our endearment be forgotten, but let me have in this great distress your pity and your prayers.' The following day, and the day after, he wrote again, giving details of his treatment and progress, and at last a kind reply came from Mrs Thrale, offering to come if he should send for her (which he did not), but making no proposal for his coming to Bath. 'I sincerely wish', she wrote in her journal, 'the continuance of a health so valuable; but have no desire that he should come to Bath, as my plan is mere retirement and economy, which alone can shorten the absence that destroys my health, consumes my soul, and keeps me to mourn *his* distance to whom only I wish to be near.'[10] She was, indeed, herself slowly sinking into a decline through sheer unhappiness, made more bitter by her regret at having given up Piozzi.

It is clear enough from his letters that Johnson realized at last the extent of the breach between them; but he still hoped; he still wrote almost daily, describing his health and his miserable condition. The 'black dog' of melancholy was his chief enemy, and how could he avoid it when so many of his old comforts had been snatched away? Levett had died the year before, 'a man who took interest in everything and therefore was very ready at conversation'. Of the friends who had meant so much for so many years, Goldsmith, Garrick and Beauclerk were all dead; Anna Williams was slowly dying; Mrs Desmoulins and her daughter had moved away; Boswell was in far-off Edinburgh. 'When I rise my breakfast is solitary, the black dog waits to share it. . . . Dinner with a sick woman you may venture to suppose not much better than solitary. After dinner what remains but to count the clock, and hope for that sleep which I can scarce expect. Night comes at last, and some hours of restlessness and confusion bring me again to a day of solitude. What shall exclude the black dog from a habitation like this? If I were a little richer,' he told Mrs Thrale, 'I would perhaps take some cheerful female into the house.'[11] But he was not richer, and cheerful females, alas, were hard to come by.

The only remedy, as he had so often insisted to others, was to avoid solitude and idleness. He watered his tiny garden, where there were saplings transplanted from Streatham, plucked and dried leaves in order to ascertain the weight lost in the process, translated the *Catiline* of Sallust, wrote letters, conferred often with his doctors and carried out experiments on himself in an effort to relieve his various ills. His chief misery was a bronchial asthma so severe that he often dared not lie down at night, but slept fitfully in a chair. Opium, which 'being a cheap drug, is everywhere genuine', gave him sure relief, but also produced effects which made him afraid of it. Sir John Hawkins later maintained that he took it 'in large quantities' and was sometimes intoxicated by it, but Johnson's diaries and letters show that the disagreeable results often outweighed the benefits. 'Frequent opiates', he found, '. . . kept me waking in the night, and drowsy the next day, and subjected me to the tyranny of vain imaginations.'[12] Gout came and went, sometimes receding until he could move quite freely, at others attacking his feet so painfully as to make him 'helpless as an infant'. There was for a time considerable alarm over a 'sarcocele', or cancerous swelling of the scrotum, but this subsided of its own accord and proved to be a 'hydrocele', and therefore harmless. The most mystifying of his troubles was an increasing dropsy, which, since it was not yet recognized as a symptom of heart-failure but regarded as a malady in its own right, he treated with copious diuretics, painstakingly measuring his intake and output of fluids. If he fasted, or kept to a vegetable diet – dining, for instance, only on a dish of peas or a gooseberry tart – his asthma and dropsy improved; but being the man he was, he could never keep for long to a moderate régime. When Mrs Thrale had feared that he sometimes fasted to excess, he replied with a lecture on *genius* (in the contemporary sense of 'disposition', 'temperament') which was a shrewd summary of one aspect of his own character: 'Have you not observed . . . that my *genius* is always in extremes; that I am very noisy, or very silent; very gloomy, or very merry; very sour, or very kind? And would you have me cross my *genius*, when it leads me sometimes to voracity and sometimes to abstinence?'[13] And so, dosing himself as well with squills (diuretic) and mercury (purgative) and subsisting 'by opiates', he laboriously followed what Fanny Burney described as 'his strange discipline – starving, mercury, opium'; but always rising 'superior both to the disease and the remedy, which commonly is the most alarming of the two'.

He needed, desperately needed, more than medicine. Loneliness was the great affliction; solitude, and the quiet house, in which nobody conversed over the teacups or quarrelled in the kitchen. What he longed for was congenial company and conversation, and to this end, in the unusually severe winter of 1783, he established a modest 'club' in Essex Street off the Strand, where the members were to meet three times a week and each time they missed a session, forfeit threepence. This Essex Head tavern was now kept by Sam Greaves, the Thrales' servant who had accompanied them to France, and whose trade the club would encourage. A large miscellaneous company was soon enlisted, but at Johnson's first attendance his asthma increased so alarmingly that he could hardly get home, and then was too ill to move for more than eight weeks. 'The asthma, however,' he wrote to Boswell, 'is not the worst. A dropsy gains ground upon me; my legs and thighs are very much swollen with water. . . . My nights are very sleepless and very tedious. And yet I am extremely afraid of dying.'[14] But a fortnight later there was a sudden and miraculous relief: his surgeon had made an incision in his thigh and drawn off twenty pints of water, and by April he was out and about again, returning thanks in St Clement Danes Church for his recovery, planning to attend the club, ordering new clothes and writing to Mrs Thrale with renewed cheerfulness. 'The dropsy . . . is quite vanished, and the asthma so much mitigated, that I walked today with a more easy respiration than I have known, I think, for two years past. I hope the Mercy that lengthens my days, will assist me to use them well.'

What better use could he put them to than in taking a jaunt with Boswell to Oxford, to stay with Dr Adams in his old college? Boswell at last was in London again and full of schemes. He would be done with Edinburgh; he would bring his wife and children to London and practise at the English Bar; there were a thousand things to discuss as they rattled away from London in the coach – even, in a confidential moment, the reprehensible behaviour of Mrs Thrale, whom Boswell was pleased to find out of favour, since Johnson declared, 'Sir, she has done everything wrong, since Thrale's bridle was off her neck.'[15]

These pleasant weeks in June, when once again Boswell was constantly in the company of his 'great Philosopher', were full of tea-drinkings and dinners in various colleges and so rich in memorable conversation, all freshly recorded, that it puzzles us how he managed to sleep at all. There was 'something exceedingly pleasing in our leading a College life, without restraint, and with superior elegance'. But Dr Adams, that amiable clergyman who had been Johnson's nominal tutor at Oxford and who now, in his late seventies, was Master of the College, provoked Johnson one night at supper to an outburst which cast a curiously Calvinistic light on his death-fear obsession. Johnson had mentioned his horror of death, at which Dr Adams expressed a mild surprise. 'JOHNSON: It is necessary for good upon the whole, that individuals should be punished . . . and as I cannot be *sure* that I have fulfilled the conditions on which salvation is granted, I am afraid I may be one of those who shall be damned (looking dismally). DR ADAMS: What do you mean by damned? JOHNSON: (passionately and loudly) Sent to Hell, Sir, and punished everlastingly.' Boswell heard Adams murmur, 'I don't believe that doctrine', but Johnson was 'in gloomy agitation, and said, "I'll have no more on't."' Clearly the conversation never recovered after this startling glimpse into his private inferno. How the aged Countess of Huntingdon, still at seventy-seven enlarging her frontiers and establishing Calvinist chapels all over the country, would have rejoiced to hear him subscribe in terror to her inexorable doctrine of election and damnation!

The fortnight in Oxford on the whole, however, put Johnson into a happier frame of mind as his health improved. He was not even particularly cast down when a scheme he had been cherishing, of spending the coming winter in Italy, came to nothing. (He had hoped to escape the English weather and the worst ravages of his asthma, but an application made by his friends for the increase in his pension, which would have made this possible, had been refused.) Now he and Boswell had a last eleven days in London together, and a final dinner by themselves with Joshua Reynolds, which Boswell had an uneasy foreboding might be their last. When it was over, he accompanied Johnson in Reynolds's coach to the entry of Bolt Court. 'He asked me whether I would not go with him to his house; I declined it, from an apprehension that my spirits would sink. We bade adieu to each other affectionately in the carriage. When he had got down upon the foot-pavement, he called out, "Fare you well"; and without looking back, sprung away with a kind of pathetic briskness. . . .'[16]

This was the end of a day ominous in another aspect, for there was already in the post a letter from Mrs Thrale which would provoke an outrageous response in Johnson and make any further friendship between them impossible. It was now more than six months since the poor lady's sinking health had alarmed her physicians, who had at last been able to persuade even Queeney that unless Piozzi were recalled, and the marriage allowed, she might never recover. It seems probable that Johnson had heard that

Piozzi was to return to England, but that the marriage was at last to take place he had no suspicion. The horrified arguments of her friends, his own 'expostulations' and the daughters' implacability must by now, he would suppose, have done their work. But it was no longer so. Piozzi, postponing his return until he was sure that he was to be no more rejected, was now on his way from Italy, and Mrs Thrale had written a circular letter to the executors and guardians to tell them that her daughters preferred to have their own establishment at Brighton, in view of her impending marriage.

When Johnson broke the seal he found also a personal letter from Mrs Thrale, begging his pardon 'for concealing from you a connection which you must have heard of by many people, but I suppose never believed. Indeed, my dear Sir, it was concealed only to spare us both needless pain; I could not have borne to reject that counsel it would have killed me to take. . . .'[17] Until he wrote kindly, she told him, she felt as though she were acting without a parent's consent.

Johnson did not write kindly. He wrote angrily and brutally, in a letter which has become as famous as his earlier chastisement of Chesterfield:

Madam,

   If I interpret your letter right, you are ignominiously married; if it is yet undone, let us once talk together. If you have abandoned your children and your religion, God forgive your wickedness; if you have forfeited your fame, and your country, may your folly do no further mischief. If the last act is yet to do, I, who have loved you, esteemed you, reverenced you, and served you, I who long thought you the first of human kind, entreat that before your fate is irrevocable, I may once more see you . . .[18]

Mrs Piozzi (formerly Mrs Thrale)
painted by an anonymous artist during her
honeymoon in Italy

It is greatly to Mrs Thrale's credit that she was able to reply to this insulting outburst with reason and dignity, desiring 'the conclusion of a correspondence which I can bear to continue no longer. The birth of my second husband', she told him, 'is not meaner than that of my first, his sentiments are not meaner, his profession is not meaner. . . . Farewell, dear Sir,' she concluded. 'You have always commanded my esteem . . . but until you have changed your opinion of Mr Piozzi – let us converse no more. God bless you!'[19] To this, as we would hope, Johnson was able to reply with chastened affection:

What you have done, however I may lament it, I have no pretence to resent, as it has not been injurious to me. I therefore breathe out one sigh more of tenderness, perhaps useless, but at least sincere. I wish that God may grant you every blessing . . . and whatever I can contribute to your happiness, I am very ready to repay for that kindness which soothed twenty years of a life radically wretched. . . . The tears stand in my eyes.[20]

But what could he possibly contribute to her happiness? Mrs Thrale was rapturously preparing for her honeymoon in France and Italy, and the long *amitié amoureuse* was over.

The punitive ostracism which pursued Mrs Piozzi, as she now was, for having made what proved to be a singularly successful and happy marriage, seems strangely inexplicable to us today. Her friends, almost to a man, were as scandalized as if she were a duchess running off with the second footman. In Johnson's case, as well as all the usual prejudices, there was a deeply and selfishly emotional involvement. He could not lose

Gabriel and Mrs Piozzi, happily married and living in Streatham Place:
sketches by George Dance in 1793

all that the Thrale connection had meant to him without a roar of pain. It was a deplorable reaction; but in the moment of shock he was incapable of concealing what he felt. Though decency had been hastily restored by his second letter, there could be no more communication between them – ever, ever. 'I drive her quite from my mind,' he told Fanny Burney, with evident distress. 'If I meet with one of her letters, I burn it instantly. I have burnt all I can find. I never speak of her, and I desire never to hear of her more. I drive her, as I said, wholly from my mind.'[21]

Nowadays we are more inclined to take Mrs Thrale's side in the affair, and to see Johnson's first reaction as unpardonable. Perhaps it is Anna Seward after all, who knew them both and never greatly cared for Johnson, whose summing-up touches at least the surface of the truth. 'He loved her', she told Boswell, 'for her wit, her beauty, her luxurious table, her coach and her library.' A little harsh, perhaps, but what woman could hope for a more dazzling constellation of attractions? We know now that Johnson's feeling for Mrs Thrale had also its depths and its complexities; for him she was also the wielder of power and the possessor of secrets; and to mislead him at last and abscond into an alien world was the one unspeakable betrayal he could not forgive. Again it is Anna Seward who, of all their acquaintance, is the most reasonable in conclusion: 'I do not approve of either, but I think it unfair that one should be considered a saint and the other a demon.'

From the moment of this shattering débâcle Johnson finally admitted to himself that he had not long to live. It was not that the will to survive was any less; as he had said to Boswell in Skye, 'However bad any man's existence may be, every man would rather have it than not exist at all'; but he knew there was little room for hope. He turned reluctantly to those final duties which he knew would reproach him at the last if they were left undone – composing a Latin epitaph for Tetty ('beautiful, elegant, ingenious and pious'), ordering a stone to be laid on her grave at Bromley and the same for his father and mother in Lichfield, and his brother Nathaniel. Then there was the question of his will; this he was always tempted to put off from day to day, but at last, with Hawkins's help, he laboriously completed it, so that Frank and his family should not be destitute.

In the hope of improvement from country air, he set off in July 1784 on a round of visits – to Lichfield, Ashbourne, Lichfield again, Birmingham and Oxford – which was more like a tour of farewell to the people he had loved, and the places, perhaps above all, in which his past was rooted. Lucy Porter was still alive in Lichfield and Hector in Birmingham; John Taylor was busy rebuilding his house and going to bed at nine, so that Johnson was struck, not for the first time, with the strangeness of their enduring friendship, since 'his whole system is so different from mine that we seem formed for different elements'. Taylor's routine was boring and the weather bad, yet he lingered on through the 'gloomy, frigid, ungenial summer' and the kinder autumn until sleeplessness and physical misery drove him in mid-November back to London. 'He returned from Lichfield', Dr Brocklesby observed, 'swollen, dejected, and giving himself up for a dead man.'[22] Yet he still believed that in London he might recover. 'The town is my element,' he wrote to this devoted and beloved physician, 'there are my friends, there are my books to which I have not yet bidden farewell, and there are my amuse-ments.'²³ But not even the town or his friends could avail him any more. His breathing grew daily more difficult, the dropsy advanced, and in the intervals when he could rise from bed he set about burning great masses of private papers. For this unhappy act of self-obliteration Sir John Hawkins was partly responsible. Like Reynolds, Langton, Burney and many other friends he sat often at Johnson's bedside, and being aware that some paper-burning had been going on, quietly pocketed a volume of the private diary. The theft was observed and reported, throwing Johnson into such an agitated state that Hawkins was obliged to return the notebook, and apologize. From that day until the end, alas, the fire in his room continued to reduce his most private memoirs to ashes.

A few days before the end, by what subconscious process we can never know, the fears that had haunted him all his life mysteriously receded, and he appeared, as Fanny Burney was told at the door, 'perfectly resigned to his approaching fate, and no longer in terror of death'. The change was as ineffable and complete as though he had secretly experienced some inner miracle. For as many years as anyone could remember, his 'horrour of the last', his fear of a punishing God, had been so obsessive that it seemed as though, of all the passages in the Bible that he so resolutely studied, only those spreading terror through the Commination Service had had lasting effect. '*It is a fearful thing to fall into the hands of the living God.*' The arguments of friends and the more comfortable doctrines of the Church had never reassured him. '*The day of the Lord cometh as a thief in the night; and when men shall say, Peace, and all things are safe, then shall sudden destruction come upon them. . . . Then shall it be too late to knock when the door shall be shut; and too late to cry for mercy when it is the time of justice.*' He had never, until this final hour, been absolved from his terror of that '*extreme malediction which shall light upon them that shall be set on the left hand. . . .*' And now, no one knew how or why, it tormented him no more.

He had pressed Dr Brocklesby to tell him the whole truth, and learning that he was indeed dying, refused to take further medicine, not even his opiates, since 'though they ever lulled my bodily pains, yet they usually filled my imagination with horrors and visions . . . and I should be loth to die in that state.'²⁴ Brocklesby had thankfully witnessed the change from fear to serenity, when 'He one morning in rapture of exultation said, "My friend, I am fully persuaded that to be a good Christian is the sheet-anchor of our hope. There is nothing that will stand the test in the hours of trial but a firm confidence in the truth of the Christian religion."'²⁵ The terror of divine vengeance had dissolved at last.

On December 13th the stertorous breathing worsened and the pain in his dropsical legs became so unbearable that he implored Frank to bring him a lancet, with which he scarified his legs in three places, immediately afterwards snatching up a pair of scissors from a bedside drawer and plunging them into the calves of both legs. After this desperate alleviation he became easier, and slept.

Mrs Desmoulins, who once more was an inmate of the house, sharing with Frank the long-drawn vigils of the sickroom, noticed about seven o'clock that the raucous breathing had stopped. Together they approached the bedside and found that he was dead.

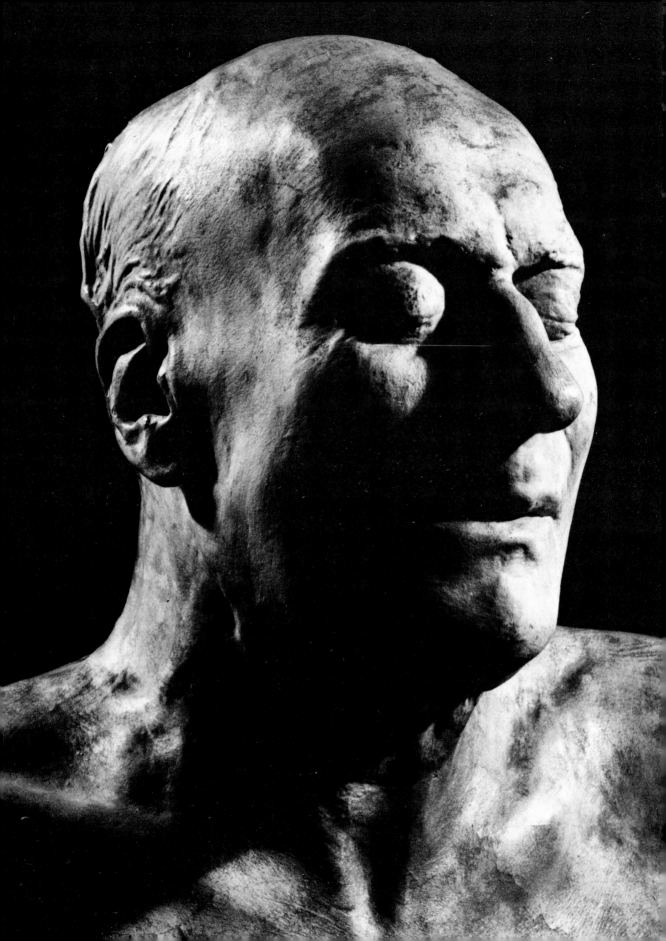

Select Bibliography

ANDERSON, ROBERT. *Life of Samuel Johnson, LL.D.*, 1795.

BOSWELL, JAMES. *Life of Johnson, together with Boswell's Journal of a Tour to the Hebrides and Johnson's Diary of a Journey into North Wales*, edited by G. Birkbeck Hill, revised by L. F. Powell, 6 vols., 1934–64.

BOSWELL, JAMES. *The Private Papers of James Boswell*, Yale edition: *Boswell's London Journal*, 1950; *Boswell in Search of a Wife*, 1957.

BOSWELL, JAMES. *The Correspondence and Other Papers of James Boswell Relating to the Making of the Life of Johnson*, edited by Marshall Waingrow, 1969.

BOSWELL, JAMES. *Journal of a Tour to Corsica*, edited by S. C. Roberts, 1929.

BOYLE, HENRY. *Chronology of the Eighteenth and Nineteenth Centuries*, 1826.

BRAIN, RUSSELL. *Some Reflections on Genius*, 1960.

BROADLEY, A. M. *Doctor Johnson and Mrs Thrale*, 1910. (Includes Mrs Thrale's Welsh Journal)

CAMPBELL, THOMAS. *Dr Campbell's Diary*, edited by J. L. Clifford, 1947.

CLIFFORD, J. L. *Young Samuel Johnson*, 1955.

CLIFFORD, J. L. *H. L. Piozzi (Mrs Thrale)*, 1941.

D'ARBLAY, FRANCES. *Diaries and Letters*, 7 vols., 1843.

GEORGE, DOROTHY. *London Life in the Eighteenth Century*, 1925.

HAWKINS, JOHN. *Life of Samuel Johnson, LL.D.*, 1787.

HILL, G. BIRKBECK, editor. *Johnsonian Miscellanies*, 2 vols., 1897.

HYDE, MARY. *The Impossible Friendship: Boswell and Mrs Thrale*, 1973.

JOHNSON, SAMUEL. *Works*, Yale edition: Vol. I, *Diaries, Prayers and Annals*; Vols. III, IV, V, *The Rambler*; Vol. IX, *A Journey to the Western Islands of Scotland*.

JOHNSON, SAMUEL. *Letters*, edited by R. W. Chapman, 1952.

KRUTCH, J. W. *Samuel Johnson*, 1944.

LANSDOWNE, Marquess of. *The Queeney Letters*, 1934.

NORTHCOTE, JAMES. *The Life of Sir Joshua Reynolds*, 2 vols., 1818.

PIOZZI, HESTER LYNCH. *Anecdotes of the late Samuel Johnson, LL.D.*, edited by Arthur Sherbo, 1974.

PIOZZI, HESTER LYNCH. *Thraliana*, edited by Katherine Balderston, 2 vols., 1941.

READE, A. L. *Johnsonian Gleanings*, 11 vols., privately printed 1909–52.

REYNOLDS, JOSHUA. *Portraits by Sir Joshua Reynolds*, edited by F. W. Hilles, 1952.

SHAW, WILLIAM. *Memoirs of the Life and Writings of the late Dr Samuel Johnson*, edited by Arthur Sherbo, 1974.

TINKER, C. B. *Dr Johnson and Fanny Burney*, 1911.

TYSON, M. and GUPPY, H., editors. *French Journals of Mrs Thrale and Dr Johnson*, 1932.

WAINGROW, MARSHALL, editor. *The Correspondence of James Boswell*. (See under Boswell, James)

WALPOLE, HORACE. *Letters*, edited by Peter Cunningham, 9 vols., 1906.

OPPOSITE The death-mask bust of Johnson, originally owned by his surgeon, William Cruikshank. It was Sir Joshua Reynolds, apparently, who 'immediately after the Doctor's death, ordered Mr Hoskins in St Martin's Lane, caster of figures to the Royal Academy, to make a plaster-of-Paris cast from his face'.[26] The bust is now in the National Portrait Gallery.

Chapter 1

1 Boswell, *Life*, I. 34.
2 Sir John Floyer, physician.
3 Johnson, *Diaries, Prayers, Annals*.
4 ibid.
5 Daniel Defoe, *The Compleat English Gentleman*, first published 1890.
6 Johnson, *Diaries, Prayers, Annals*.
7 L. C. Henry and R. MacKeith, 'Samuel Johnson's Childhood Illnesses and the King's Evil', in *Medical History*, Vol. X, 1966.
8 Johnson, *Diaries, Prayers, Annals*.
9 Boyle, *Chronology*.
10 Johnson, *Diaries, Prayers, Annals*.
11 Marc Bloch, *The Royal Touch: Sacred Monarchy and Scrofula in England and France*, 1973.
12 Lord Macaulay, *History of England*, Ch. 14.
13 Mrs Piozzi, in her *Anecdotes*, later improved this to 'a lady in diamonds and a long black hood'.
14 R. Crawfurd, *The King's Evil*, 1911.
15 Johnson, *Dictionary*, 1755.
16 Johnson, *Diaries, Prayers, Annals*.
17 ibid.
18 ibid.
19 Now in the National Portrait Gallery.
20 Johnson, *Diaries, Prayers, Annals*.
21 ibid.
22 Mrs Piozzi, *Anecdotes*.
23 Johnson, *Diaries, Prayers, Annals*.
24 ibid.
25 Mrs Piozzi, *Anecdotes*.
26 George Irwin, *Samuel Johnson, a Personality in Conflict*, 1971.
27 Mrs Piozzi thought it had been 'her old maid, Catherine', but Catherine Chambers was only a year older than Johnson, and entered his parents' service in 1724, when Johnson was fifteen.
28 J. L. Clifford, *Young Samuel Johnson*.
29 Mrs Piozzi, *Anecdotes*.
30 Anon., *A General Description of All Trades*, 1747.
31 B. C. Middleton, *A History of English Craft Bookbinding Techniques*, 1963.

Chapter 2

1 Johnson, *Diaries, Prayers, Annals*.
2 Boswell, *Life*, I. 44.
3 Waingrow, 50.
4 ibid., 49.
5 Oliver Goldsmith, *Citizen of the World*, Letter 12.

6 Boswell, *Life*, I. 67.
7 *Weekly Journal or British Gazeteer*, Apr. 14th 1716.
8 Boswell, Life, I. 67.
9 Cornelius Ford had a remote connection with Chesterfield through his wife's great-niece's marrying Chesterfield's younger brother. Such tenuous relationships were not unimportant in the eighteenth century, but there is no evidence that Johnson, even at the time of his famous letter to Chesterfield, had any inkling of this one. (A. L. Reade, *Johnsonian Gleanings*, III. 151–3.)
10 Robert Anderson, *Life of Samuel Johnson*, 20.
11 Mrs Piozzi, *Thraliana*, 171.
12 Quoted in Hugh Phillips's *Mid-Georgian London*, 1964, 142.
13 *The Connoisseur*, Jan. 31st 1754.
14 Johnson, *Life of Fenton*.
15 *Gentleman's Magazine*, Sept. 1731. A nice gloss on the speech of the time, when 'clergy' would be pronounced 'clargy'.
16 Boswell, *Life*, II. 460.
17 William Shaw, *Memoirs of Dr Johnson*.
18 Professor H. C. Wyld.

Chapter 3

1 Boyle, *Chronology*.
2 A. D. Godley, *Oxford in the Eighteenth Century*, 1908.
3 Douglas Macleane, *History of Pembroke College*, 1897.
4 George Whitefield, *A Short Account of God's Dealings with the Rev. George Whitefield*, 1740.
5 R. Graves, *Recollections of William Shenstone*, 1788.
6 Boswell, *Life*, I. 94.
7 Nicholas Amherst, *Terrae Filius*, 1721.
8 Boswell, *Life*, I. 60.
9 ibid., I. 272.
10 ibid., I. 70.
11 ibid., I. 74.
12 ibid.
13 ibid., I. 63.
14 ibid., I. 66.
15 ibid., IV. 94.
16 ibid., I. 68.
17 ibid., IV. 373.
18 Hawkins, *Life*, 21.
19 C. E. Vulliamy, *John Wesley*, 3rd edn, 1954, 142.
20 Boswell, *Life*, I. 85.

Chapter 4

1 Waingrow, 91.
2 Northcote, *Reynolds*, II. 161.
3 Boswell, *Life*, III. 389.
4 ibid., I. 94.
5 G. Birkbeck Hill, *Johnsonian Miscellanies*, II. 49.
6 Boswell, *Life*, I. 95.
7 William Shaw, *Memoirs of Dr Johnson*, 33.
8 Wine, usually port, mixed with sugar and oranges.
9 Boswell, *Life*, I. 96.
10 ibid.
11 Original letter in Pembroke College.
12 Joseph Cradock, *Literary and Miscellaneous Memoirs*, 4 vols., 1828.
13 Mrs Piozzi, *Anecdotes*.
14 Hannah More, *Memoirs*, II. 16.
15 Madame D'Arblay, *Diary*, I. 65.
16 Boswell, *Life*, V. 126.
17 ibid., I. 99.
18 Johnson, *Diaries, Prayers, Annals*, 36.
19 Hannah More, *Memoirs*, I. 251.
20 Boswell, *Life*, I. 103–5.
21 Johnson, *Rambler*, No. 15.
22 A. L. Reade, *Johnsonian Gleanings*, I. 1.

Chapter 5

1 Hitchin, *A True Discovery of the Conduct of Receivers and Thief-Takers in and about the City of London*, 1718.
2 Walpole, *Letters*, V. 267.
3 Boswell, *Life*, I. 110.
4 Boyle, *Chronology*, 82.
5 Boswell, *Life*, II. 299.
6 Lord Bristol in two marriages had fathered twenty children, so he presumably knew what he was talking about.
7 William Lecky, *History of England in the Eighteenth Century*, 3rd edn 1883, I. 482.
8 Hawkins, *Life*, 53.
9 Boswell, *Life*, IV. 395.
10 Mrs Piozzi, *Anecdotes*.
11 *Rambler*, No. 107.

Chapter 6

1 Taylor was capable of taking vigorous action when it suited him. According to the historian of Pembroke College, he 'left his estates to his shoe-black and page, William Brunt, to spite his relatives whom he overheard, when in a grave illness,

discussing the distribution of his property. The boy, the son of a vendor of besoms, swooned at hearing the news.' But he was, in fact, a remote poor relation who had been educated at Taylor's expense and was living in his house – whether in a menial capacity or not we do not know. He was sixteen at the time of his inheritance, which promoted him to the landed gentry and made him a county magistrate at the age of thirty-one. (Thomas Taylor, *Life of Dr Taylor*, 1910.)

2 Mrs Thrale's Welsh Journal, in Broadley, 164.
3 Boswell, *Life*, III. 148.
4 ibid., IV. 15.
5 Mrs Piozzi, *Anecdotes*, 113, 114.
6 Hawkins, *Life*, 315.
7 Boyle, *Chronology*, 91.
8 Johnson, *Letters*, I, No. 12.
9 Chesterfield himself was writing political squibs at this time, under the pseudonym of Geoffery Broadbottom.

Chapter 7

1 Walpole, *Letters*, VIII. 260.
2 Boswell, *Life*, I. 166.
3 ibid., I. 165.
4 Clarence Tracy, *The Artificial Bastard*, 1971.
5 Boswell, *Life*, I. 163, n. 1.
6 Johnson, *Letters*, I, No. 19.
7 Mrs Piozzi, *Thraliana*, 161.
8 Johnson, *Miscellaneous Observations on the Tragedy of Macbeth*, edited by Arthur Sherbo, in the Yale edition of *Works*, Vol. VII.
9 Boswell, *Life*, I, 70, n.2.
10 Chevalier de Johnstone, *A Memoir of the 'Forty-Five'*, Folio Society, 1958.
11 Boyle, *Chronology*.

Chapter 8

1 Boswell, *Life*, I. 186.
2 Johnson, *Plan of the Dictionary*, in *Works*, Vol. II (Introduction by Arthur Murphy), 12 vols., 1820.
3 ibid.
4 Johnson, Preface to the *Dictionary*, ibid.
5 Hawkins, *Life*, 175.
6 Madame D'Arblay, *Diary*, II. 327.
7 Boswell Papers, Yale edition: Apr. 20th 1783.
8 Dr George Cheyne, *Essay of Health and Long Life*, 1724.
9 Lady Knight's memoir of Anna Williams's account, in *European Magazine*, Oct. 1799: G. Birkbeck Hill's *Johnsonian Miscellanies*, Vol. II.
10 Mrs Piozzi, *Thraliana*, 176.
11 Mrs Piozzi, *Anecdotes*.
12 Boswell, *Life*, I. 194.
13 W. J. Bate, Introduction to *The Rambler*, Yale edition.
14 *Rambler*, No. 14.
15 Hawkins, *Life*, 219.

16 Chesterfield, *Miscellaneous Works*, 1777, II. 491.
17 Chesterfield, *Letters*, edited by Bonamy Dobrée, 1932, III. 1167.
18 Boswell, *Life*, I. 261.
19 Chesterfield, *Letters*, I. 421.
20 Boswell, *Life*, I. 238.
21 *Rambler*, No. 18.
22 Johnson, *Diaries, Prayers, Annals*.

Chapter 9

1 Hawkins, *Life*, 401.
2 Johnson, Preface to the *Dictionary*.
3 Johnson, *Plan of the Dictionary*.
4 Johnson, *Letters*, No. 70.
5 ibid., Nos. 77, 78.
6 ibid., No. 103.
7 ibid., No. 57.
8 ibid., No. 56.
9 Johnson, *Diaries, Prayers, Annals*.
10 Johnson, *Letters*, Nos. 78–84.
11 A. T. Hazen, *Johnson's Prefaces and Dedications*, 1937.
12 John Wesley, *Journal*, July 6th 1746.
13 Dr James Grainger.

Chapter 10

1 *Rasselas*, Ch. 44.
2 Arthur Murphy, 'An Essay on the Life and Genius of Samuel Johnson, LL.D.', in G. Birkbeck Hill's *Johnsonian Miscellanies*, Vol. I.
3 *Journals of Captain Cook*, edited by J. Beaglehole, 1955, Vol. I, cxxxiii.
4 'Loplolly': eighteenth-century naval slang for ship's doctor's medicine. 'Loplolly man': surgeon's mate.
5 Mrs Piozzi, *Anecdotes*, 154.
6 J. Northcote, *Reynolds*, I. 118.
7 Horace Walpole, *Letters*, III. 481.
8 The text of Johnson's report, as published in *The Gentleman's Magazine*, is given in Boswell, *Life*, I. 407, n. 3.

Chapter 11

1 Boswell, *London Journal*, 305.
2 Fanny Burney, letter to Mr Crisp, Oct. 19th 1782.
3 Boswell, *Journal of a Tour to Corsica*, edited by S. C. Roberts, 83.
4 Charles Churchill, *The Ghost*, quoted in Boswell, *Life*, I. 320.
5 Walter Raleigh, *Six Essays on Johnson*, 1910.
6 Waingrow, 268.
7 Hawkins, *Life*, 423.
8 Boswell, *Life*, I. 480.
9 Sir Joshua Reynolds, in G. Birkbeck Hill's *Johnsonian Miscellanies*, II. 228.
10 Boswell, *Life*, II. 15.
11 Johnson, *Letters*, No. 150.
12 ibid., No. 157.
13 G. Birkbeck Hill's *Johnsonian Miscellanies*, II. 391.

14 Arthur Murphy, in ibid., I. 423.
15 Arthur Malone, Preface to his *Shakespeare*, 1790
16 Arthur Murphy, in G. Birkbeck Hill's *Johnsonian Miscellanies*, I. 409.
17 Johnson, *Diaries*, March 29th 1766.
18 Waingrow, 24.
19 Mrs Piozzi, *Thraliana*, Sept. 18th 1777.
20 Rocque's *Map of London, Westminster and Southwark*, 1746.

Chapter 12

1 Mrs Piozzi, *Thraliana*, 159.
2 ibid., 171, 172.
3 ibid., 52–3.
4 Arthur Murphy, in G. Birkbeck Hill's *Johnsonian Miscellanies*, I. 423–4.
5 Mrs Piozzi, *Anecdotes*, 102.
6 ibid.
7 ibid.
8 ibid., 72.
9 Mrs Piozzi, *Thraliana*, 83.
10 *Dr Campbell's Diary*, edited by J. L. Clifford, 61.
11 ibid., 68.
12 Mrs Piozzi, *Anecdotes*, 89.
13 Sigmund Freud, *Civilization, War and Death*, edited by J. Rickman, 1939.
14 Mrs Piozzi, *Anecdotes*, 129.
15 ibid.
16 *Boswell in Search of a Wife*, 155.

Chapter 13

1 Mrs Piozzi, *Anecdotes*, 122.
2 ibid., 97.
3 *Boswell in Search of a Wife*, 166.
4 ibid., 167.
5 ibid., 169.
6 ibid., 353, 354.
7 Boswell, *Life*, II. 42.
8 Reade, *Johnsonian Gleanings*, Vol. II.
9 Johnson, *Diaries*, 119.
10 Joseph Jean Hecht, *The Domestic Servant Class in Eighteenth-Century England*, 1956.
11 Boswell, *Life*, II. 464.
12 ibid., II. 79.
13 ibid., II. 149.
14 Boswell, letter to Reynolds, 1781: *Reynolds Portraits*, in Boswell Papers, Yale edition.
15 Mrs Piozzi, *Thraliana*, 1.
16 ibid., 310.
17 ibid., 312, 313.
18 ibid., 313.
19 Johnson, *Letters*, Nos. 279, 280.

Chapter 14

1 Johnson, *Letters*, No. 294a.
2 Marquess of Lansdowne's *Queeney Letters*, 6.
3 Johnson, *Letters*, No. 311.1.
4 ibid.

5 ibid., No. 307.1.
6 ibid., No. 311.1a.
7 Mrs Piozzi, *Thraliana*, II. 625.
8 Johnson, *Letters*, No. 313a.
9 Boswell, *Life*, II. 215.
10 *Boswell for the Defence*, 197.
11 Boswell, *Life*, II. 228.
12 ibid., 100.
13 Boswell, *Journal of a Tour to the Hebrides*, 175.
14 ibid., 244.
15 Boswell, *Life*, II. 268, 269 n. 1.
16 Boswell, *Journal of a Tour to the Hebrides*, 11.
17 ibid., 24.
18 Johnson, *Journey to the Western Islands of Scotland*, 40, 41.
19 E. Cloyd, *James Burnett, Lord Monboddo*, 1972.
20 Russell Brain, *Some Reflections on Genius*, 112.
21 Johnson, *Journey to the Western Islands of Scotland*, 85.
22 ibid., 96.
23 ibid., 50.
24 ibid., 101.
25 ibid., 83.
26 Boswell, *Journal of a Tour to the Hebrides*, 79.
27 ibid., 231.

Chapter 15

1 Johnson, *Letters*, II. No. 373.
2 Mrs Thrale's Welsh Journal, in Broadley.
3 ibid., 219.
4 Donald Greene, *The Politics of Samuel Johnson*, 209.
5 Mrs Piozzi, *Anecdotes*, 132.
6 M. Tyson and H. Guppy, *French Journals*.
7 Boswell, *Life*, IV. 289.
8 M. Tyson and H. Guppy, *French Journals*.
9 Greene, *Politics of Samuel Johnson*, 216.
10 Johnson, *Letters*, II, No. 477.
11 Johnson, *Diaries*, 264, 294.
12 Frances Reynolds, in G. Birkbeck Hill's *Johnsonian Miscellanies*, II. 251.
13 Johnson, *Sermons*, No. 11.
14 Gerald Howson, *The Macaroni Parson*, 1973.
15 Frances Reynolds, in G. Birkbeck Hill's *Johnsonian Miscellanies*, II. 284.
16 Johnson, *Letters*, II., No. 523.

Chapter 16

1 Mrs Piozzi, *Thraliana*, I. 488.
2 Johnson, *Diaries*, 304.

3 Johnson, *Letters*, II, No. 717.
4 Mrs Piozzi, *Thraliana*, I. 498.
5 Quoted in full in Mary Hyde's *The Impossible Friendship*.
6 Waingrow, 35.
7 Mrs Piozzi, *Thraliana*, I. 541.
8 Fanny Burney, *Diary*, Oct. 1782, quoted in C. B. Tinker's *Dr Johnson and Fanny Burney*, 151, 152.
9 Johnson, *Diaries*, 358.
10 Mrs Piozzi, *Thraliana*, I. 568.
11 Johnson, *Letters*, III, No. 857.
12 ibid., III, No. 77.
13 ibid., II, No. 686.
14 ibid., III, No. 932.
15 Boswell, *Life*, IV. 277.
16 ibid., IV. 339.
17 Johnson, *Letters*, III, No. 969a.
18 ibid., No. 970.
19 ibid., No. 970, 1a.
20 ibid., No. 972.
21 C. B. Tinker, *Dr Johnson and Fanny Burney*, 184.
22 Waingrow, Letter from Dr Brocklesby, 26.
23 Johnson, *Letters*, III, No. 1029.
24 Waingrow, 33.
25 ibid., 94.
26 Preface to *The Beauties of Johnson*, 7th edition, 1787.

Acknowledgments for the Illustrations

The producers of this book wish to express their thanks to all those indicated by the list below, who have kindly given permission for items from their collections to be reproduced here.

Abbreviations used are:

BM The Trustees of the British Museum, London
Courage Ltd. Reproduced by permission of Courage Limited, Brewers, London
JBM Johnson's Birthplace Museum, reproduced by kind permission of Lichfield District Council
JH The Trustees of Dr Johnson's House, Gough Square, London
LL London Library, London
Mansell The Mansell Collection, London
NPG National Portrait Gallery, London

A page number in italic type indicates a colour plate.

Jacket subjects. (front) Unfinished oil by James Barry; NPG. (back) LEFT to RIGHT, TOP Oil by Van Loo, *c.* 1742; by permission of the Trustees of the Shakespeare Memorial National Theatre; photo Crown Copyright. Oil by anon. artist; the Hyde Collection, Somerville, N.J. CENTRE Oil by Allan Ramsay, 1765; NPG. Oil, studio of Reynolds, *c.* 1770; NPG. BOTTOM Oil by Robert Edge Pine, *c.* 1771; Courage Ltd; photo Witty. Oil by George Willison, 1765; Scottish National Portrait Gallery; photo Tom Scott.

Endpapers Details from Rocque's *Plan of the Cities of London and Westminster and Borough of Southwark*, 1746. Reproduced by Harry Margary, Lympne Castle. Original, Guildhall Library, City of London.

Frontispiece Oil by Sir Joshua Reynolds, 1783. Haverford College, Penn.

page 8 Drawing, anon., 1782. The Trustees of the William Salt Library. Photo: Peter Rogers.
11 Dean and Chapter of Lichfield Cathedral. Photo: Rackham.
12 Engraving from *The Complete English Traveller*, 1771. The Trustees of the William Salt Library. Photo: Peter Rogers.
15 Engraving by E. Finden. From *Johnsoniana*, published by John Murray, 1835. Lent by Margaret Lane.
19 From *King's Evil* by Raymond Crawfurd, 1911. LL.
21 JBM. Photo: Rackham.
24 St Bride Printing Library. Photo: Freeman.
26 LEFT Sketch, 1829. Album lent by Captain H. E. Widnell. RIGHT Engraving by C. J. Smith from *Johnsoniana*.
31 Oil, by Josef van Aken, 1726–30. London Museum.
32 *A Midnight Modern Conversation* by William Hogarth, 1732–3. Sir John Soane's Museum. Photo: Witty.

33 Engraving, 18th c. Birmingham Libraries, Local Studies Dept.
36 LEFT Photo: John Crampton. RIGHT From *Johnsonian Gleanings*, Vol. 6, by A.L. Reade, 1909. LL.
37 Detail of *The Marriage Contract* by Hogarth, 1745. National Gallery, London.
41 Engraving, 18th c. Pembroke College, Oxford.
43 'Artium Baccalaureus', from *Oxonia Illustrata*, MS. Wood. 276ᵇf. XIX. 18th c. Bodleian Library.
46 Oil, after John Opie. Pembroke College, Oxford.
50 Coloured plaster bust attributed to L. F. Roubiliac, *c.* 1750. NPG.
55 Pembroke College, Oxford. Photo: Studio Edmark.
59 JBM. Photo: Rackham.
62 LEFT Oil by T. Kettle, 1762. RIGHT Oil by H. W. Pickersgill, 1822. Both NPG.
65 Hyde Collection, Somerville, N.J.
66 *St James's Park and the Mall*, anon. *c.* 1743. Reproduced by gracious permission of Her Majesty the Queen.
68 Engraving by Sutton Nicholls, *c.* 1725. London Museum. Photo: Freeman.
69 From *London Tradesmen's Cards of XVIII century*, 1929. LL. Copyright Batsford.
71 TOP Watercolour by Rowlandson and Pugin, early 19th c. BOTTOM Oil after Canaletto. Both London Museum.
72 Watercolour by Rowlandson and Schultz, *c.* 1798. London Museum.
74 LEFT *The Distrest Poet* by Hogarth, 1736. Sir John Soane's Museum. Photo: Witty. RIGHT Reproduced from a copy. JBM. Photo: Rackham.
83 Oil, *c.* 1740. By permission of Sir Rupert Bromley. Photo: McGeorge, Rhodesia.
84 Oil by J. Woolaston, *c.* 1742. NPG.
86 LEFT Oil by John Opie, *c.* 1780. JBM. Photo: Rackham. RIGHT From *Johnsonian Gleanings*, Vol. 6. LL.
89 From a copy. JBM. Photo: Rackham.
91 Engraving by P. Begbie, 1775. London Museum. Photo: Freeman.
94 Oil by James Roberts. Heather Professor of Music, Oxford University.
96 *The Press Gang* by T. Rowlandson. Photo: Mansell.
99 Oil by anon. Italian artist, *c.* 1770. NPG.
101 Oil by Jean-Baptiste van Loo, *c.* 1742. Hanbury-Williams Collection.
102 Oil, studio of Reynolds, 1769. Tate Gallery. Photo: Witty.
105 LEFT Engraving by Jean Daulle, mid-18th c. RIGHT Engraving, anon. 1797. Both BM. Photos: Folio Society.

107 Drawing, 1746. London Museum.
112 From *Old and New London*, Vol. 1, by G. W. Thornbury, 1873. LL.
117 Made by John Flaxman, 1783. From a copy, JBM.
119 Oil by Allan Ramsay, 1765. NPG.
120 Pastel by Francis Cotes. By permission of the Duke of St Albans. Photo: Witty.
124 *The Quarrel with her Jew Protector* by Hogarth, 1732. BM. Photo: Freeman.
127 LEFT and RIGHT From the 1st edition of Johnson's *Dictionary*, 1755. LL. Photo: Witty.
129 Engraving by C. J. Smith from *Johnsoniana*, 1835.
130 Oil by Joshua Reynolds, 1756. NPG.
131 LEFT Oil by Nathaniel Dance. RIGHT Self-portrait by Reynolds, 1753-4. Both NPG.
132 Drawing, anon. JH. Photo: Witty.
134 From Johnson's *Dictionary*, 1755, 1st edition. LL. Photo: Witty.
138 JBM. Photo: Rackham.
139 JH. Photo: Witty.
142 Unfinished oil by James Barry. NPG.
145 Chalk sketch attributed to Reynolds. NPG.
147 LEFT Coloured engraving by John Cleverley, 1772. RIGHT H.M.S. *Deal Castle* by T. Hearn. Both by permission of the Trustees of the National Maritime Museum.
150 *The Cock Lane Uproar*, engraving, 1762. Guildhall Library, City of London.
153 From *Old and New London*, Vol. 3, by G. W. Thornbury, 1873. LL.
157 Oil by R. Houston, *c.* 1768. NPG.
159 LEFT Oil, after Reynolds, 1768. RIGHT Oil, studio of Reynolds, *c.* 1770. CENTRE Wax medallion by T. R. Poole, 1791. All NPG.
161 Oil by Jean-Baptiste van Loo, *c.* 1742. By permission of the Trustees of the Shakespeare Memorial National Theatre. Photo: Crown Copyright.
162-3 Oil by John Collett, 1760. From the collection of the Earl of Jersey. Photo: Royle Publications Ltd.
164 Oil by George Willison, 1765. Scottish National Portrait Gallery.
166 Woodcut. The Trustees of the William Salt Library. Photo: Peter Rogers.
168 Engraving by E. Finden. From *Johnsoniana*, 1835.
173 ABOVE *The Lady's Last Stake* by Hogarth, 1759. Albright-Knox Art Gallery, Buffalo, N.Y. Gift of Seymour H. Knox. RIGHT Engraving from a portrait by Reynolds. From *Johnsoniana*, 1835.

175 Water-colour by W. H. Brooke. JH. Photo: Witty.
176 Oil by John Zoffany. By permission of the Earl of Shelburne. Photo: Anthony Miles.
180 Oil by Reynolds, *c.* 1781. The Hyde Collection, Somerville, N.J.
182 Engraving by E. Finden. From *Johnsoniana*, 1835.
187 LEFT Silhouette. JBM. Photo, Rackham. RIGHT Oil by Reynolds, Tate Gallery.
189 Oil by Robert Edge Pine, *c.* 1771. Courage Ltd, London. Photo: Witty.
190 Oil by Reynolds, 1774. By permission of Lady Teresa Agnew.
193 TOP *Gin Lane* by Hogarth, engraving, 1751. BM. Photo: Freeman. BOTTOM *The Procession*, engraving in the Mansell Collection. Photo: Mansell.
199 ABOVE Oil by Reynolds, *c.* 1779. By permission of the Earl of Shelburne. Photo: Anthony Miles. RIGHT Engraving, 1772. BM.
205 ABOVE Pencil sketch by Sir Thomas Lawrence. NPG. LEFT Engraving by T. Trotter. Mary Evans Picture Library.
207 Oil by Reynolds, 1775. Courage Ltd, London. Photo: Cooper-Bridgeman Library.
208 Oil by Allan Ramsay. Ashmolean Museum, Oxford.
210 Engraving by E. Finden. From *Johnsoniana*, 1835.
211 Sketch, anon. National Galleries of Scotland. Photo: Tom Scott.
213 Engraving by Charles Grignion, 18th c. BM. Photo: Freeman.
214 Engraving, 18th c. Mary Evans Picture Library.
219 Oil by Allan Ramsay, 1754. Tate Gallery.
221 Oil, after Reynolds. NPG.
222 Engraving by P. Mazell after a drawing by I. Donowell, 1778. Royal Pavilion, Art Gallery and Museums, Borough of Brighton.
223 From Mrs Thrale's *Welsh Journal*. The Hyde Collection, Somerville, N.J.
229 Oil by Reynolds, *c.* 1772. Pembroke College, Oxford. Photo: Thomas Photos, Oxford.
232 ABOVE Oil by E. F. Burney. NPG. LEFT Engraving, 1777. BM.
235 Oil by Reynolds, 1785. NPG.
238 Engraving, after Bourjot, 1795. London Museum. Photo: Freeman.
244 Oil, anon. Italian artist, *c.* 1785. NPG.
245 LEFT Pencil sketch by George Dance, 1793. RIGHT Pencil sketch by George Dance, 1793. Both NPG.
248 Death-mask bust, plaster, 1784. NPG. Photo: Witty.

Index

255

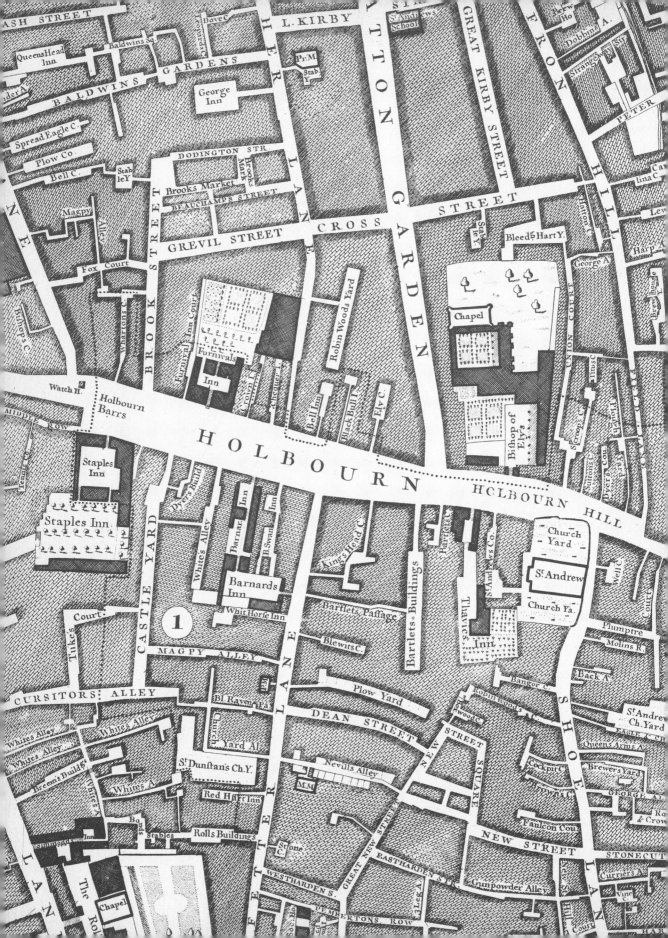